Liz Claiborne

Liz Claiborne

THE LEGEND, THE WOMAN
BY ART ORTENBERG

TAYLOR TRADE PUBLISHING
Lanham ▪ New York ▪ Boulder ▪ Toronto ▪ Plymouth, UK

Published by Taylor Trade Publishing
An imprint of The Rowman & Littlefield Publishing Group, Inc.
4501 Forbes Boulevard, Suite 200, Lanham, Maryland 20706
http://www.rlpgtrade.com

Estover Road, Plymouth PL6 7PY, United Kingdom

Distributed by National Book Network

British Library Cataloguing in Publication Information Available

Library of Congress Cataloging-in-Publication Data

Ortenberg, Art.
    Liz Claiborne : the legend, the woman / Art Ortenberg.
        p.   cm.
    Originally published: St. Louis, Mo : Missouri Botanical Garden, 2009.
    ISBN 978-1-58979-494-8 (cloth : alk. paper)
    1. Claiborne, Liz, 1929-2007. 2. Fashion designers—United States—Biography. I. Title.
TT505.C52O78 2009
746.9'2092—dc22
[B]
                                                                    2009043275

Designed by Tracey Cameron and Michelle Leong

♾™ The paper used in this publication meets the minimum requirements of American
National Standard for Information Sciences—Permanence of Paper for Printed Library
Materials, ANSI/NISO Z39.48-1992.

Printed in the United States of America

With gratitude, this work is dedicated to the trustees of our foundation:
Bill Conway, Bob Dewar, Alison Richard and Jonah Western.

PROLOGUE

LIZ CLAIBORNE ORTENBERG died at the end of June 2007. When it became known that Liz Claiborne, the design visionary and corporate leader, had died, the acclaim she received was thunderous and came from every part of the globe. A great woman had died, a woman of extraordinary accomplishment and influence. The accolades related to the central role she had played in building a remarkably successful, happy and ethical company, a company whose sales were well over a billion dollars the year she retired, whose products had achieved a national ubiquity that left an enduring imprint. She had anticipated and responded to a lasting economic and cultural change in the America of the 1980s, when significant numbers of women entered the workplace and reached professional heights heretofore denied to them. She created clothes that were appropriate for working women. The clothes were professional looking and comfortable, not intended to beguile or to dress a woman up in man's clothing. Liz strove for perfection. She shaped an apprenticeship that equipped her with the technical and visual skills necessary to implement her vision. As she often said, she had been educated "to see," and to bring to life what she saw. During the fruitful, learning years at the company, she never failed to devote her professional self to communicating with the women she sought to dress. And I, who admired her without reserve, who trusted her love of beauty, her talent and her vast technical skill, was privileged to be her partner, her lover, and perhaps most importantly, a person dedicated to doing what I could to assure that her vision would be realized.

Liz loved the beautiful and "seeing" for her meant just that, responding to the "beautiful." This fragment from a speech she gave in 1991 reads like a poem: "As a small child I was taught," she said, "to respond to the graceful utility in my surroundings—the arrangement of flowers, table settings, napery and flatware, the lines of furniture, the rugs underfoot, wall hangings, the house one lives in, the way one wears one's hair, carries one's body— my entire life seemed to be immersed in things visual." For Liz, this came to mean that "seeing" was the beginning of the process; making what you had seen come to life was the art.

During those early years in Brussels, her development, supervised by her banker father who ran the American branch of the Morgan Guaranty bank, formed a private person who had to learn how to project herself to her broad public. She was taught as a small child to speak softly, to speak when asked to speak and to be the receiver of opinions, not the dispenser of private thoughts. She and her brothers were taught that table manners and disciplined, polite behavior were required of people of privilege. Privilege and civility were the two faces of the same coin.

The broad public knew very little, in many cases, or perhaps nothing, of who this Liz Claiborne person had been and why she merited the newspaper coverage that followed her death. I, her husband of almost fifty years, have determined to write a narrative of Liz's broader life. My hope is that you will get to know Liz, the Liz of our early life together, the Liz of the company, the Liz of the wonderfully adventuresome years after we left the company, the Liz who loved wild creatures and wild places, and the Liz who had been found to have cancer and fought it heroically.

Her battle with peritoneal carcinoma, a nine-year struggle, began in May 1998. This is an extremely rare disease, afflicting less than 10 percent of women diagnosed with ovarian cancer. It attacks the lining of the stomach— the peritoneum—and subtly "seeds" its surface with tiny, malignant cells. Statistically, it is the equivalent of a death sentence: three to five years of life if treated. Total remission is extremely rare, as rare as 20 percent of those treated. The discovery of the disease does not necessarily indicate that the cancer has just appeared; it may well have established residence a few years earlier. But much of the grimness described above was either described less clearly to us at the time, or we, as a great number of new patients are prone to do, heard only optimistic words.

Liz was victim to a primary peritoneal carcinoma. That meant that there were no tumorous growths. The critical fact that we came away with was that, indeed, the cancer was treatable. On July 6, 1998, the treatment began.

Liz's coming to terms with her disease, a disease she was determined to outlive, inspired her and those who knew her well to live fuller, more productive lives. She had inspired me since the day I met her, but never more than when she determined that she would not be beaten down. "She loved life," Dr. Tom Weiner, her oncologist in Helena, Montana, told me recently, "and she loved living."

She died on a Tuesday morning, June 26, 2007. We interred her ashes the following Saturday on a lonely knoll about a mile and a half from the main cabin at Triple 8 Ranch, our favorite ranch in Montana, a place Liz adored. As I stood there and watched the lacquered Liz Red urn with Liz's ashes disappear into the earth, I knew that I must write about Liz, the inspirational Liz whom I loved.

I hope with all my heart that readers of my narrative will also come to be inspired by Liz and the life she lived.

. . .

After her death, I was deluged with letters from a vast variety of people: friends, of course, many people whom Liz and I had met through the work done at our foundation, many of her colleagues at the company, so many, indeed, that I was unable to respond to them all. Some, however, were so moving and so to the point that I decided to share them more broadly. The letters are enduring evidence of how Liz affected the lives of others. That gift of adding value to the lives of such a broad diversity of people was as natural for Liz as breathing. I include a few now, some excerpted.

The first appeared in a biannual newsletter written by Ken Wolff, Vietnam War Marine veteran and director of the Grounded Eagle Foundation, Kraft Creek Road, Condon, Montana. Ken is one of the most effective birds-of-prey rehabilitators in our country. He is a man of bone and muscle and outdoor-living skills. Jody, his wife, is soft-spoken and tenderhearted, expert in growing garlic and monitoring wounded birds, and a person who enjoyed Liz and whom Liz similarly enjoyed, despite the vastly different lives they had led.

We met Ken and Jody in 1986, our first summer as part-time residents of Montana. He had spoken at a Veterans of Foreign Wars meeting in Seeley Lake, a town about thirty miles south of Condon, and disabused his audience of the necessity to go to war in Vietnam.

We thought that this was a singular thing to do, so we called him and encouraged him to form the Grounded Eagle Foundation. The following is excerpted from the Spring 2007 issue of *The Raptor Room News*, a publication that is part diary, part advocacy and mainly about birds of prey.

"One special and courageous woman, Liz Claiborne. I watched Liz suffer from cancer for a decade. She never stopped smiling. Liz was one of the toughest people I have ever met, generous, gracious, unbelievably strong and determined, with a smile that melted icebergs. It was both an honor and a great pleasure to have shared some time and space with Liz."

This letter is from Katy Allgeyer to *The New York Times*. It appeared in the January 13, 2008, issue of the *Times Magazine*. Katy's letter was her way of commenting on an essay that Rebecca Johnson, a contributing reporter, had written for the magazine's "Lives Worth Living" issue. Liz Claiborne had been a part of its annual compendium of notable deaths for 2007. Ms. Johnson had ended her piece by highlighting the inspirational quality of Liz's life. Katy, a former Liz Claiborne knitwear designer, and now a feng shui expert, wrote:

"I had the privilege of designing for Liz Claiborne from 1983 to 1989. When Vogue *published a knit ensemble (skirt, shell top and long cardigan) in the mid-1980s, it was the first time Claiborne's line had ever made the pages of fashion's bible, despite—or perhaps because of—being the average American woman's favorite designer label. Most designers would have savored the moment alone, but Liz wrote me a personal note congratulating me for getting 'us' into* Vogue *with my knitwear designs.*

"I was proud to be part of her team, and I learned as much from her as to how to treat others as I did about design."

Ray Minella, the writer of the third piece, was the lead man at Merrill Lynch when the company went public. Ray and his small crew of assistants traveled with me to a number of large cities: San Francisco, Los Angeles, Dallas, Chicago, Boston and New York. Our job was to make the case for large investment groups to recommend Liz Claiborne Inc.—New York Stock Exchange symbol to be LIZ, offering price to be determined—as worthy of being in the portfolios of their clients. The audiences were generally skeptical. Despite the company's impressive track record (30 to 40 percent growth in volume, year after year, a similar growth in earnings and the high respect we had earned among both stock analysts and large retailers for our managerial skills and product excellence), the skepticism remained. Two big negatives were against us: first, we were an apparel company, an industry sorely disliked and distrusted for its reputation of breeding shoot-from-the-hip, disorganized, certainly-not-thoroughly-honest managers; and second, the last successful public offering of an apparel company was that of Levi Strauss in 1977. We were seeking a much higher premium over earnings than had Levi Strauss.

This was considered a dubious strategy. But Ray had a stroke of genius: he sold the obvious. "This isn't an apparel company," he said. "This is the first pure play that responds to the new demographics: millions of women entering the work force." On June 6, 1981, the company went public. The offering was a success. Liz Claiborne Inc. became the second most successful company that sold its shares to the public in the 1980s, second only to Microsoft.

This is what Ray wrote to me a number of weeks after Liz's death:

"Dear Art: I have been carrying this card around with me for some time, on flight after flight, hoping that I would find something profound and comforting to say in the wake of Liz's passing. I haven't. I've heard it said that if it wasn't for death, life wouldn't be so precious, but I don't think that's true. For someone like you, who was lucky enough to find the love of your life, I suspect you would have been happy just to enjoy her company forever and that life's relative shortness was unnecessary in making life sweet and meaningful.

"Liz was surely a wonderful person: talented, energetic, beautiful, vivacious. She had all the great virtues, but the smaller ones, too. I think she was the most famous and least impressed with herself person I ever met. I'm sure it was a joy to wake up in the morning, knowing you had the rest of the day to be with her. And as wonderful as that

was, it must now be awful not to have her to share every day with. I can only imagine...

"I guess there is one comforting thing I can think of...it's as much as you were proud of her, as much as you looked forward to spending every day with her, that's how much she loved you, was proud of you, and looked forward to every day she had with you. I think that's as good as it gets. And you did that for her, and I think that's worth more than anything."

I have done much of the writing of this narrative in our beautiful apartment on Fifth Avenue in Manhattan, where Liz and I shared a small study. The apartment itself overlooks Central Park, now in full bloom. I think of this apartment as Liz's most adored place as her life and health ebbed. It is here that I keep these letters. It is here that I keep photographs, documents, every remembrance of Liz and our life together that I have searched out and found this past year. I have mounted on my study wall a collage of some of these photographs, many of Liz alone at one point or another in her life, many of the two of us over time, many of Liz in a group. They all, for me, and I would imagine for many others, show Liz as captivatingly beautiful. She was lithe and boyish of build, graceful in movement, capable of "creating" herself with a turn of her head, or the velocity of a smile, or a gesture, all unrehearsed, all spontaneous. The photographs are mute reflections, however; they tell us nothing of Liz's selflessness, or that she gave of herself to those she loved and demanded nothing in return. Time was her ally then; her confidence and wholeness became more a fixed part of her as she lived her life. She grew as an integrated, whole person with each passing year. And I, as life insists, grow older. Yet I live with this ageless Liz every moment of every day and will do so until I too die.

I have interviewed many people who knew Liz well. I have used their comments, recollections, insights and feelings about Liz as honestly as I know how. I feel that I have faithfully done the research as Liz would have wanted me to do. I have had access to a mountain of photographs, many taken by Liz, many taken by others, some by me. I have a record of communications, faxes, e-mails and letters that I feel will help me as I try to bring Liz back to life. I feel it's important for me to revisit my life with Liz, those times that remain acutely remembered and those times, particularly the difficult years of her illness, so deeply engraved in my mind that my every thought was captive to her struggle for life. But as my speaking with others who were deeply involved with Liz opened new insights, I became convinced that the story of Liz is an important one.

Thus, this narrative. I hope that you will see why I feel it's important for you to know about Liz. Knowing about her, I feel that you will be inspired to accept that what we have perceived as the outer limits of courage, integrity, endurance and determination are far short of what we are all capable of; that kindness, humility and love of beauty are critical to the molding of a civilized life, of a civilized world. I also feel that Liz's example will convince you of the great human potential in all of us, that life is a gift to be treasured and that how you live it matters. She showed us all that striving to do better, be better, matters.

CHAPTER ONE

DURING THE EARLY hours of June 25, Liz knew her struggle was ending. She had asked Sharon, her night nurse, when I would be there.

Liz was ready to die. She would finally breathe her last in the bed where she had lain for the past six weeks, in room 252, 10th floor North, New York-Presbyterian Hospital. She wanted nothing more than to be released from that hospital bed that held her body captive for so many weeks. Liz was seventy-eight years old. I was eighty. She had shared her life with the disease since 1998, discovered when she was sixty-nine, I, almost seventy-two. Despite the accumulated years, we never thought of ourselves as elderly people.

The room had two large double-hung windows overlooking what I ruefully called "Pebble Beach." The beach was actually the top of an adjoining building. Staff had attempted to make it look beach-like by scattering granite pebbles on its surface. That surface had been Liz's view of the world for quite some time, a dreary final view for someone who had been a creature of the pleasures of seeing. I had done my very best to enliven room 252. There was a bulletin board on the wall facing her bed. I had thumbtacked photographs of her grandson, her puppy, anything meaningful or diverting. We had watched movies together on the room's DVD player. She and Sharon had watched a Bette Davis movie that evening.

It was humid, warm to the point of discomfort. Those days at the end of June that year were sticky, but clear and rainfree. Nonetheless I found them stifling, full of gloom.

I had called early that morning and, after speaking with Sharon, I told her how I appreciated her presence. I could feel her distress. She told me that Liz had asked when I would be there. Sharon told Liz that I was on my way. Liz smiled. She thanked Sharon for being with her throughout the night. Liz had spoken of her years of living with cancer, of fighting to live on. But the struggle was over. She was now ready to die. She asked Sharon if she would be coming back that evening. Sharon said she would not. Liz then shook Sharon's hand and thanked her for hearing her out.

"She was something, that lady," Sharon later told me when I spoke with her by phone. And then she repeated, after a moment or two, "She was something, that lady."

I came, my last morning in room 252, kissed Liz as I did every morning and sat next to her on her hospital bed. Elisa Haber, her day nurse, who would be with Liz until 8:00 PM, had also arrived and was taken aback at the change in Liz since the last time she had seen her.

Liz opened her eyes and, as always, reached for my hand. "I'll be leaving you soon darling," she said. "I know," I said. "It's OK. It's alright." She closed her eyes and fell back. She dozed off, her body going limp one moment, twitching and irritated the next. I did what I could to soothe her, but my eyes were flooded and accepting her dying was beyond me. I stroked her hand and sat blindly, it seems, for hours. I watched over her, knowing that she was anxious beyond description to be released from the physical distress she had suffered for so long.

"It's alright," I kept saying. "It's alright."

Elisa, quietly sobbing, lightly wrapped Liz's legs with gauze to absorb the weeping of fluid through her tissue-thin skin. From time to time she shifted Liz about in bed to keep her as comfortable as she could. Poor Liz had become impatiently edgy and frustrated; she so badly wanted it all to end.

Liz's doctors stopped by the room during the day and into the evening. Dr. Mark Pasmantier, Liz's primary oncologist, ordered that Liz was to receive morphine as soon as she felt pain. Her bronchial tubes were giving way. The fluid seeping into her lungs was beginning to cause pain.

Dr. Raymond Sherman, a kidney specialist who shared quarters with Dr. Barry Hartman, our internist, had been called in to help correct a low albumin count. He failed to do so, but in the process had become Liz's new friend. He demanded nothing of her. She felt he was her one ally. He spoke calmly and soothingly. When he left her room, her spirits were up. But this day was different. She spoke with him for a few moments and then slept.

By two in the afternoon, Liz was put on morphine to be applied every three hours.

I held her in my arms as she slept. My mind had become an endless hole of emptiness. I could in no way envision a life without her, mortally ill, helpless, whatever her condition.

By five o'clock, we changed the dosage of morphine to every two hours. Liz was now utterly defenseless. The morphine dosage was strong enough to take her life quickly. She suddenly opened her eyes and reached up for me. "Please, please let me go," she pleaded.

"Soon, soon, darling. I promise you, very soon."

I held her to me, my beautiful, ravaged wife. The morphine had taken over. She sank back, comatose as she would be to the end. I released her, for the very last time.

• • •

Liz and I had left the company at the very end of 1989, or, as I often put it, the company left us. We had semi-retired a year earlier, working as a couple alternate months of the year. I now believe that this part-time approach was an unrealistic, self-indulgent strategy. It was a strategy that could not help but demoralize many of the sportswear design staff and in no positive way prepare the company for the years ahead. The design staff felt afloat. The young designers, try as they did, did not think and "see" as Liz did. It became clear that the team we had helped put into place so that all bases were covered could not work together as a team. Operations and merchandising had taken a back seat to sales. In our absence one person dominated and that person was Jerome Chazen. Chazen, who joined the company in April 1977, was by far the senior member of the new team. He was a large shareholder. He had strong relations with many of the members of the board. He was the most experienced and most qualified to be chairman of the board.

We tried to engineer our travel plans so that we could attend periodic board meetings, an obligation neither of us found productive and that Liz found emotionally draining. We had planned 1989 as a year of getting away, keeping busy, crammed with movement to new places and excursions to be with Liz's family. Among many other things, it was the year that Liz met her first terrifying blizzard. We had flown around the world in March, a trip of 26,000 nautical miles, sixty hours in the air. We had chaperoned Liz's mother and close family from Wivenhoe in East Anglia, England, where Liz's brother Louis lived, to Brussels in Belgium for a sentimental family lunch. We had explored eastern Montana in September, dragging a horse trailer with us, had been stunned by the ragged beauty of Utah in October with Liz's oldest brother, Omer, and his wife Jeanette. I will be describing all of these activities in much greater detail later, but for now I will concentrate on the events as they relate to our departure from the company.

• • •

We were planning to end this fascinating and adventurous year with a journey to Machu Picchu.

This is the sequence of events. No matter what one's sightseeing plans may be, one must first arrive at the major airport in Lima, the capital of Peru. It was a brilliantly clear late afternoon as our driver lunged forward through the ominously happy and laughing people strewn about the streets. Hands were thrust in our open window, begging. Our driver swatted them away and grinned a gap-toothed grin at us. Flowers were everywhere. The air was saturated with a mysterious scent: offal, perfume and the aroma of unrecognizable foods being simmered. How to be enthralled and terrified simultaneously was a state of mind we had come to accept.

Our hotel was safely hidden in the exclusive Miraflores section of Lima. Once in our suite, Lima was no longer ominous. It was a city where wealth created a deluded but pleasure-filled reality. We dined well, slept well and flew off to Cuzco the next day where we readied ourselves for the jaunt to Machu Picchu.

Cuzco, once the administrative center of the Inca Empire, sits in the southeastern part of Peru. It is the regional capital and had, at that time, a population of about one hundred thousand people. Cuzco is perched in the Peruvian Altiplano at an altitude of 11,000 feet. We were booked into the Hotel Libertador, a medieval Spanish hotel, more of a hacienda than a hotel, actually three appendages surrounding a one-hundred-square-foot patch of garden. We had been driven there from the tiny airport, taken immediately to a bar on the lower level of the hotel and given a local, therapeutic concoction to counteract the vertigo that attacks at this new altitude. (Whether this is custom or therapy remains unresolved.) The drink is called "coca tea," derived from the leaf of the coca plant indigenous to the southeastern part of Peru. Its color is a pale, insipid green Liz felt to be unattractive, but the drink itself was fine, bland but calming enough to permit Liz to walk about, to photograph local peoples who were perhaps more curious about us than we were about them. Then we went back to the hotel, to bed and were up early for the planned trek to Machu Picchu.

We had long had Machu Picchu, a wonder of ancient Peru, in our must-see folder. Machu Picchu, or Old Mountain in the ancient Incan language, was built in the fifteenth century as a religious complex. It sits high in the Andes, contains the wreckage of many ancient temples of worship and had become, to our dismay, a super major tourist attraction. Visiting Machu Picchu was my idea, not Liz's. She saw nothing of interest in ancient rocks scattered forlornly over a moonscape, a moonscape difficult to get to at that.

It requires a train ride of about six hours to get to Machu Picchu. The morning train leaves at 6:00 AM and climbs over serpentine uphill tracks for about six hours. Then you and a trainload of howling youngsters and grouchy oldsters are at Machu Picchu. The train trip back down, possibly more terrifying than the trip up, takes four hours. But when we took a cab to the train station and approached the ticket window, we found ourselves at the end of what seemed an enormous line of screeching children and overstuffed adults carrying bulky baggage. No conversation was necessary. Liz and I wheeled about and reentered the cab. So we never made it to Machu Picchu. Only the guidebooks, breathlessly read, formed the basis of our imagined trip. All of this had been a somewhat farcical end to a very serious year.

We had gone to a great deal of trouble to spurn the wonders of Machu Picchu only to end the trip back at our Cuzco hotel.

The concierge at La Libertador was not surprised to see us. We were far from the first American tourists to have a change of heart at the train station. We were told that a phone call from New York awaited us. I suspected we would be asked to vote on a controversial subject, one in which we were in the minority. "Can't it wait until the next board meeting?" I asked. The answer was negative.

"Hold on, we'll get back to you."

• • •

My mind drifted from that small suite in Cuzco to past times, to the road we had traveled together over the years and that had brought us to this room, this time and this event. My thoughts became focused on the Liz who I had come to know in all of her uniquely-Liz facets. I hear her again as she describes herself.

"I loved art," she often said, "and I loved sewing. So I would become a designer." She became *the* designer of her time.

This is the story of Liz during the golden years before the intrusion of the disease and Liz, the afflicted, the Liz who finally failed as we all do and will, but whose failure was a tribute to life and the living of it. She lived her life, mindful always that life is a glorious gift on which we spend all our strength until our bodies give way.

I began my journey into the past in August 2007, meeting three times with Liz's gynecologist and thus far a total of eleven times with her oncologist. It had become clear to me that, however I dedicated the rest of my life, I must start with a refocusing on my years with Liz. I had been so intensely absorbed in her losing struggle with the disease for the last ten months of her life, from the end of August 2006 until her death, that I had completely blotted out the details of the beginning. I had thought of nothing else during those many months other than getting her well, willing her to be well and cured. I had to retrace the events of the beginning when the cancer was discovered.

I have spoken with scores of people since then: nurses, manicurists, dental hygienists, friends with whom we spent substantial time during the good and bad times of Liz's treatment, family and whoever I felt might give me an insight that my closeness to Liz and my focus on my relationship with her might have caused me to miss.

The Liz of the company years grew dramatically as a spokesperson, as a self-assured, vivacious, commanding human being. As Ray Minella pointed out, she was "the most famous and least impressed with herself person" he had ever known.

The Liz of the adventuresome, cancer-free years, 1989 to 1998, was a person growing in poise, confidence and articulation. She somehow grew more beautiful as time passed. She was slender and active, stood five feet six inches tall and weighed about one hundred twenty pounds; her voice a honey contralto, with a hint of magnolias, her stride firm and graceful. She was all charm and sunbeams.

The Liz of the cancer years was no less forceful a person, but with time, her magic blend of uniqueness, courage, elegance and kindliness became who she was. As her weight fell away she became frail in frame, but far from frail in spirit. Her smile never lost its power.

"I used my smile as a little girl as a way of putting others at ease: my duckies, for instance, or my pony," she told me once, early in our marriage, as she recounted memories from her childhood in Brussels. "I was no novice at speaking softly. I always spoke softly to my duckies. They were so easily frightened. There wasn't much for me to do during the day in our house in Waterloo, a suburb of Brussels, so aside from riding my pony, gardening, helping my mother or watching her sew, I fed my duckies. I loved it when they came waddling toward me and I would say 'here duckie, duckie,' and there

Liz with her duckies and earlier with her pony in Brussels, in the 1930s.

The children—Omer, Liza and Louis, 1931; Omer Villere Claiborne and Louise Fenner Claiborne with little Liza, 1935.

they were. And then I fed them corn out of my hand. I was thrilled."

I think of her love for animals as my mind's eye sees her again in Central Park after we had moved to Fifth Avenue in New York City in 2001. It was late March and Liz was feeling just great. She had undergone radiation in January and had not had chemotherapy for months. We loved our new apartment overlooking the park; we loved our morning walks together, dodging people and dogs as we power-walked—yes, she power-walked.

She stopped at the Alice in Wonderland monument. This was her favorite place in the park. This particular morning we watched a young woman and a group of children she had in tow. They, like virtually all children who saw this monument, adored this life-sized Alice and her zany friends: the Mad Hatter, the March Hare, host of the tea party, the Cheshire Cat and the Dormouse. The children crawled all over the bronze figures, rubbing the worn surfaces, laughing and shouting joyfully. They became, as I imagine the sculptor hoped, living parts of the life-sized monument. "Isn't that marvelous," Liz asked. "How much those children are enjoying being here with Alice. They love them. Good for whoever made this possible." She read aloud, "In memory of my wife Margarita Delacorte who loved all children. George Delacorte."

Standing beside Liz, this glorious, hopeful morning in the park, led to more memories. Liz did not make a point of loving all children, but she loved seeing the beautiful interaction between young people and the places

22

they felt were put there specifically for them. Whether it was one-on-one or Liz with a group at a fitting or working on color ranges, it was to Liz very much alike. It was fun play, as in the park now; as it had been in Bilbao.

As though we traded thoughts, we both arrived at the same recollection: our trip to Bilbao, Spain.

"Do you remember that fabulous room?" she asked. "Of course I remember it," I said.

On October 19, 1997, the week of the opening of the museum to the public, we had stood in the atrium of the shining new Guggenheim Museum in Bilbao. Bilbao was an aging port city in the process of reinventing itself. It had been an industrial center; now it was to become a modern city, a technological center and, significantly, a cultural center. The museum became the first strong statement toward fulfilling that objective. The city sits a few miles inland of the Bay of Biscay, in northern central Spain. It is the largest city in Basque country.

"Museum" seems to me now much too grown-up a word for what I'm sure children perceived as a teetering funhouse. Huge blocks of silver and bronze titanium, Tinkertoy oblongs, rectangles, rhomboids and lopsided squares wrestled with one another and had created an outer shell in a state of lasting tension for this magical building. Frank Gehry, the architect, had created a free-flowing building. We were entranced. We remembered the effect that the building had on the townspeople of Bilbao: pride and awe for the grown-ups. But for the children we watched on that bright October afternoon, the effect was sheer joy and wonder.

Memory may create a fictitious past, but Liz and I remembered alike the long rectangle of an installation just to the right of the atrium. It was a room about fifty feet long and thirty feet wide. The floor was the only element you could safely identify as a level plane. The walls were made of brightly painted interlocking shapes, sloping, dipping and falling away.

Triangles ingested triangles, wainscoting snaked around the room in traffic-light yellow and other electric colors. And in this uncertain jungle of shapes, children hooted and roared laughter, ran about, touching the walls where they could, hugging one another.

"Almost like clothes," Liz said. "Clothes on a hanger are dead and flat. Clothes on a confident body in motion are alive and full of energy. So it is with this space."

We remembered that day in Bilbao as we stood in front of Alice. "How glorious that day was," Liz said. "How unforgettable."

I've been remembering the Liz of the not-yet-bloated company and her vigorous enjoyment of working with her young assistant design staff. She and they, whether it was one-on-one, or Liz with a group at a fitting or working on color ranges, seemed to me to be at play. Serious play, of course, but I could easily see how much she loved the interaction.

I recall one especially significant morning, the morning of our twenty-fifth wedding anniversary, July 5, 1982. We had been a public company for a little over one year. It was a day of great satisfaction. It had taken courage, skill and good fortune to bring us to this room. As usual we would be having dinner with a number of our staff. Liz's son, Alex, had flown in from California to join us.

We had started the day on a happy high note, with a brisk walk from our apartment on 56th Street to our offices, fifteen minutes away, at 1441 Broadway. We walked as always, hand in hand.

Monday mornings were allotted to the design staff, this one for a color meeting. Liz started today's lesson. "Today we're going to spend some time learning how to condense a color, to compact the essence of a color, so to speak, by squinting at it."

She narrowed her eyes, held up a color at arm's length and squinted as she gazed ahead. "Squinting," as Liz had said, was evidently the most effective way of "seeing" the particular subtleties of a color.

She asked, "Well, Betty, what do you think? Is there too much green in the color?" Betty took the color from Liz, held it up, and copied Liz's squint. "I don't think so. Liz, I think it's fine as is and it looks right as part of the range."

"You may be right, Betty. Chris, Kathy, Tracy, what do you think?" And then, when some consensus had been reached, she turned to me and asked, "Well, darling, what do you think?" I had my faults, but Liz trusted my color sense.

Chris broke in before I could answer. She was our designated color-matcher. This was all vital-to-know material. "Liz, where did you learn to squint?" she asked. "I see how it focuses my eye and it works. But you taught me. Where did you learn your special way of seeing?"

Liz stood against the table, spread her arms out and leaned in, resting her body on her palms. Her many silver bracelets slid down each arm and

Liz with her design staff, 1982.

rested on her flattened hands; her fingers were illuminated by lacquered red manicured nails. Liz would wear as many as three or four silver bracelets on each wrist. But essential to the look were her manicured nails. Liz Red they were called, the derivation of which Chris was to make clear.

"OK, but be prepared to be bored to tears," Liz said. "Do you know why I spell so strangely? I don't think it's strange. I think English spelling is strange, but that's because French was my first language. So where words are similar in English and in French, I tend to spell the word in the French way. 'Familly,' for instance. In French, the word is *famille*."

I was leaning against the back wall of the design room, wondering why Liz was unrolling her life's story in response to a simple question. But I could see that it was important to her to tell her story. After all, this day was a signal day in her life. And so she went on.

"Everything that's happened in my life has brought me to this table and this long-winded explanation. I was born in Brussels and didn't speak a word of English until I was ten years old. That's when the war began and we left Belgium. I spent the summer in New Orleans being tutored, being readied to go to a real American school. It was horrible. English grammar and spelling were particularly horrible for me. And then we moved to Mountain Lakes, New Jersey. That's down the road from Morristown. I did sort of go through primary and secondary schooling, though only until my sophomore year. I took the same European history course three times and never got to American history. How bizarre, the French would say, but that's what happened.

Liz, who never graduated high school, in New Jersey, circa 1945.

And I did take every art course that was given. I never graduated. But I had been educated at home, more or less. Like a homeschooler. And when the war ended, we went back to Europe."

I thought about the events of the last weeks at the company. What might have happened to focus Liz's mind so determinedly on her past and the full value of that past? She had had a run in with one of our partners during a short budget meeting; just the four of us. Something was said that really nettled her. Liz lost patience and, for once, control. She picked up a pencil and threw it at the offender. In our industry that isn't much. Designers have been said to throw shears. The incident troubled her. We didn't speak about it. There had been no apologies. The short meeting became even shorter.

That was the only time in the thirty years I had known her that anger and frustration had moved her to violence, pencil-throwing violence.

I realized that she had been more private in her thoughts than was the norm for her. It now seemed to me that she felt an urgency to connect more intimately with her design staff. I settled in to listen further.

"My father was the head of an American bank in Brussels, a banker who loved paintings, beautiful buildings, landscapes. He was a man of immense pride, easily hurt, vulnerable. After all, he knew he was a direct descendant of the first and second governors of Louisiana. He needed obedience and respect. My mother came of an old Creole family that had had tons of money, still did, but not nearly as much as before the crash. It was rumored that her father was off the wall and had to be kept locked up in a closet. Imagine that, my grandfather locked up in a closet. Nevertheless my mother, beautiful and delicate, made the best of things. She was a wonderful seamstress. She loved making clothes. I loved watching her."

Liz stopped for a moment, sipped a drink of water and sat down. One of the staff had pulled a chair over so that Liz could at least sit if she were going to ramble on. And ramble on, she did.

"Now, where was I?" Liz asked. "Oh yes, the war ended and back we went to Brussels. I was first sent to a convent, racier in many ways than our raciest high schools of the time. My father thought that a finishing school was just the right thing and that a convent would properly finish me. But there was a wonderful art history teacher and I immersed myself in that. The next two years my father allowed me to go to a painter's studio to study serious painting. He thought I should become a serious painter, a proper activity for a woman."

Well, I thought, Liz rarely spoke at this length on any subject. And Liz's father, always regarded as a man of very strongly held opinions and prone to voicing them, was then still alive. After years of separation they had reconciled. It was not a dramatic, effusive reconciliation. He would have considered any spontaneous show of affection excessive and indiscreet. But nonetheless she knew he was proud of her. Perhaps this was her way of paying homage to him.

"My father quit the bank in 1948. I came back to the States the following year, spent the summer in New Orleans with my Aunt Clarisse, my father's sister. That's where the tedious tutoring took place and where I read about the *Harper's Bazaar* design and sketching contest."

Oh yes, I thought, the famous *Harper's Bazaar* contest, an annual event that elicited sketches and designs from young people all over the country to be adjudged for originality of design concept and skill at sketching.

"Well, to everyone's horror, I won. I designed a military-look coat. It was even produced and sold at Lord & Taylor. The grand prize was a trip to Paris and a visit to the studio of Jacques Heim, the designer, and a week of visiting with French couturiers. Well," she again sipped from her water glass, "wasn't that something?"

I could see she was getting a bit worn out, but the staff people were entranced. They could listen to Liz forever.

"So the next year was spent studying at the Academy of Art in Nice in the south of France. There was a wonderful teacher. He took me into the countryside on a painting trip and told me, 'Now I'm going to teach you how to see.' And he did."

And now Liz stood up again and said, "Squinting is just a way of seeing."

Liz, as she often did after making a point, emitted a wide, happy smile.

As I listened I wondered if Liz would tell the story of the stoplight. Her mother and father, having just returned from Europe, were driving back to

Liz and her mother Louise Fenner Claiborne leave for Paris, 1949. Liz and Jacques Heim—toast to the winner, Paris, 1949.

Harper's

ORIGINAL DESIGN CONTEST *Winner: Elisabeth Claiborne*

Elisabeth Claiborne received the **Grand Award** in the **Original Design**

Contest . . . a trip to Paris, via Air France, as guest of the famous couturier

Jacques Heim for ten busy days. Miss Claiborne's designs were entered through **A. Harris,**

Dallas and were judged the winning entry over twelve other national finalists.

Miss Claiborne is just 20 . . . is from New Orleans, Louisiana . . . attended

St. Timothy's School . . . in Baltimore and studied art in Brussels . . . Her winning

coat design will be manufactured by Linker & Herbert for the Jacques Heim Jeune Fille

line and will be found in stores throughout America.

The twelve other finalists who competed for the grand award are:

Betty La Mothe, Wilmington, Julius Garfinckel;

Norma Jeanne Stothers, Kansas City, Kan., John Taylor's;

Jean Cordes, Carmel, N. Y., Country Shop;

Evelyn G. Wong, Chicago, Carson Pirie Scott;

Joy Rosenblum, Youngstown, The Higbee Co.;

Joan Block, Springfield, Mass., Manhattan Shop;

Verna Gamble, Jensen Beach, Fla., Nina Ray Swift;

Dolores Gayle Martin, Virginia Beach, Thalhimer Bros.;

Betty McGarr, Flushing, N. Y., B. Altman;

Jean Andre, Worcester, Mass., Jordan Marsh;

Bonnie Bartell, Eugene, Ore., Frederick & Nelson;

Phyllis Yampolsky, Phila., John Wanamaker.

New Orleans. Omer Villere Claiborne did not drive. His wife handled that chore. At a stoplight, soon after the trip began, Liz announced to her mother and father, "I'm getting out here. I'm going to find work in New York. I'm going to be a designer."

Omer Villere Claiborne was unfazed. He got out of the car, opened the trunk and put Liz's suitcase on the sidewalk. He handed her a fifty-dollar bill.

"Good luck," he said and got back into the car and closed the door. The light changed. The car drove off. But that's not what Liz was now saying.

"When we got to New York I struck out on my own. My whole life had prepared me. I was now ready to go through my apprenticeship, just as you all are doing now. I had been very fortunate. My father and mother had made me aware of beauty and determination. I owed so much to them for the schooling that they had exposed me to. I had been encouraged to take classes in art and to study with painters. I had been encouraged to find my life in the visual world."

I was leaning against the back wall of the design room. It had become clear to me why Liz had unrolled her life's story in response to a simple question. She needed to make sure that certain feelings she had carried for years would be shared beyond her sharing them with me. It had become necessary to share herself with young, talented people.

Color meetings, line-planning meetings were daily events in the late 1970s and throughout the early 1980s. This day's opening of her heart was not. It had been a onetime performance.

• • •

I've been thinking about Liz Red ever since I began this narrative. I vividly recall the lacquered Liz Red urn in which Liz's ashes were buried. I remember other incidents that indicated to me that for Liz, Liz Red fingernails were as necessary as breathing. I asked Chris Brook if she remembered how Liz Red came into being. Here is what she answered:

"Liz Red was slightly to the yellow/orange side of red, definitely not the bluer direction and not in the middle either. It was warm and inviting and looked great with black and white houndstooth check. Flattering to the skin unlike the bluer, colder reds. She liked the yellower, warmer side of all the colors and very often we looked at lab dips together. Regardless of the color, her comments were to add yellow (even to

black). Liz Red was not a dark, overly bright or flashy color but on the lighter, softer side. It was like a tomato. It was also the color she wore on her nails (always, as far as I can remember), and her hands were very distinctive. The color looked great next to her tanned skin and was a trademark of hers as much as the glasses she wore. You couldn't help noticing her hands because of her rings and the bracelets that made noise as she moved. She had a tendency to softly touch our hand or arm, which was extremely memorable, and was a sign of either approval or sympathy, depending on the situation. I can vividly picture the color. We knew the kind of red she liked so we referred to it as Liz Red because she really disliked all other reds. Of all the colors, I think she had the strongest opinion about this one."

Liz wore Liz Red nail polish to the very end. She wore rings and bracelets as long as her fingers and wrists could support them.

• • •

The evening of our twenty-fifth wedding anniversary, Alex appeared at the dinner table precisely on time. He had moved to California in 1979 at the age of 25, and had the distinction of almost earning his living as a jazz guitar player. In 1979 the California guitar-playing constituency was possibly larger in number than either of the major political parties, so that skill was only one component of getting work. Showing up on time was as important as keeping your strings taut. And so he appeared at dinner on time.

Alex is slender and loose-limbed. His brownish hair is quietly receding, but thick enough so that the passage of time seems to have had little overall effect. His expressions are mobile and youthful. All in all, his general appearance is much like that of his father, Ben Schultz, whom Liz divorced when Alex was a baby. He's tall, about my height, and radiates sociability. He's good company. And so it was that night.

A number of Liz's staff joined us, somewhat solemn. They knew that Liz had been uncharacteristically open about her inner thoughts at the meeting that day. A number of my staff joined as well. This was an even more serious, schedule-minded group. We did not permit schedule talk that evening. We were merely going to enjoy being together. We quickly became a happy group who shared time and space and purpose with one another. It had been, lack of schedule discussion notwithstanding, as productive a day as the company had ever enjoyed.

Liz toasted and surprised us all. She lifted her glass and said, "Cheers. To we happy few, to all of us." We applauded.

• • •

Liz, without effort, emitted the same quiet energy on our quarterly Hong Kong trips. The company was now in motion, the Liz Claiborne label was dominant and our product was one of which we were all proud. The team was in Hong Kong to check pre-production samples, follow work-in-progress both as to quality and scheduling, tightening control of the mysteries of import and export fees, required documents, availability of quota, a world too arcane even for a PhD.

But key was the presence of Liz. Our suppliers loved her and she respected them. She taught by demonstrating, by putting her body into the work. She would crawl on a cutting table, pins in her mouth, cutting wheel in hand (the small rotary cutting wheel that perforates the pattern paper to indicate changes to be made in the pattern). She would place a pin here, a pin there and then look up and say, "See, just a little more slope on the shoulder and a little less bagginess under the armpits." And then she would beam at the onlookers. And all of her students, in this case the factory's cutters and patternmakers, would beam back and applaud. It was as if she had been born to demonstrate, to show how this or that is done, to teach.

We visited our Hong Kong office a number of times to walk the floor, comment on the wisdom of the feng shui architect, hear the complaints of the quality control people, discuss strategy with the office director and the product merchandisers.

Every morning of a Hong Kong trip, weekends included, we met the staff for an early breakfast at a corner table in the veranda. In the Peninsula Hotel the staff knew us well. Liz and I always booked rooms 505 and 506, called the "Gate of Heaven." From the late 1970s on, the suite had been our working and living home in Hong Kong.

Breakfast was routinely scheduled for 7:15 AM. Only Liz could break the schedule. I could feel the tension at the table as though all were straining at the leash. We were all "Liz people," whether from New York or from Hong Kong. At the time Liz arrived, the group was usually finishing their tea or coffee and ready to go. And then, this muscular, proud group was released, and like a pack of hungry carnivores, they dashed out of the hotel, briefcases in hand and burst into the flow of Hong Kong traffic. Liz and I sat alone. Claudia Wong, if this were during Claudia's tenure as director of our Far East operations, left to be sure our automobile was waiting out front.

We were both very happy and we were both having fun. To the outside world the company was a marvel. It seemed ready to go on forever. But we knew then, happy as we were in Hong Kong, that our hearts might well take us elsewhere.

• • •

And now we are back in our small suite in Cuzco, one of the many elsewheres to follow. It is December 1989, the end of a long, happy travel year. Liz and I continued to sip our coca tea. Liz was quiet. She rarely cried, but I could see tears forming. I was angry at myself. I blamed myself for having encouraged growth and more growth, despite her evident distress. But more than anything I was now angry at the board itself for its lack of consideration and respect for Liz, she who had made all the pomp and circumstance possible. We had lived through a number of brilliantly successful years, years of self-realization for Liz, years of pride and self-validation for me. And we had permitted the blanketing of the country with our clothes. We had permitted, I perhaps even encouraged, the use of the name of Liz Claiborne on a number of new product lines. All the while, as Liz grew in poise, in authority, in her ability to sell herself as she presented her clothes and the thinking that conceived them, the foundation on which all of our efforts rested was eroding, becoming less capable of carrying the weight of so much responsibility.

Our relationship with Jerome Chazen, from the time he joined the company, sixteen months after we were in motion, had been uneasy. The need to retain a Claiborne taste level and quality, a Claiborne design independence and a Claiborne culture did not seem to be nearly as important to him as it was to us. As painful as it would be, particularly for Liz, to blind herself to the future of her company, the need to end this sour and unproductive relationship drove our decision.

"I've had it, darling," she said. "Let's just resign. I feel like a fifth wheel at the board meetings. The first board meeting we didn't go to they voted themselves a clothing allowance, and when I let Jerry know how tacky and unlike us that was, he just shrugged and said, 'It's a different company now.' It certainly is, and it breaks my heart."

I put my arms around her and said, "I'm sorry, darling. I carry a lot of responsibility for the way we structured this company. Much of this is my fault."

"No, that's wrong," she said. "We did great things together, all of us. We had some wonderful times. We did something very important. But now, certainly for me, it's over."

I called New York and cast our negative vote. I said that we would be resigning from the board and retiring from the company.

• • •

We closed the last page of what had been a glorious time in our lives. Few are as fortunate as we had been. We were always mindful that together, and with a lot of help from our colleagues and friends, our lives had enjoyed blissful fulfillment.

I feel no less alone despite my gratitude for the years we were together. I write now about the Liz who was now essentially Liz Ortenberg, the person tempered by her self-awareness and thus knew who she was and sculpted the person she would become.

I think particularly about the value she placed on active engagement in the world she found so entrancing. I think of her visceral pleasure in working with young, open-minded people who had been encouraged to draw their conclusions from evidence they had gathered themselves. I recall her pleasure as I remember an evening in Nairobi in 1987, an evening I will describe in greater detail, when we and others formed our personal foundation, the Liz Claiborne Art Ortenberg Foundation.

It was through the foundation that we were able to recompense those idealistic conservation biologists who nurtured the rich abundance of life on our lonely planet. Through our foundation and the funds derived from our years at the company, we would demonstrate our reverence for the variety of living things that time had sustained. Even though we had no articulated strategy for how we would dedicate our lives after we left the company, it is clear to me now that there was a rationale behind the purchase of our villa in St. Barts in 1984 and our first ranch in Montana in 1985. This is how that came about and some of the events that followed.

Montana Highway 83, at its southerly junction with Montana Highway 200, Clearwater Junction by name, is approximately 2,200 miles from 1441 Broadway in New York City, Liz Claiborne headquarters, and on a straight line a bit more than 6,800 miles from the "Gate of Heaven." You know you're at the junction when you see a huge brown and white plastic cow on the northeast corner. It's about forty-five square feet and is actually there to announce the presence of a gasoline station that shares space with a general store. It also announces that this is livestock country. There's more to Montana than mines and trees and horses and wheat.

The highway runs north for about ninety miles, through densely forested land punctuated by tamaracks, lodgepole pine, groves of Douglas fir, here and there a stand of Ponderosa pine. Highway 83 is a two-lane road for the most part, considered by many to be the second most beautiful highway in the country, second only to California's Route 1. It winds past dazzling lakes that sit like a string of pearls to the west.

It was late June 1986. Liz and I had bought a plantation-style house in St. Barts in 1985. We were in the process of adding a wing and of making other adjustments, aesthetic as well as practical. And here we were, no long-term strategy discussed, looking for another home, this one in the American West.

It's surprising, as I think back over those events, that we never really planned these homes as part of our exit strategy from the company. Consciously or not, we were arranging a future life, independent of the company. I've often speculated as to what inner needs propelled us to St. Barts, to Montana, and the later wanderlust that highlighted our lives.

I know that I never felt I had a secure starting point. I had been born and brought up in Newark, New Jersey. My father had emigrated from Russia to Canada where he spent years as a peddler. My mother was born in Poland, a poor peasant girl who had worked in the fields and finally followed her three elder sisters to the United States. My parents met in Newark. My father's days in Canada had come to an end. They fell in love and were married. He was a handsome man, medium height, with long, full black hair, and vigorous, trusting and decent. My mother was a slight, pretty, timid, frightened girl, from whom all bad news was shielded. She became a seamstress. My father became a self-taught upholsterer, was ambitious enough to open his own shop, and lived out his life as a typical Jewish secular humanist, widely read, always in search of meaning. He was a lonely man who rarely found another person he could talk things out with, not even his too callow and self-involved son.

I was lucky, though. We lived across the street from a public library. The library became my second home. I found my reality between the pages of the books I devoured. There was no adventure story too romantic or implausible for me. There was no story of heroism and far-off places and far-off times that I found wearisome. I had traveled Montana with Bernard DeVoto. I had sailed the Caribbean with Nelson as he pursued the French fleet through Jamaican waters. I had sailed the southern oceans with Ross and Cook and Weddell. I had crossed the twenty-eight miles in the *James Caird* dinghy with one sail screaming in the wind as Frank Worsley, against all odds, brought Shackleton and the never-give-up Tom Crean from Elephant Island to South Georgia. I had searched for the Northwest Passage with Franklin and mourned with Mrs. Franklin when the crew and captain were found dead.

Liz, though, was rooted in her family's background. She collected our homes as a connoisseur would collect beautiful paintings. She loved to travel. She loved New York. She loved Montana and St. Barts and Fire Island. Life, for Liz, had become exhilarating.

We were now driving a rented car north from the Clearwater Junction to Tranquillity Lodge. Kim Baker, later Kim Brindel, my administrative assistant at the company, a person who was immensely important to our lives, avid and efficient in all undertakings, was a subscriber to Andrew Harper's *Hideaway Report*, a luxury travel newsletter. She had found Tranquillity Lodge, which was listed by the *Report* as the Hideaway Lodge of the Year. She made a number of calls and discovered it might very well be for sale. A Montana lodge seemed to all of us, Liz, me and Kim, just the perfect refuge. It was isolated and, according to Andrew Harper, until now, undiscovered. It turned out to be precisely as described.

Kim's centrality to our lives became more and more apparent over time.

We passed through Seeley Lake, a logging-dependent community of about two thousand people, the largest town nearby to Tranquillity. At Seeley Lake you knew you were in a valley, the Mission Mountains sloping downward to the west and the Swan Range dominant to the east. The Swan River cuts through to create the valley. I drove twenty miles further north to the thirty-four-mile marker, made a left turn and, after driving four dust-covered roads, we were at Tranquillity. It was aptly named. I knew the moment we parked the car that we had found our mountain paradise. The ranch house faces the softly eroded, breathtakingly awesome Swan Mountain Range. Fifty feet east of the lodge sits a larger-than-a-pond, much-smaller-than-a-lake body of water, which we later called Tranquillity Lake, regardless of its size. This is all-rugged, bewitching country, take-it-or-leave-it honest country. We phoned Earl McClane, the representative of the owners of the lodge. Earl was acting on behalf of a group of doctors from the Scioto Valley in Ohio who were using Tranquillity as a rest-and-rehabilitation lodge and retreat. The group had a problem. They were losing money, despite their paying Jerry and Roger Watson, the managers, very little, and possibly because too many dollars were going into liquor, a sure way of retreating. McClane and his wife flew from Ohio the following day, she enthusiastically carrying a suitcase full of Liz Claiborne clothes. We sat at the bar until well into the night and agreed on a price. That was June 30, 1986. The actual closing was one month later.

Tranquillity became our base in Montana, from which Liz would continue to develop her interest in working with young people, both at the elementary school in Condon, the local small post office town, and Seeley Lake, where we had a more ambitious program in place by 1988.

. . .

Liz frequently pointed out that she had had no formal education. But she had had built-in advantages that these rural young people did not have. And she discovered at the company that she enjoyed teaching and that good teachers, and good programs, involved parents. And we were the parents of our company. I didn't have to be sold. I loved being considered a part of these communities. Looking back, our work at the elementary school in the Swan Valley and the larger, more comprehensive program at the Seeley Lake Elementary School were to be essential components in our second careers in community-based work.

We had urged the Seeley Lake school board to create a preschool program, a means of giving Seeley Lake children a head start and relieving their working parents of the responsibility of day care. The children were to develop learning skills, social skills, and a sense of being a part of a greater, though largely homogenous, community.

We were extremely lucky that a young teacher, Sheila Devins, was available to get the program going and supervise it, as she continued to do, right through 2007. But the preschool program was only one component of a total school program. It basically stands alone, but forcefully creates a learning and teaching environment that is holistic in approach. The children are taught "everything" and they are taught to work with one another and help one another. We considered that aspect of preschool work valuable and worth emulating in the higher grades.

The post-preschool program in 1988 was aimed at enriching the full curriculum—math and science and music and the arts—and to foster a more intimate understanding of the natural wonders of the Seeley Lake landscape. The objective was to include the entire community in the work being done at the school. We planned events in which parents, teachers and students interacted to lay the groundwork for making Seeley Lake a more vibrant community. The town offered little to its young people once they had completed the required years of schooling. And as the young left the area, Seeley Lake became a less interesting place to live. We hoped that that the program would bring vitality and community to the town. We hoped that this program would encourage the children to think critically and not accept what was handed down to them as unassailable, objective truth.

This philosophy of teaching and learning was to become the driving objective of the Montana Heritage Project. Teachers would learn to use the community as classroom. We planned to introduce site-based learning strategies, give teachers and their students the freedom to integrate community research, the study of regional literature, and challenging writing assignments. This course of study, we felt, would cut across the lines of traditional single-subject study.

I find it surprising that this modest approach to open-minded thinking and learning is still regarded with suspicion by so many adults. It became the backbone component of the Montana Heritage Project. The trick, we believed at the time, was the willingness to be completely inclusive.

There are innumerable pathways to the creation of the Montana Heritage Project. No single person dominated, no single idea energized the program. The most obvious beginning point for Liz and me was at Triple 8, a second ranch that we had bought in 1990.

Triple 8 is located in Canyon Creek, Montana, just east of the Continental Divide and twenty-one miles from Helena. We bought Triple 8 because Liz had found the horseback riding in the alpine setting of Tranquillity to be overly constricting.

"Tranquillity," Liz told me, "lacks a wide open view. It has trees, beautiful trees, but I'd like to ride in more open country." We hired a real estate group that specialized in ranches that were an integral part of the surrounding landscape. A livestock ranch was for sale. It consisted of 3,300 rolling acres, a fresh stream running through the property, and mountains in the near distance. It seemed to us that the ranch had extraordinarily propitious feng shui. Thus the name Triple 8, a name that contained numbers that assured fortunate days ahead.

The owner had two sons, now grown and married with children on the way. The ranch was not capable of supporting three families. We bought it on sight. The main house was in a valley. That wouldn't do. Tom Moore, our long-term architect, was at that time a victim of advanced prostate cancer. We asked Tom to help site the main house and a number of sleeping cabins. He was far too ill to supervise the full year of construction, but Triple 8 was planned consistent with Tom's original siting. There will be more about Tom as the story continues. He had been the major intelligence behind the design and redesign of all of our homes until his death.

Construction began in 1990 and was completed in 1991. Tom never saw the finished product: a main family cabin, with living room area large enough to accommodate a small meeting, a dining room and a wonderfully efficient kitchen built to Liz's specifications, a kitchen in which she would work happily for years to come. The interior materials were all ruggedly beautiful: leather chairs, slate tabletop, stone floor, sliding semicircular doors opening to a magnificent 180-degree southerly view. We strung out four individual sleeping cabins, lined up east to west, to the south of what is still called Cabin A. We lived in Cabin B and the other three cabins were to be for guests and our children.

Liz's son Alex had come to love the outdoors. Living in California had made him a desert lover. He loved Jasper National Park, wildflowers, hiking and photography. We hoped that Neil and Nancy, my son and daughter from my previous marriage, would become lovers of the outdoors as well. They had grown up in Oak Park, Illinois. My former wife moved west, closer to her parents, after our divorce in 1957. Neil was then five years old, Nancy was three years old, and, as another proof that you can't engineer the future, neither ever came to love Triple 8 as we did. Triple 8 is where Liz is buried and where I will join her. But I've gotten much too far ahead of myself.

We were ready to divide our time between Triple 8 and Tranquillity by early summer, 1991. Ownership of Triple 8 is what put us on the Helena side of the Continental Divide. If you start your drive from Tranquillity to Triple 8 at Clearwater Junction, turn left and head east by northeast for about sixty miles, past Ovando, past the turnoff to Helmsville, home of the annual local rodeo, rodeos which Liz came to love, particularly when the bucking broncos bucked-off their riders. And then on and through Lincoln, a town about the size of Seeley Lake. Lincoln has the distinction of servicing the Blackfoot River, a destination point for trout fishing when the river was less polluted. It's a slow drive through Lincoln and then, about ten miles further on, you're at the juncture of Highway 200 and Montana Route 279, Lincoln Road. And now you're on a glorious, intoxicating drive through the Flesher Pass to the top of the divide with miles and miles of open, heavily treed land below you. The road traversing this landscape lies in serpentine coils, descending so sharply that the eye can absorb only a slice at a time. You're looking westward, back to the plateau-flat land over which you've just driven. The road sign indicates forty-nine miles to Helena. Triple 8 is at the twenty-one-mile marker. The drive from Tranquillity to Triple 8, at a no-nonsense pace, takes about two hours.

Had we not bought this ranch, a mere twenty-five-mile drive to the heart of Helena, it's doubtful that the Montana Heritage Project would have been developed. Nor, unrelated as it may seem, could we have held a fundraiser there for Dorothy Bradley in 1992. But that's where Marc Racicot entered the story. Liz was restrained in her political enthusiasms but not for this race. The governor's seat was at stake. Marc Racicot, Republican attorney general of the state, was Dorothy's opponent. Dorothy was a member of the state's legislature. She was progressive, slender, youthful and attractive and her positions on education spending and abortion were consistent with those held by Liz. So we had a smash of a fundraiser. Dorothy was introduced by the distinguished governor of Oregon, Barbara Roberts, a woman with an authoritative voice and the volume to carry it far into the hills.

Dorothy Bradley lost in a very close race. I felt she would have won, had she been tougher on her opponent. But Marc Racicot, it turned out, would become as responsible for the Montana Heritage Project as were Liz and I. Unprincipled person that I am, or was, according to Liz, I felt it necessary to get to know the new governor. We were in the conservation business and, like it or not, we had to befriend him. I found Marc knowledgeable and decent. He moved with grace, like a hunting creature. There was very little sideways to Marc. Once you knew he had been an all-star basketball player at John Carroll University in Helena, his quickness was no surprise. He never told me the astonishing record he holds to this day: the most assists in a single college basketball game—thirty-two. Astonishing! I enjoyed Marc's company. We never talked politics. Liz felt differently. She found his politics disagreeable. But she agreed that he had charm and that it was necessary to work with him.

Marc and his wife, Theresa, accepted an invitation to dinner at Triple 8. That evening at dinner, late in 1993, was the beginning of the marriage between our work in Seeley Lake and a Montana rural-town initiative that had taken place in 1944. Marc had brought along a copy of a book called *Small Town Renaissance: A Story of the Montana Study* written by Richard Waverly Poston in 1950. The book described the program, how it came to be and how it expired.

Marc had grown up in Libby, Montana, one of the small towns that had participated in the study. The needs perceived in 1944 were just as vital in 1993 as they had been fifty years earlier. The fulfillment of the original objectives—the necessity of making life in rural Montana towns more interesting and more exciting, a place for the children of the community to return to when their education was completed—remained unfulfilled though half a century had passed.

At dinner that evening in 1993, Liz and I were in agreement that the time was right to reclaim the original objective of *Small Town Renaissance*. We had already initiated a prototype of such a program in Seeley Lake. We described the work underway there to Marc. He was enthusiastic.

The Montana Heritage Project, in short, was an initiative that Liz and I conceived to teach the young people of Montana to see their own communities as valuable subjects of study. A number of high schools from various parts of the state would be invited to research the history of their own communities through studying archives, old letters, oral interviews, whatever relevant materials could be found. A specific subject would be chosen; the subject of middens, for instance, as described below.

The students would thus learn the history of the communities they lived in and explore how that history was affected by national and international events. But paramount would be an understanding of the cultural beliefs and practices that shaped the unique character of their communities. And most important, teachers were encouraged to invite student participation in subject matter selection. A product would be produced for the community, a product that students, teachers and community members generated. Ownership of the program was to be shared.

We all felt that a partnership with the Library of Congress was also important. Two of its departments, the American Folklife Center and the Center for the Book, spearheaded the Library's involvement. I had been a trustee of the Library, selected in 1986. My becoming a trustee was solely due to the fact that I was Liz's husband. The senatorial election in 1986 gave control of the Senate to the Democrats. The majority leader was Senator George Mitchell of Maine, as pleasant and congenial a person as you will ever meet. Bespectacled, with eyeglasses as large as those Liz wore, always smiling with perfectly arranged teeth, he was as gracious a party leader as desired. Since one of my responsibilities at the company was meeting legislators in Washington and working on trade issues, I made it my business to get to know Senator Mitchell. At that time, the Democratic Party was generally positive on trade issues, but not George Mitchell. He had grown up in Waterville, Maine, at that time a textile town. He told me that his mother had lost her job at the Lockwood Cotton Mill in the 1950s when the textile industry was moving south. In those days the beneficiary was Spartanburg, South Carolina. George never forgot.

As Senate majority leader, George could fill vacant trustee seats for the Library of Congress. One seat was open in 1986. I'm pretty sure that finding a famous woman to fill that seat was considered desirable. So George approached Liz. Her fame made her a natural choice. He called her directly. It took Liz a nanosecond to answer. "I'm sorry, Senator Mitchell," Liz said.

"I'm very flattered and very happy that you're our majority leader. But you don't want me. I'm not the big reader in our family. Art, my husband, is our reader and has been for years and years."

The Liz connection was essential. Without it I doubt that I would have become a trustee of the Library of Congress. That was the key that enabled us to bring the Library to the Montana Heritage Project.

Liz and I met with Jim Billington, the reigning Librarian of the Library of Congress, who gave the development of the program his blessing. We formed a working committee that included Governor Racicot; the head of the Office of Public Instruction, Nancy Keenan; the presidents of the University of Montana and Montana State University; the director of the Montana Historical Society and the library department heads. By the end of 1994, we were ready to go into action, find a director for the project and begin enlisting schools. Just as in the original Montana Study, the program was community based: one high school class, led by a teacher dedicated to the program, would create its own teaching and learning agenda. For instance, one school examined a huge midden (a refuse heap) just outside of town and traced the contents to early town usages. The class then studied the use of middens historically in Montana, in other parts of the country and globally. The question of waste disposal was then studied in its largest sense. This, remember, was in the mid-1990s. The final product in this case was a museum collection and a number of essays and slides shown and read to the community.

I could describe many more, but that would be a stand-alone book. It's a staggering realization that we worked in a dozen towns, each producing a product every year. Eventually, over five thousand students participated in this program.

To coordinate this effort we went on a search for a field director. Liz and I insisted on being a part of the search "working group." We got lucky. We hired Michael Umphrey, former principal of St. Ignatius High School, part-time ambulance driver, part-time town backbone when in a jam. St. Ignatius is an old mission town of about eight hundred people in the northwestern corner of Montana. Michael was well-read, had well-formed ideas about education and was a die-hard fan of John Dewey. We were in motion by the summer of 1995. The success of the program was largely due to Michael's hard work, knowledge and devotion. Even with the input of the Library of Congress, it's a rare person who could administer a program across a state as huge as Montana, with towns so far-flung.

• • •

Dr. Bill Conway is a man of greyhound elegance, with eyebrows out of proportion and quizzically aslant and an aquiline nose; a man as elegant in movement as he is in intellect. In 1982, he noticed that the Liz Claiborne Foundation, the charitable arm of the newly public company, had become the sole funder of *Nature*, a program created by the Public Broadcasting Service. Liz had been approached by the producers of the program, and she, a long enthusiast of animal life, pledged our share of the company's allotted charitable moneys, $100,000. We were the first donors to make available the funds to show the program weekly in the metropolitan area of New York. How proud we were. Bill, then general director of the Bronx Zoo, wrote a letter to Liz. He said he would be calling her soon to talk about the program and about the zoo's field programs as well. "We not only entertain and educate," Bill wrote. "We work throughout the world to conserve wildlife. Our field group is Wildlife Conservation International. I believe we have the most dedicated, capable, and best trained scientists in the field. Let's talk about how we can get you and your husband involved."

We met with Bill, were enchanted by his words, his appearance, and a touch of British intellect in his manner of speaking. He spoke slowly, reflectively, and, we thought, with forceful intelligence.

Liz was an easy sell; it might have been the memory of her duckies and her ponies, infused with her lifelong love affair with beautiful creatures. Conserving tigers became a major objective of the foundation. Jaguar conservation followed. In time she captured in her camera lens as many of the large African cats as she could safely find: lions, leopards, cheetahs. Elephants, in Liz's mind, were in a special, elevated category. It was their behavior that she considered transcendentally beautiful.

I was an easy sell as well. Liz's enthusiasm was sufficient reason for me to become enthusiastic, and the upper strata social group that seemed to be running this show was very appealing to a Newark native, delighted to be accepted in high society.

We became modest donors to the zoo, targeting our funds to its field-work. We continued to fund *Nature* through the company. I remember how pleased Liz was when she would tell me about the number of people who thanked her for the *Nature* series.

"A cabdriver turned around and said to me, 'Are you Liz Claiborne? I recognize you from a picture I saw of you.' I nodded, and he said, 'I just want to thank you for that TV program. My whole family watches it.'"

"Isn't that wonderful?" I said.

"It's more than wonderful," she said. "It's rare that people are as lucky as we are. We can indulge our passions and even get happy feedback."

• • •

In February 1987, it was time to see Africa and animals for ourselves. With the help of Bill Conway, a trip to East Africa was planned. We were given the mandatory important donor treatment. Our safari was charted from the day we arrived in Tanzania to our final departure from Kenya. Our guide was Jim Murtaugh, the curator of the Central Park Zoo, fresh from St. Catherine's Island off the coast of Georgia, where he had been studying—actually mainly chasing—translocated ring-tailed lemurs. Lemurs are indigenous to Madagascar, but they can be found in zoos and in habitats like St. Catherine's Island, where a small group of ring-tails had been raised so researchers could study their behavior without traversing half the world. Lemurs became another deep affection of our foundation.

Jim spent four years as curator of the Central Park Zoo after the 1987 trip. He was in his early forties, the son of a highly principled and intellectually rigorous father. We felt that Jim was made of material that would work well for the foundation, and we were right. He thinks things out methodically and is thoroughly honest. He also has an excellent memory. We hired him to be the program director of the Liz Claiborne Art Ortenberg Foundation in 1991. As our chaperone on the trip to Africa in 1987, a description of which follows, Jim was at the table with us when the foundation was formed. His intelligence and rigid adherence to the facts in the case, as he saw them, were and are valuable assets.

He is now considerably older, of course. If anything is to be said of his appearance, he is pleasant looking, with such intensity of concentration that even a cheerful "good morning" startles him. Everything else about Jim is medium: height, hair recession, weight, tenor of voice, demeanor. He is still program director, a walking encyclopedia of past foundation activities. His skill at pronouncing unpronounceable Malagasy names is formidable.

More theoretical than practical, more thoughtful than active, Jim remains with me now that Liz is gone. He admired her. I believe he was even devoted to her. He told me once, "I don't know anyone who can read people as well as Liz does. She doesn't fuss, but I can tell."

• • •

The 1987 trip was a wondrous adventure for Liz, me and Jim, as well.

The trip began in February 1987. We were still with the company at that time, but not firmly dedicated to daily work. We were now in our one-month-off routine from the office, just the perfect time for our first adventure in the wild. The weather was forecast as probably dry. Elephants were on Liz's mind. She was fascinated by the clan-like social life of the African elephant. We met Jim at Heathrow in London and flew to Nairobi, the capitol of Kenya, home then, as probably now, of an airport that radiated bedlam, full of beggars, hawkers of anything, even your own luggage. Translating the Kenyan shilling into dollars defied the most skilled mathematical mind. No one met us. Liz, as always, was fascinated and I, as always, bordered on paralyzing agitation, and failure as purveyor of macho. Not one hustler or beggar backed away.

Nevertheless, we made it to our hotel and chartered out the following day to the world-famous Maasai Mara and our tented camp, Kichwa Tembo, or "Head of the Elephant" in Swahili, the lingua franca of Kenya. The Maasai Mara (the Mara being the river that runs through the Serengeti) is situated at the foot of an escarpment in southwestern Kenya. The Kichwa Tembo safari camp is leased from Maasai chieftains and is consequently exclusive; a perfect setting for Liz and her cameras. The camp lay directly in the path of Africa's legendary migration of hundreds of thousands of wildebeest, zebra and a tasty assortment of ungulates. The migration begins in October, as countless hordes of animals head south in search of rain. In April they return, once more crossing the Mara River.

But the safari camp, Kichwa Tembo, serves a purpose more exquisite and moving than experiencing the surging migration. It is a quiet place where a person can sit alone in early morning stillness and watch an elephant clan lumber by, displaying all the grace contained in tribal caring for one another.

Liz was awake at five o'clock in the morning. She had left our tent and was seated on the top rail of a bench close to the border between the camp and the reserve.

Giraffes undulated by, regal, detached, swaying in beat to a song only they could hear.

One short moment later, an elephant clan, tightly clustered, slowly and quietly ambled by. In the lead was the matriarch, the oldest female in the clan, she who was responsible for the route the clan was walking, responsible for the safety of each member, she who halted as all the elephants halted when a calf had stumbled or fallen to its knees. The safety of the clan was all that mattered. If the clan came under attack from humans or a group of predatory animals, she shielded the clan and burst forth to confront the attacker. Her life might be forfeit to that one great responsibility.

It was at this moment, sitting on the top edge of the bench, camera in hand, that Liz had her epiphany. That is when elephants became Liz's religion. The family structure of the elephant clan became the symbol of natu-

Elephants—elephants—elephants, Kichwa Tembo Camp, Maasai Mara, 1987.

ral family ties, the way life should play out, the instinctive guardian role of the matriarch. Liz never unlearned that lesson. She would do what was required of the matriarch.

A close recounting of the many inspiring stops we made would require another book, so breathtaking and secure were Kenya and Tanzania in 1987. We spent a few days in Tanzania at a coffee plantation, getting a sense of how some Tanzanians lived with the land. We drove to Lake Manyara National Park for viewing. Manyara is a freshwater lake whose environs offer excellent viewing of elephants, leopards, baboons and hippos. A few years later Liz and I purchased a slice of land that created an elephant corridor from the lake to the park. You can still see the sign: "This road has been built with funds donated by the Liz Claiborne Art Ortenberg Foundation." We never seemed to make a public point of the work we had made possible in the field of conservation. But this was just one of many projects, some of which I'll highlight further on in the narrative. That corridor still exists and is critical to elephant movement for water. The purchase of the corridor established our relationship with that great elephant biologist, Iain Douglas-Hamilton. He became a friend and grantee of the foundation. He remains a champion of elephants.

Liz, Jim and I also spent a few nights in the Ngorongoro Crater, an extinct volcanic crater about two thousand feet deep, filled with game. Whatever created the crater trapped the wildlife living there at the time. It is now an area where wildlife flourishes and humans are the species who find the crater hostile to their pursuits.

We left Tanzania in an ancient DC-3, so energized by all we had seen that we overlooked becoming terrified at the shortness of the runway, where a scattering of Maasai women were clutching their babies to their breasts, dodging the grunting aircraft as it barely went airborne before the runway ended. We landed at Amboseli National Park, then a "must" stop in any safari agenda. There was a stunningly beautiful lodge. Somehow the blend of African and western forms, sinuous and functional, worked remarkably well. There was no color; all the interiors were black and white. But more important to us, this was where we met Dr. David Western, known by everyone as Jonah. Jonah was in charge of the Wildlife Conservation Society programs in East Africa. It was his on-the-ground research and conservation work that led to the establishment of the park.

Jonah was to become central to our lives. He also was to become a close friend, a person ranked among the three or four African elephant experts in the world. He grew up in Tanzania. His father, an Englishman, was in the insurance business. He allowed Jonah to run loose among the Maasai and Jonah did. He joined them in their meat-eating orgies. He spoke Swahili as well as Maa. He was trusted. And then one day his father was killed by a charging bull elephant. His mother returned to England, took her two sons to be educated in London, knowing that without a doubt Jonah would return, doctorate degree in hand, to Africa. His older brother, Martin, a notable wildlife photographer, is still close to Jonah. He lives in England.

It was this Jonah we met in Amboseli. He is among the most far-ranging and multi-talented conservation biologists in the world. Jonah was chairman of the African Elephant Rhino Specialist Group, a committee of the International Union of Conservation of Nature (IUCN), a fifty-year-old organization of scientists. In the 1970s and 1980s, Jonah played a vital role against the poaching of elephants for the value of their tusks. He was also among the most outspoken and professional advocates of the banning of the ivory trade under the auspices of the Convention on International Trade in Endangered Species of Wild Fauna and Flora.

I am astonished at how little he has changed these past twenty years or more. He is a tallish, slender man who moves with energy and purpose, each joint seeming to unwind as he strides forward, always forward. He is a man who reasons carefully and rarely finds less than three sound arguments to support his position. There is a sharp clip to his discourse. His words follow smoothly. His positions are always backed by solid reasoning and solid factuality.

We left Amboseli and spent the next evening in Nairobi at Jonah's home, also very much the home of Shirley Strum, professor of anthropology at the University of California, San Diego campus, author, baboon specialist, accomplished and attractive wife of Jonah Western. She is an engaging and lovely person. That she is a baboon specialist, having spent twenty-five years in the field among her social but rambunctious primates, renders her no less engaging. She and Jonah enjoy a good solid partnership that has produced a daughter, Carissa, and a son, Guy, who inherited the very best of the two of them. Liz liked and trusted Jonah and Shirley and was always pleased to use our friendship as a basis for reliable work in the field that she could fully support.

The evening of our visit, we arranged to have dinner at the famous Norfolk Hotel, Kenya's answer to comfortable ex-pat interactive living. The hotel was fronted by a long, not overly narrow veranda that was open to the street. The veranda permitted viewing of the political and social hierarchy in Nairobi. Those seated closest to the railing, sipping a fruit and gin concoction, were considered upper tier. Those wandering by on the outside walk, checking to see who was chatting with whom, were considered people on the way up, or often, people on the way down.

We had reserved a table in the Ibis Room restaurant and joined the significant people on the veranda for a pre-dinner drink. Our safari together had not been confined to viewing alone. We had become aware of our growing passion for the wildlife we had viewed. We had discussed our funding of the PBS series and how gratifying that had become. We were prepared to discuss the details of starting our own foundation. Finally we were beckoned to dinner. We walked through the long lobby, entered a large rectangular-shaped garden that served as the conduit to various amenities: a breakfast room, the Lord Delamere Terrace bar, and off to the left, in the back corner, the Ibis Room.

In 1987, the Ibis Room was a well-kept secret, about thirty feet square, dimly lit, elegant period furniture. There were five of us: Liz, me, Jim, Jonah and Shirley. We ordered our dinner, and then plunged into the heart of the matter. What would the next steps be to start the Liz Claiborne Art Ortenberg Foundation? This foundation would be ours, away from the company. We had three trustees: Liz, me and Jonah. The time spent in the field, the time spent with Jonah and our developing appreciation of what would later be known as biological diversity had prepared us. Liz and I fully understood that the educational work we were doing, the Montana Heritage Project for instance, would become separate and our personal responsibility. Liz and I would compensate the foundation for that work. But the raison d'être of our foundation was the protection of wildlife and wildlands. Zoos, we all felt, were fine for human entertainment, but were jails for animals. They extracted the wildness from an animal's behavior and that animal was no longer what nature had intended it to be. We wrote the mission statement at the table with all of the above in mind.

It was February 13, 1987. The statement read:

"The Liz Claiborne Art Ortenberg Foundation is dedicated to the survival of wildlife and the wildlands on which all life depends."

The statement was simple and direct. It could be faulted as paying little attention to the people who actually lived with wildlife: local peoples who depended not on wildlands, but on cultivated lands, and who suffered the consequences of wildlife invading their gardens and fields. At times more than crops were lost. Lives were lost.

For Liz and me, new to the world of creature conservation, the Ibis Room declaration was perhaps a bit naïve. Over the years we became more sensitive to the needs of the people who live with wildlife and who are dependent on natural resources for personal sustenance. But the evening in the Ibis Room marked, for the rest of our lives together, the beginning of our personal commitment to preserving wildlife around the world.

Ten years later, in the early spring of 1998, our board, now enlarged, met for the purpose of adapting our mission statement to the changing circumstances of the times. The wild places of the world had diminished. There were more people and consequently there was less habitat for wildlife. We agreed that our mission statement was in need of repair. Unless local people could find some benefit in living with wildlife, wildlife would disappear. Wild animals would be confined to zoos, or, if land was available, to reserves. Tourism became one answer, but in the long run, uncontrolled tourism could create havoc and disrepair in places animals frequented. And too often tourism is uncontrolled. The outlook for free-running wildlife was bleak in 1998 and has grown bleaker since.

As it has since 1998, our mission statement now reads:

"The Liz Claiborne Art Ortenberg Foundation is dedicated to the survival of wildlife and wildlands and to the vitality of the human communities with which they are inextricably linked."

The word "inextricable" carries a heavy, singular meaning, "a tangle from which the parts cannot be separated." The use of the word signifies not only the life force that humans bring to this world, but also the life force brought by wildlife and the many resources of nature. The word protects the whole.

The following programs were adopted while Liz was alive. There were a number of species that the Durrell Institute had identified as endangered in

Madagascar, from rare tortoises to lemurs to pond ducks and numerous others. Our funds and encouragement had not only preserved the species but had been critical for developing young Malagasy scientists.

Funding had also been instrumental in the Russian Far East, where we had worked with field scientists as well as village inhabitants to keep the four hundred Siberian tigers that had been identified on the ground alive and reproducing. Poaching had to be severely controlled, both of tigers themselves and the tiger prey base: ungulates, wild boars and small rodents. Working with the hunting community we were able to maintain stability in animal numbers for years. We had invested over $800,000 in each of these programs.

They could only be successful if local peoples were a key part of the programs. Liz was an enthusiastic advocate of the need for balance. That balance was reflected in programs we supported in the field. The work done in Madagascar was typical of our insistence on durability and professionalism in the field.

As I reread these lines, it becomes clearer to me why I chose this point to begin the story of Liz's new life, as well as mine. I realize looking back that many things, not just how we felt about the misdirection at the company, but also the acquisitions of our homes in the American West and our world travels, led us to this path. This was a new life that added immeasurably to the talents and sensibilities of the Liz we already knew. She, who loved life, loved life even more deeply now. She was becoming more expansive, more an advocate as well as a teacher and doer. Even the growth of the company, her final compromise, enabled our adventures.

• • •

The Ibis Room meeting went beyond the formation of the foundation. Jonah described the poaching threat under which elephants lived. He covered the issues in the ivory trade and the groups involved. Jonah educated us as to the value of organized action to save elephants from extinction. Elephants were being killed at the rate of nearly five per hour. It was clear to Jonah and painfully clear to Liz that an ivory trade moratorium was crucial to elephant survival.

Liz, who normally would shut her mind to acronyms—CITES, the Convention on International Trade in Endangered Species, for instance—was alert and involved. She listened carefully to the facts of the ivory trade. "Jonah, what can I do to help?" she asked.

"First," he said, "I'll get you more material to read. We're pushing for a total ban on trading in ivory. With any luck we may get that in place in two years. I'll look to you then to go public and urge designers and retailers to avoid designing and selling objects made of ivory."

"Let me know when," Liz said. "I'll do what I can. But you have to realize that I'm a very private person. My name isn't private. I am. But I'll do what I can."

"Deal," Jonah said.

Private person or not, Liz became engaged as she had promised she would.

This is from an Associated Press story dated October 18, 1989:

"About 70,000 elephants are killed each year, according to William Conway, general director of the New York Zoological Society. He said the African elephant population has fallen from 1.5 million ten years ago to 625,000. Last week, major retailers pledged not to sell ivory and clothing designers said they would not use it in a campaign organized by designer Liz Claiborne.

"Taking the pledge were such stores as Macy's, Lord & Taylor, Nordstrom, Marshall Field's, and the Federated, Allied and Carter Hawley Hale chains, and designers Oscar de la Renta, Dana Buchman, Linda Allard and Bill Blass. A statement issued on their behalf read, 'We believe that ivory must be kept out of fashion and in the possession of the magnificent creatures for whom it was originally designed.'"

A total ban on the trade in ivory became policy in 1989.

Unsurprisingly, a number of African countries ignored the ban. In 1991, loopholes were created so that all members could sign on. Over one hundred countries did so. This was to be a Pyrrhic victory, perhaps not even as positive as a Pyrrhic victory.

Liz had carried out her end of the deal. She had concentrated her efforts on the buyer, not the seller. But elephants continued to be slaughtered. The ban on the sale of body parts, the reason for being of CITES, was to prove to be largely ineffective.

• • •

There was more we could and did do for elephants. The foundation, Liz, our elephant programs and Jonah's determined work in the field endured throughout the years ahead.

She was to say, many years later, in front of her last audience at the company she had founded, "If we can't save these magnificent animals," and then she stopped, her voice had left her. There were tears in her eyes. She smiled a moment later, and said, "I'm sorry. I get so emotional about this. But if we can't save these magnificent animals, we can't save ourselves."

• • •

Bjorn Figenschou is still as tall and in love with Patti Moehlman, golden jackal biologist, as he was in 1988. Then his base was Tanzania. He was our guide on our second trip to Africa. He is Norwegian born, a man of Viking mindset, slim, muscular, and protective of his wards—us. He had arranged a fascinating safari for us. He had an excellent crew and treated his workers as equals. Patti, solid and well proportioned, came along with us for much of our safari time. She was an amazingly adapted field biologist. Liz and I came to be in awe of Patti. She had every skill necessary to work in the field: she could dig a jeep out of six inches of mud. She could look under a hood of a reluctant vehicle as all of the men in the group shook their heads dolefully from side to side. Patti would step forward and with a ten-cent piece tighten or loosen this or that, and magically the vehicle purred contentedly and began to move forward. Nobody commented. Patti was blonde, had wide-set grey eyes, and an open, attractive face. She was fun to be with. Liz admired Patti. She was a woman who knew how to do things, practical, yet still a whiz at knowing and loving jackals.

Bjorn reintroduced us to some of the places we had visited the year before: the Ngorongoro Crater, where we had camped for four days and nights, the Lake Manyara corridor area and Arusha, the main safari entry and exit town. New to us was Tarangire National Park, with its assemblage of animals awaiting us. It was July, dry-and-vaulted-blue-sky time. The animals were dependent on the Tarangire River for water. Second only to the Serengeti in concentration of wildlife, Tarangire provided a rich tableau of elephants, stalking lions, zebras, buffalo, gazelles, eland, and many more species, ungulates, predators small and large. Bjorn and company provided three dazzling days of viewing, intimate dinners over a campfire and terse talk about the fragility of animal reserves. Tarangire has survived. The reserve has been well maintained and remains a major source of income for Tanzania.

. . .

The year 1989 was tumultuous, a year in which the desire to visit everywhere seemed to possess us. Elsewhere had begun to summon us. We no longer played an active role in the daily operations of the company. We had become board members, observers more or less, not players. So we planned to roam the world, perhaps circle it in our newly acquired Gulfstream III. It didn't take too much contemplation to conclude that flying around the world is precisely what we wanted to do. We laid out a sensible itinerary with our pilots and were airborne in mid-March: Anchorage, Alaska, for an overnight stay, the sky brilliantly clear, a trouble-free sea, and then to Cold Bay in the Aleutians the following morning for refueling. The weather remained clear and we had the satisfaction of providing that week's entertainment for the dozen or so local children of the military families that had been assigned to this refueling tarmac for a short course of duty. It was a gay time for all. The next leg of the trip was a long drone in the air with a stop at the northern Japanese island of Hokkaido, the refueling village of Sapporo. The refueling was fast and colorful, so much so that we returned for the same purpose five years later. The next two stops were like hometown visits: Seoul in South Korea where the Liz Claiborne office staff stuffed us with soju and kimchi until we were reeling from the alcohol and the garlic.

I'm afraid that we might have offended our office staff in Taipei, Taiwan, the following day, but nonetheless it was a marvelous visit. We were quartered at the venerable, palatial Grand Hotel, once the headquarters of the Kuomintang, built by Chiang Kai-shek to impress his cosmopolitan wife and the cosmopolitan world. We found it stiff and overblown, but nonetheless a sumptuous feast for the eyes and the imagination. And, I'm afraid, torture for the body. The backs of the heavy wooden sitting chairs all sloped toward the front of the seat. Liz eventually became disenchanted with the beauty of semi-ancient Chinese craftsmanship. She was delighted to make it to our suite at the Peninsula Hotel in Hong Kong the following day and enjoy old friends and reminisce about old times. We were now far enough over the hill so that martinis, single malt scotches, old friends, old times and old remembrances made for a soothing evening. Singapore, our next stop, where Liz and I had been feted a number of years earlier at an apparel fair, was as fulfilling as had been Hong Kong. We next flew to Bangkok in Thailand, again in luxury, and now we were ready for new adventures.

Kathmandu, the capital of Nepal, was indeed new and adventuresome for us. The city itself boasts numerous large, sprawling boulevards. No traffic patterns were discernible. People were everywhere. It seemed they whirled about in a huge kaleidoscope: people of every description, color and age, either sauntering or pushing a bicycle or pushcart or merely standing and looking. At the perimeter of any boulevard we would find ogee-shaped doors behind which were lovely gardens and whitewashed modest homes. We stayed at the largest and grandest hotel. The hotel was grand and old in its own colonial style, far from the swank of Hong Kong or Singapore. Our suite had a huge walk-around terrace from which we could see miles in all directions. Off in the distance were terraced fields and further away you could begin to see the shapes of the foothills to the mountains. We were all so enamored of the landscape that we stayed in Kathmandu for three days, awakening at about five each morning to go to the airport and stand in line to board a plane that would circle Mt. Everest. One hour of standby and then a young woman would come out, shaking her head and saying, "Flight cancelled today. Disappearing mountain." No further explanation was offered. And then she would walk off. The sky above was the answer—mist, low clouds, even a bit of rain. After three early mornings of "disappearing mountains," we decided to forego that adventure and perhaps fly over Everest on our way to Karachi, a mandatory refueling stop in Pakistan. We did get a glimpse of a snow-buried peak of Everest on our way to Pakistan.

Once we had landed in Karachi we were immediately surrounded by a dozen Pakastani boys, each kneeling and pointing an AK-47 at our plane. Pakastani airspace, it appeared, was not so easily accessed.

It took three hot hours, but our pilot got the clearance and off we flew to Antalya, in Turkey, a lovely tourist city on the Mediterranean coast. I took a photograph of Liz that afternoon in Antalya that I now find heartbreaking. She is sitting on a low stone wall, the bay behind her. She sits quietly, smiling her carefree smile, dressed in pale blue denim jeans and a pale blue chambray shirt. The back of the photograph reads, "Sitting on Good Luck Bridge, Antalya, Turkey. April '89."

The Anatolian portion of Turkey is a landscape of varied beauty: beaches to the sea, the foothills and highlands of the mountains to the north, coves and inlets and ancient village towns. Our next stop was Izmir, modern-day Smyrna, where we visited the ancient site of Ephesus, home of the Temple of Artemis now in ruins. Istanbul, next stop, was exciting, with mysterious paths and byways that led to lovely tiny squares where hot Turkish coffee, so strong that it seemed to thin your hair, was offered and gossip was the recreation. Istanbul is also the home of the still glitteringly gorgeous Hagia Sophia, translated as Holy Wisdom, a masterpiece of architecture vying with the Blue Mosque, Topkapi, Suleiman's Mosque and others for an enduring central place in history. These structures are now not only precious and strikingly gorgeous, but vulnerable to the corruption of time.

We next flew on to Paris and then to the Azores and St. Maarten and then, New York. The trip consumed a month of our time. Africa would have to wait.

We decided the year was young and there was ample time to stay on the move. We sat in on another board meeting, feeling misplaced. We became further convinced that we should accept an invitation from the people at ARCO Drilling and Mining Company (Atlantic Richfield Oil Company) to fly to Alaska with George and Betsy Frampton. George was the president of The Wilderness Society. I was a member of the governing board.

The four of us left New York, stopping in Fairbanks for the evening. The following morning we enplaned to travel to Deadhorse on Prudhoe Bay, an inlet of the Beaufort Sea in northern Alaska. The weather in Fairbanks had been sunny and warm, typical July weather. Deadhorse was warm enough, but storm clouds were gathering to the northwest.

It was this trip that convinced me that the Antalya bridge name was indeed applicable to Liz, that our lives were somehow protected by the gods of future good things. The point of that trip, since we agreed that no trip should be pointless, was to visit the Alaska National Wildlife Refuge and camp on the northern slope of the Brooks Range. The North Slope was then and still is considered a rich source of hydrocarbons, and the fight to protect the foothills of the Brooks Range was then underway. Bleak as the slope looked, it fronted the wildlife-rich Brooks Range. The famous acronym, ANWR (Arctic National Wildlife Refuge), has since become widely known.

The public relations staff of ARCO met us. It was the staff's job to take us or ship us into the field so that we would witness all the measures taken by ARCO to preserve caribou habitats. Our first stop would be the northern slope of the Brooks Range, and then after a day of camping, we would all return to Deadhorse.

The following morning, Andy, our helicopter pilot, flew the four of us to the northern slope for our camping experience and waited in a heavy rainstorm with his rotors spinning. Liz, destiny's child in this case, opted to get back on the plane. Neither she nor I were aware that Deadhorse, our intended return destination, was slowly closing in due to this passing storm, and Kaktovik, a last ditch alternative, had zero ceiling and zero visibility.

Betsy and George, grim adventurers, would not hear of leaving.

So off Liz and I and Andy went. Once aloft and flying north, Andy delivered the bad news; Deadhorse was now temporarily closed. The other bad news, but of no concern to Andy, was that Kaktovik was also closed.

I did my best to appear casual, although terrified. One terrified person aboard was enough. Liz appeared merely restless.

Andy smiled knowingly. "You see, I live on Kaktovik. I'll put us all down on the ground safe and sound. You'll see."

Kaktovik was a northern base erected to watch for missiles possibly flung by the Russians in the general direction of the United States. Liz, not aware that fate had a much longer life plan for her, pointed out to Andy that Kaktovik sounded as perilous and socked-in as Deadhorse. Deadhorse, with its more sophisticated landing equipment, should open in a few hours, Andy explained.

"Why didn't we just wait on the ground?" I asked. "It sounds like Kaktovik is risky."

"No problem," said Andy. "My wife will talk us down. When I'm flying and the weather's not so good, she gets out her radio telephone, listens for the sound of the chopper and has her own skillful, never-fail way of knowing just where I should set down."

Fine, I thought. There was nothing more to be said. So hand in hand, eyes shut, Liz and I landed on the cement surface of Kaktovik, zero visibility, zero ceiling.

It strikes me now how beautiful both Liz and I thought the postage stamp tarmac village of Kaktovik was. It was so ramshackle, so full of discarded house items, just lying about. Liz commented that the landscape and the objects strewn about seemed the equivalent of action sculpture; their beauty lay in just being there. All of it could be placed in one corner of the landing field. Throw in a number of rusting refrigerators, discarded toilets, a shanty shack here and there and then, perhaps not as incongruous as it may sound, a few Harley-Davidson motorbikes in gleaming condition. The total population, we were told, was about sixty persons. Andy motorbiked us to the center of the village where our waiting time would be spent. Here was a two-story building, perhaps twenty feet across and twenty feet high, cobbled together of aging planks. This was the Waldo Arms, the local hotel. One entered by climbing three wooden steps, pushing aside a cotton-printed curtain, Hawaiian multicolored print as I recall, leaning against a single-hinged door, and announcing oneself. The proprietress, an aging Inuit woman (the population was all Inuit), looked up, grinned through a maze of icicle-like teeth and said, "Come on in. Coffee, tea, beer?"

Andy was right. Here we were, safe and sound. The proprietress offered us a number of ancient *New York Times* to read while we waited for the weather to improve so that we could fly back to Deadhorse.

The weather improved. We had spent three hours in Kaktovik and were now on our way to Deadhorse. Andy assured us that he had clearance to use his judgment for landing in Kaktovik and assured us that he would have George and Betsy safely back the following morning. We indulged ourselves in a heavy protein dinner at the Deadhorse 24/7 cafeteria. And then to bed, eyeshades tight, earplugs in.

We were both amazed at George and Betsy's good humor when Andy dropped them off in Deadhorse around noon the following day. ARCO had scheduled a field trip for the four of us to walk along the pipelines and judge for ourselves how caribou-friendly they were. Afterward we were to visit Endicott Island, an artificial island built in the Beaufort Sea a few miles off the northern shore, not far from Deadhorse. It had been built in 1987 and was used for petroleum production. We voiced our concerns about dumping and were assured that precautions had been taken that were more than adequate. Two years later, under the management of British Petroleum, serious dumping did take place.

We left Deadhorse the following morning, all four of us stuffed into a Cessna 186 flying in blizzard conditions, with a bleary-eyed pilot at the wheel.

Twenty-four hours of light each day can be disruptive to sleep. Our position fixings were dependent on a plane about thirty miles ahead of us, weaving through the Atigun Pass of the Brooks Range. Finally, remarkably, we flew into clear weather. We had exited the pass and ahead was Fairbanks, Alaska.

• • •

We flew to Missoula, and drove up to Tranquillity, took a collective deep breath, and readied ourselves for an August trip to Wivenhoe, Louis's home, to be followed by a sentimental afternoon in Brussels, as Liz would say, *en famille*. Omer Villere Claiborne, the patriarch of the family, had died in 1988. This trip would bring together much of his family, and even though it would not be by any means an explicit memorial (he would have despised that) it was to refresh certain memories for Liz's mother. We stopped in Santa Fe, picked up Omer and Jeanette, made a stop in Gulfport for Liz's mother and then flew off to Stansted Airport in England.

I have a magnificent photograph of the assembled family sitting in front of Jackie and Louis's home, Wrabbe House. Louis is kneeling at one end of the group. Liz stands behind him, obviously wonderfully happy. Next to her stands Omer, glass in hand, then Michele, Louis's daughter, holding her child, and at the end of that row stands Andrew, Louis's son. Jackie's head is barely discernible as she leans over Michele, Jeanette is to her left and there I stand, comparatively small-headed, it seems, for a person of so many opinions. To Jeanette's right stands Michele's newest beau, and then Corinne, Andrew's wife, and Jake, Michele's eldest son.

And, of course, Louise Fenner Claiborne dominates the scene. She is smiling, a soft gentle smile, one arm around Michele's youngest boy and the other around one of Andrew's two little girls.

The following day in Brussels might have been anticlimactic, but it wasn't. We were given a history lesson by Louise. She stood in front of the restaurant after our meal and pointed out how different everything was, how many buildings she had known years ago that were no longer standing. It saddened her greatly. She felt that the square had lost its character. Liz and her brothers stood beside her, their eyes misting. Where are the signposts of yesteryear, she seemed to be asking? She seemed to be saying, but only inwardly, "I'm a stranger in the city where I gave birth to my children."

Despite the all too inevitable sense of loss that Liz's mother experienced, the trip was a great success. Louise and I had become fast friends and would so remain. We flew to Gulfport. Louise was fatigued and ready for rest and remembrances.

The following day we flew with Omer and Jeanette to their home in Santa Fe. They live on the famous Canyon Road, famous because of the large number of shops that make it their home. The shops carry, it is believed, authentic native objects: handwoven Navajo rugs, antique tribal pottery, hand-hewn native furniture, jewelry, silver objects—if you can think of a category that was native to the Southwest, you could find it somewhere on Canyon Road.

Omer has a shop in which he sells authentic Mexican and native furniture. He carries an assortment of other objects, but his main business is furniture. They have a beautiful home, designed mainly by Omer, located behind the store. All of this: the shop, the home, the objects to be sold, and now Pete, Omer's beloved German shepherd, show extraordinary good taste. Jeanette's daughter, Leslie, a young woman devoted to Omer, runs a shop in Soho in which she sells whatever she can of Omer's inventory. She has adopted the surname of Claiborne. She had become Liz's only family in New York.

Before we left Santa Fe, we made plans with Omer and Jeanette for an exploratory trip to Utah in October. But in the meantime we were anxious to get back to Tranquillity and stay put. For Liz, nonstop movement was far from a popular pastime.

One week of horseback riding and hiking and we were ready for eastern Montana. Roger Watson, our general manager at Tranquillity who handled the bar, the horses and the rigs, hitched the horse trailer to our 4 × 4 Ford truck and loaded our horses. Jerry Watson, his wife, ten years older than Roger, tall, cheerful, dark-haired and a person in command of her kitchen and herself, came with us. They were both fine riders and good companions. Liz was fond of Jerry. They enjoyed working together in the kitchen, riding horses together and generally chatting about past hard times, mainly hard times that Jerry had endured.

We drove east, first stop Livingston, about thirty miles east of Bozeman, famed for its french-fried onion rings, available only at the Livingston restaurant. We gorged ourselves, determined that the onion rings were overrated and drove about sixty miles west to the Gallatin Gateway Inn. That would be our evening stopover. Roger pastured the horses and we then did what any sensible Montanan does late in the afternoon: we found the bar. There, to our pleasure, we met David Quammen, an author whom we admired, arm in arm with the director of the Nature Conservancy, Bob Kiesling, best described as irrepressibly imaginative and energetic. Bob was also one of the owners of the Windbag Saloon, a restaurant in Helena, soon to be well known to you. He left the conservancy after a while, being a better idea person than manager, I guess. Conservation misses people like Bob. We have problems making full use of people who can't help being "Lone Rangers."

Bob and David Quammen were in their forties then, or that's what I would have guessed. Liz and I had read David's book, *The Flight of the Iguana*, a humorously and knowingly written account of iguana life in the Galápagos, among other subjects. David, wiry haired and bespectacled, was seemingly born with a delightful grin that presaged delightful talk. Grin and wise talk were immediately liked and admired, and within a week David was asked to become a board member of our foundation. He accepted.

The Gallatin Gateway Inn and the Libertador Hotel in Cuzco may be in practically the same time zones, but they are in totally different worlds. Our last trip of the year, already described, would take us far south to Peru. I was enticed by what I had read about Machu Picchu, and Liz was enticed by the colors and traditions of altiplano living. Cuzco was far more interesting to Liz than ruins. Remember, her father had introduced her to magnificent Romanesque and Gothic churches, all still standing in their original glory. I also looked forward to the fulfillment of my lifelong yearning to visit Ushuaia.

I had started this recollection of 1989 with our December trip to Peru and our resignation from the company. We had found additional meaning in the work of our foundation. It was the end of our company life, and truly another compulsion to give our lives to the work of our foundation.

• • •

The year 1990 brings to mind a charming anecdote that I'll wedge in here. I have on my shelf a white leather-bound company phone directory. The only marking on the cover, bottom right side, is the logo name, "Liz Claiborne," and above the name, spaced over the small "o" and "r" of Claiborne, is the sliced logo triangle. All the print is in black. It is a most elegant phone directory. It was published in July of 1990, just as the contents had been renewed as they had year after year while we were at the company. Liz would go nowhere as the year began without her 1989 directory which was replaced as soon as 1990 was available. She had no plans to call anyone. She was merely so proud of the arrangement of the contents, that she would mention it in any company, at any time. She would say, "I love our company's directory. It's all done by first names. Just like a family. And each letter is separated by a yellow sheet with the appropriate letter on a tab. Isn't that terrific? I just love that."

And I would ask, "Can you give us an example?"

And she would say, "Sure. I memorize the first and last name every year." And then she reached into her bag and pulled out a piece of paper and read, "Abby Novak—extension 3348—Collection/Sport." And then she read, "Zuzel Prieto—extension 6165—Human Resources."

I would say, "I thought you said you had memorized the names."

"Oh, I really meant that I had written them down and memorized which bag I carried them in."

Either way, Liz loved her company's phone book, and I really believe that what she missed most about our leaving the company was not receiving her annual update. But she rarely failed to mention her phone book when talking to someone about the bygone days.

It's been a while since we had referred to this antique way of communicating. I once told her that modern companies don't bother with paper, that phone books were the equivalent of sending smoke signals. You communicate electronically, first name, last name, department, it's all the same to the computer. It sorts and resorts. The only thing it doesn't do is make saleable product.

She shrugged and said, "That's another reason for leaving."

• • •

Africa did wait but not very long. In February of 1990 we journeyed back to Africa, this time to see Shirley Strum and her "Pumphouse Gang," a baboon group Shirley had been studying. She was now faced with a new problem. The Pumphouse Gang had run out of living space. Shirley had been on the ground in East Africa for more than twenty-five years and was an acknowledged baboon expert. Wild, hungry creatures, baboons can be uncontrollable. They are exploiters of easy-to-reach food, and had made home farming tough for local people. Here, in the highlands of Kenya, we had a prime example of human and animal conflict. The baboons had to go. The only feasible answer was translocation; corral the group, tranquilize them, and then haul them off to where habitat and tolerance might exist. Translocation of wildlife is rare, the cost being high and the outcome uncertain. The Pumphouse Gang was moved to the Laikipia Plateau, in northern Kenya. Shirley had found a receptive rancher who would let the baboons run free on his ranch. Shirley also needed a hand to recompense the local peoples for the inconveniences of baboon field study. The thought was that the Liz Claiborne Art Ortenberg Foundation might help fund dwellings for teachers at the local school. Letters had flown back and forth from 1988 on. Liz and I agreed to fund Shirley's work. We made a number of grants, the first in 1988.

In retrospect I find it revealing that Liz and I, not possessed with a driving affection for primates, should have funded baboon work to the extent we did. The reason, I am now sure, is that both Liz and I funded people who we believed were serious, knowledgeable, and who would be determined, even in the face of setbacks, to keep at it, to endure. That had become one of our most unshakable golden rules—support talent and determination.

Shirley is best known for her book that was published in 1990, *Almost Human*. The book clearly demonstrates the affinity between baboons and humans. From bullying to appeasing, from forming relations dependent on fear to those dependent on trust, baboons and human beings are remarkably alike. The binding elements of trust and predictability are key to the social behavior of humans and baboons. The book has been a standard in the field and has been published in seven languages.

Our 1990 safari was to take us to the Laikipia Plateau to visit a school and walk the baboon range with Shirley. It was our misfortune to hit bad weather and rain out of season. Thus far, this safari trip had not been as energizing as our first two trips. We had visited the Mathews Range in northern Kenya. Liz, for once, was not aglow. "I love safaris, darling," she said, "but you'll have to get used to the fact that I'm not an intrepid traveler. Heavy, wet brush, and nonstop flies are not for me." They weren't for me, either.

We were off to meet up with Shirley.

Liz and I, a half a world away from Seeley Lake, Montana, were the guests of honor at a dance performance of the schoolchildren, young, on the whole, grinning boys and girls who were wrapped in cloths of clashingly brilliant colors. They danced and sang and jumped and twirled to much drum pounding and shrieking. They were thanking us. We had provided a five-year grant. The grant money was to be used to create living quarters for children so they could stay at school overnight and not be faced with the uncertainties of getting to school every day. The grant also was to supply material to cement the schoolroom floor, to keep a steady supply of paper and crayons on hand, to purchase books, to pay the schoolmaster's salary and to support Shirley's liaison staff member.

The children knew that schooling was important. They also knew, boys and girls alike, that education was their only road to a fuller life.

The weather had cleared. It was sticky-hot in the sun. The children had danced barefoot, stomping and jumping up and down. The elders were seated on wood chairs, forming a circle around the children, unsmiling, but not completely displeased. You send a child to school; you remove a child from the field.

One year later the school had received the paper, crayons and rudimentary books. The new floor was being installed. Until then the children wrote on discarded corrugated egg-carton cardboard or whatever could be found. The immediate results of this intervention were positive. "Intervention" has become jargon for outside involvement in local problems. A small boarding facility was ready by 1994 and, as a result, the very first students in the area did well enough in exams to get a place in secondary school.

As well-intentioned outsiders, we responded to the voiced needs of the local people. Shirley was our translator. Shirley's field assistants were her translators. Local politicians had a heavy hand in the selection and order of amenities that we brought to the school. But as we all learned, there's much more to it than that. There is the need for constant monitoring, for evaluation of the people who are carrying out the planned programs—the headmaster, the teachers, the students, the suppliers of materials—a consortium of implementers, implementing programs that made sense to Westerners.

The neat bundle frayed; the headmaster developed a drinking problem, drought pressured the children to skip school and work the farm, suppliers delivered shoddy material. Nonetheless, Liz and I determined we would do it again. Perhaps we would be more flexible and patient. Perhaps we would select the key players more carefully. Perhaps Shirley would be less trusting of her own assistants in the field. There are many perhapses. Liz and I never second guessed the intent of the program. We had learned the importance of failure. The program had not failed. There were unquantifiable residuals, but all in all, life for those involved had been improved. More important, we had learned that success, as quantitatively defined in the business world, is a rare outcome. The lexicography of conservation of animals and the balanced welfare of peoples in undeveloped parts of the world is not the lexicography of the business world. There is no knowable bottom line. There are desired outcomes, but they are never permanent. Liz wasn't the least troubled. She had learned, perhaps more readily than I, that small, temporary victories were a measure of success. "You'll have to get accustomed to settling for less than the big payoff," she said. "And anyhow, you know the first law of conservation as well as I do: winning is temporary. It's losing that's often permanent."

...

I started my journey to gain a better perspective of who Liz was, who I was, as me, Art, and as a part of her life. I find that this everyday, intense time I spend working on this narrative makes her absence less real, creates, for me, a world in which Liz is omnipresent. And I understand more clearly the meaning to both of us of our foundation work. We were indeed different people than we had been in the company days.

In late December of this past year, I received this e-mail from Ian and Jane Craig, old friends from Kenya. Ian and Jane had found out that Liz had died when David Quammen recently visited Lewa, their wildlife conservancy. He was working on a piece for *National Geographic* that was to be based on elephants and Iain Douglas-Hamilton. (The article did appear in the September 2008 issue of the magazine.) David passed on the sorry news about Liz. In part their e-mail read:

"The seed that you both planted in Il Ngwesi twelve years ago has grown far beyond all of our wildest dreams. We are now working with fifteen different communities across Kenya, all based on the same model that was established by your very bold and ambitious support to Il Ngwesi. The lodge at Il Ngwesi remains a flagship of this principle and continues to be used as the model from which all the other community conservancies have grown. Our most ambitious program is now on the Tana River, working with a Somali community adjoining the Tana River Primate Preserve. It may interest you to know that we now employ over 1,200 people across this part of Kenya, all based on conservation… If time ever allows I would love to show you the fruits of the Il Ngwesi seed, they are something for all who have been involved to enjoy. Wildlife is now thriving under the community's stewardship. We just thought you would like to know."

The Il Ngwesi Group Ranch is located at the northwest edge of the Lewa Wildlife Conservancy and is owned by the community. The Maasai people of Il Ngwesi, about six thousand in number, have had a long and fruitful relationship with the Craig family. Liz and I were amazed, enthralled, impressed deeply by the dedication of Ian and Jane. Ian's family has owned Lewa Downs since 1924.

I don't think we had ever experienced a continuing work in progress that could come near matching the work of Ian and Jane. This spectacular ranch, about forty thousand acres in size, has managed to support a huge variety of wildlife. The Craigs have been exemplary stewards of their land and exemplary neighbors for the Maasai people.

Jonah Western had brought us to the Craigs knowing that Liz and I would grasp the open-ended importance of their work. And, of course, we did. Ian and Jane have helped manage and promote the area for wildlife conservation and upscale tourism. It was here, with the cooperation of the Craigs that Jonah was able to translocate a herd of elephants. It was important that Liz and I become champions of the premise that elephants can be translocated, given large enough habitat, access to water, and a certainty that the social hierarchy of the herd remains intact. Translocation has become a major tool in dealing with problems of animal/human conflict and loss of habitat.

The Craigs were typical of the well-established, very-much-at-home British Kenyan. I remember them in all regards: handsome, wind-blown; he blonde, early forties in age, could have been a cousin or closer to Jonah. Jane, his wife, was more rugged, with light brown hair worn in a knot, and with the authentic look of a person who had grown up farming and riding, and well acquainted with hard work. She and Patti Moehlman could have been sisters.

This is what came of that visit. We helped the Craigs establish a ranching group conservancy for the villagers, which made possible the teaching of handicraft skills. We helped to improve grazing productivity by trading the traditional knowledge of the Maasai in animal care, rotational grazing and communal sharing in the work of growing things, for the more technically oriented conservation practices that the Craigs could impart. We were able to observe the results of the translocation work Jonah had done. We shared the funding with the Kenya Wildlife Service. In a relatively short time, we had helped to create a thriving, productive community.

I so wish that Liz could have read the e-mail that I received from the Craigs. Given Liz's deep and abiding love of wildlife, as evidenced by the following photographs that she took on various trips to Africa, it was like winning a Pulitzer.

Cheetah, Okavango Delta, Botswana.

Bull elephant, Okavango Delta, Botswana.

Reticulated giraffe, Lewa Downs, Kenya.

Cheetah cub with mother, Okavango Delta, Botswana.

Lions, Okavango Delta, Botswana.

Lion devouring lechwe.

Spotted hyena, Ngorongoro Crater, Tanzania.

Leopard, Okavango Delta, Botswana.

CHAPTER TWO, 1998

IT IS AUGUST 16, 2007, and I'm sitting in the office of Dr. Myron (Mike) Buchman. He is a man in his late eighties, a gynecologist and obstetrician of formidable reputation, skills and empathy. He had been Liz's gynecologist since 1983, so he, compared to the numerous doctors who came into her life in 1998, had known her by far the longest.

I have met with him three times and was struck on all occasions by his gentle but incisive manner. Only slowly did he admit his special fondness and admiration for Liz, but there it was. He was very much aware of the love she and I had for one another and our realistic approach to the disease. He was clinically clear, and open both about the disease and his feelings toward Liz.

The cancer story began in April of 1998. Liz had had a routine Pap test. An abnormal result is suggestive of the possibility of a malignancy in the uterus and indicates that further investigation is necessary.

That's what Dr. Buchman told me this past August and what he told Liz a decade earlier.

"Further investigation could mean the confirmation that the patient has cancer cells that could require chemotherapy treatment. It's not surprising that a number of patients turn down that treatment. Not every patient is willing to pay the price for an indeterminate period of life extension. I had known Liz for a number of years. She was realistic, practical and a person of unlimited determination. She heard me out. Then she said, 'I'll speak to Art.'"

During our August talk, Dr. Buchman told me, "She knew she was loved. And that you would do anything for her. She knew she could count on you to support her all the way. And that really matters, matters a lot. I knew then what her answer would be."

"We're going ahead. We'll do what we have to do," Liz said. We had both come to his office.

One response to "do what we have to do" was more testing, a process that Liz handled well despite her impatience with "testing." But the tests were done: an MRI, mammogram and a bowel gastroscopy.

Thus far nothing alarming had surfaced. Dr. Buchman had already outlined the process. The next and vital step was to locate and identify the malignancy. The procedure requires the use of a laparoscopy. This is non-invasive. An instrument, very much like a miniature telescope in appearance, was inserted through the outer tissue of the stomach area and made it possible to get a direct look at the peritoneal cavity. A laparoscopy was performed in mid-May. It was no surprise to any of us that Dr. Buchman had gone as far as he could. It was now time to really zero in on the source and nature of the malignancy. It was also time to select an oncologist.

Dr. Buchman and Dr. Hartman recommended Dr. Mark Pasmantier, oncologist and hematologist, a man considered at the top of his field. He had deep experience in the treatment of ovarian cancer. Cancer of the peritoneum undergoes the same treatment as ovarian cancer.

It did not occur to us to seek another opinion, to shop the market, to surf the web, to deny the evidence Dr. Buchman had presented. Mark Pasmantier was selected.

• • •

We met with Dr. Pasmantier on June 9, 1998. He had seen the results of the laparoscopy and had recommended a hysterectomy, the surgical removal of the uterus. This too was no surprise. Dr. Buchman had forewarned us that a hysterectomy must be performed. The results would tell us what we had to know about the condition of the peritoneum, the membrane, as previously described, that lines the abdominal cavity and covers most of the abdominal organs. The operation was scheduled for June 16. Dr. Pasmantier, aware that the malignancy might well require chemotherapy, scheduled Liz's first treatment for July 6.

Dr. Mark Pasmantier, the man whose skill and judgment would determine the future course of Liz's well-being, had been affirmed by doctors we knew and trusted. Most decisive, at least for us, is that these were all deeply caring men of medicine, accessible, amiable, familial. It did not occur to us to search the web for more data about the disease or to solicit second or third opinions. We had learned that Dr. Pasmantier was a decent, kind man, aggressive in his treatment of the disease, and importantly, surrounded by colleagues who were accessible and experienced in the treatment of cancer. He was affiliated with New York-Presbyterian Hospital, a teaching hospital, and thereby had all the advantages of exposure to knowledgeable, accessible colleagues and the most reliable information available on any new techniques or chemicals on stream for cancer care.

Mark Pasmantier is now a man in his late sixties who had lived with tragedy, both personal and professional, for years. His wife, Catherine, a vibrant and socially involved person whom he admired and loved, had died in 1999 of cancer. He had slept in her hospital room every evening for weeks and carried on the often grim work of trying to cure, or at the least, alleviate the pain of other cancer patients during his working day. We were unaware of the burden Mark was carrying. Liz had completed her first cycle at the end of October in 1998. Catherine died in January of the following year.

That June afternoon when we met in his office we focused on the treatment he would plan for Liz. That the hysterectomy would confirm what was already strongly suspected was taken for granted.

Liz and I sat across from his desk, in two frame chairs, side by side, holding hands. We took no notes; we listened carefully and calmly. He repeated much of what we already knew. He spoke slowly, simplifying everything to be certain that we understood. Liz sat quietly as did I.

Chemotherapy would most probably begin in July, a session every three weeks. We would hope for remission at the end of the cycle. We would hope for permanent remission. He knew that in Liz he had a patient who could absorb the details without flinching. He also knew that we would prefer no surprises. He would fill in more details later: white blood cell count and the

Neupogen booster shots that might be necessary to reinforce the body's immune system, red blood cell counts, and concerns about anemia, CA125 numbers, kidney function and more. For now it would be sufficient if we understood the measuring stick for the degree of virulence of the disease: CA125.

We were strangers to the term CA125, cancer antigen 125, which we understood to be a tumor marker which is a substance that is found in greater concentration in tumor cells than in other cells of the body. In particular, CA125 is in greater concentration in ovarian cells than in other cells.

Dr. Pasmantier explained, "So think of these readings as a thermometer and that as the number spikes higher and further from the norm—35—there's cancerous activity at work. Normally, the higher the number the more exhausted or generally rotten the patient feels. I'm telling you this now because we'll be referring to that number during the chemotherapy treatment. But if we go into remission at the end of the first cycle, you're free to forget all this. That's my hope and I believe I've got good reason to hope."

There's a school of thought that believes "hope" is essential to cancer care. Liz and I would agree.

In the years to come our lives were often governed by the latest reading; the number was always a heavy substance in the air, a banshee-like screaming in my ear: "The reading is high—the reading is disappointing…" Sometimes, it whispered: "Things are looking good, cross your fingers."

There is considerably more to be known about the solid meaning of any specific CA125 number. It is a context-driven indicator. I'll go into greater detail later in the narrative.

Liz almost always seemed to shrug at bad news, beam at good news. She lived with the number, she lived with me. I became her shock absorber.

Dr. Buchman performed the hysterectomy on June 16. Liz went through the surgery well, with no complications, healed rapidly and was home on the 20th. We then met with Dr. Pasmantier on June 24. He confirmed what we had all come to expect. The consequence of the surgery was the confirmation that the malignancy was harbored in the peritoneum.

This is the essence of Dr. Buchman's report to Dr. Pasmantier: "Mrs. Ortenberg's cancer is spread around the surface of the peritoneum, the lesions are small and thus should be accessible to chemotherapy. There is no tumor of bulk…"

Mark Pasmantier's diagnosis had been confirmed. We were dealing with a treatable malignancy. Liz's disease had a specific name: primary peritoneal carcinoma, which in this case meant that the malignant cells were in seed form and thus the surface of the peritoneum could possibly be "sanded" by chemotherapy. The problem, Mark well knew, is that this is a subtle disease and the cells could hide and then suddenly reappear. No statistics were provided nor were they requested. Neither Liz nor I believed in aggregate statistics. We were tough overachievers. What we heard was that Liz had a cancer designated as "primary," and that we were shooting for total remission. Both Dr. Buchman and Dr. Pasmantier were optimistic physicians. That's what Mark told me years later. They knew that in Liz they had a patient who was both realistic and practical and would be up to doing what had to be done.

There's much talk and speculation as to what oncologists tell their patients and what their patients take away with them. We were not misinformed. We were also encouraged to concentrate on the treatability of the disease. In Liz, Dr. Pasmantier had a patient who could financially afford whatever care might be necessary, and who would be a paradigm of determination. She also had a husband who would do anything for her. We had heard clearly enough. We chose to translate what we heard to suit ourselves. We chose to believe that primary meant early. There were no grounds for that interpretation.

We were now to live life still as one person, Liz and Art, with one critical difference; Liz would become a cancer patient afflicted with peritoneal carcinoma, a rare and unpredictable disease. She determined to live her life fully, uncomplainingly, and bootstrap every resource of body and mind to deal with whatever came. We made no attempt to avoid the reality that Liz had cancer. Our expectations, to some extent fueled by our physicians, were positive, and expectations are a strong weapon in the fight against the disease.

We walked slowly home, hand in hand. At first we said nothing, our minds flooded, both of us grappling quietly with this new reality. We held hands more tightly, looking straight ahead. And then she stopped, faced me squarely and pulled me toward her, looked up at me and said, "Darling, I will do everything I can to keep our lives moving ahead. I will do everything I can not to let this disease take precious time out of our lives together."

I turned my head away but held her more closely. I didn't want her to see that my eyes were filling with tears. "I know, sweetheart," I said. "I know. We'll beat this thing back. You'll be fine."

She pulled back and smiled. "Of course I will." We walked for another moment or two and then she stopped and said, "But first we have to get ready for dinner."

We quickened our steps, changed the subject to dinner with Jon and Stephanie Reckler at our favorite uptown Italian restaurant; the food was simple, the service was personal, and just being with Jon and Stephanie was hugely comforting. Jon is a tall, reed-thin, perpetually smiling man, elegant and knowing. They are both a good fifteen years younger than we are. He is a distinguished urologist (most necessary for me) affiliated with New York-Presbyterian Hospital. He is also a close friend and colleague of our lineup of doctors. Stephanie also wears an ineradicable smile, speaks softly, firmly and is flexible about almost everything other than the upbringing of their three children: two self-sufficient (more or less) daughters, both well educated, well employed, and one son, tall and handsome, a lawyer with a brilliant future ahead, an inherited love of dogs and independence. We had never met any of this trio, but Stephanie's motherly interest in them kept us abreast of the latest news. She not only relayed the news, she helped to make it. Stephanie is a securities analyst as well as a strong, involved member of the board that supervises the Park Avenue building where they live. She has always been given to wearing the color lime, and on that basis alone, she and Liz were soul mates.

Jon and Stephanie were then and always since then the model of supportive friends.

"I've spoken with Mark," Jon said. "Naturally there wasn't much I could press him on, nor would I want to. But he did say the disease is treatable, and I could sense from the lilt in his voice that he's optimistic."

"So are we," Liz said.

We lifted our glasses to toast one another. "To Liz," they said.

"To me," she said, and as our glasses touched, "cheers."

• • •

We had planned a trip that summer that now had to be canceled. It had been designed as a northern hemisphere tour, a part of the world that is wondrous in its bleakness. Life, adapting to harsh climate and soils, was the magic that drew us north. Global warming was not then perceived as the deadly threat it is today. We fully expected to fly north and freeze life and geography as in a static picture frame. Friends from St. Barts, Pierre Monsaingeon, architect and yachtsman, and his wife Christiane, a physician, were to travel with us. The itinerary: Churchill on Hudson Bay with full confidence that polar bears were lining up for the lens of Liz's Minolta, four days in Iceland which would be a return visit, two days on the northern island of Spitsbergen, and then four days in St. Petersburg. Well, goodbye to all that; other trips would follow.

Chemotherapy 1—Taxol-Platinum 7/6/98 to 10/26/98

Four hundred seven East 70th Street is a narrow grey stone building, perhaps forty feet wide, wedged in between such mundane shops as a candy-and-girlie-magazine store, food takeouts of various ethnic fare, a sushi restaurant, and other shops that all look so similar that 407 emerges as the only building of a certain amount of taste on the entire block. The building is five stories high, is entered up three stone steps and through a double door often difficult to maneuver for the patients of the various doctors who occupy full floors or half floors within the building. There is a varied assortment of physicians: cardiologists on the first floor; dermatologists on the second; oncologists Dr. Mark Pasmantier, Dr. Morton Coleman and Dr. Julian Decter on floor three; Dr. Barry Hartman, internist and contagious disease specialist, and Dr. Raymond Sherman, a kidney specialist, share the fourth floor; and Dan Libby, a physician who specializes in respiratory problems but who also is in demand for internal medicine, occupies the fifth floor. The basement is equipped to test for potential cardiac or lung diseases: an x-ray room, a stress test room, an MRI room, and a room that contains an echogram, a sophisticated heart-inspection machine that listens and records. The lobby is disproportionately tiny, an architectural feature that I still can't figure out.

Presiding over the lobby is George Mendes, Guyanese by birth, an amiable man in his fifties, slick dark hair worn Valentino style, who never fails to display his willingness to be helpful. He sorts and distributes the building's mail, is on call for any reasonable service one of the doctors might require, and is considered by all an important asset of the building. I have known George, in a nodding way, for twelve years.

The space that Drs. Pasmantier, Coleman and Decter share could be as stuffed as a can of sardines at times. It has happened that the number of patients being treated were so numerous that chemotherapy was administered in the waiting room. There are four small rooms for chemotherapy patients, an office at the south end of the space for the nurses and their equipment, and Dr. Pasmantier's office at the other end of the space.

Dr. Pasmantier has a small administrative staff, all fiercely dedicated to him, two nurses and an efficient laboratory in the hands of excellent technicians. The glass-enclosed greeting office was the dwelling place of her lesser majesty, Myrna, scheduler, protector of the throne, entertainer of the waiting patients, and sometime tango dancer. Bills are processed in this room and the now-exhaustive correspondence winging back and forth to and from Medicare and what this or that plan approves and does not approve is often discussed with patients who are sorely chagrined at the always inconsistent decisions of the bureaucracy.

This was to become Liz's home for therapy, for remediation when dehydrated, for Neupogen booster shots and often for emotional sustenance as well. St. Peter's Hospital in Helena, Montana, would play a secondary role the first summer for Neupogen when indicated, blood tests and emergency treatment if needed.

Mark followed the NIH (National Institutes of Health) protocol for the chemicals to be used to attack the cancer: Taxol-platinum administered once every third week with a white blood cell booster ten days after a treatment.

The first treatment day was Monday, July 6, 1998.

There was little said that morning as we left our apartment. We closed the apartment door behind us: a slab of high-gloss Liz Red enamel. We locked the door, rang for the elevator, waited. The elevator arrived. High-gloss Liz Red doors, the same color as the apartment door, slid open. This was routine, unthinking busyness. I rubbed my hand over the door for good luck. Liz did the same.

"Well, this is it," Liz said, "the beginning of a new adventure." She was dressed in pale grey velour, comfortable pants, sweatshirt top. Her nails seemed aflame against the pale grey. She was without her musical bracelets. We had a car waiting. I held her hand, not too tightly, I hoped reassuringly. She smiled, ran her fingers over mine, and then put her hand on my knee. I did not see or feel any change in her. She looked out of the car window, commented on the traffic or anything of interest that she saw. We spoke of small things, neither of us displaying concern about the events of the day to come. We might have been on our way to the theater. But we knew that things unknown awaited us. We were on our way to chemotherapy session one.

George Mendes held the elevator door for us. I pushed the number 3, floor three, the stage for all that was to follow. We entered the foyer-like room, announced ourselves, sat and waited; blood was drawn to establish readiness: white count, red count, kidney function. We already had her CA125 number from blood drawn on our June visit; it was 77.

Myrna soon emerged from her cubicle, took Liz by the hand, enveloped Liz in smiles and encouragement and said, "We've got a good luck room for you. Say hello to Bari Schultz, your nurse of the day." That was our introduction to Bari, nurse of the day and nurse of many days to come.

Bari, all assurance and calm, took Liz by the hand and led her to the small room where the treatment was to be given. We both wondered how this lovely person, perhaps five feet nine inches tall, would manage to work in this tiny room. The room was nine feet long, six feet of which was occupied by a high examination table. Next to the table was a small seat for the patient and room for the doctor to examine, for the nurse to administer, for the patient to move about when needed. There was no need to worry. Bari has long, sleek black hair that she keeps determinedly out of her eyes, pockets full of various implements, yet moves like a young gazelle.

Dr. Pasmantier came into the room. Bari and I left. He examined Liz, found all in order for the treatment to begin. Myrna sent me back to the treatment room.

"Well," Mark said, "time for treatment one. You know the chemicals we'll be using. You've probably heard that Taxol has a special charm; you will lose your hair, not all at once, but hair loss will become noticeable in a few weeks and continue from there. But don't let that worry you, Liz. I'm sure you'll figure out how to look beautiful, bald or not." He patted her shoulder, turned to leave the room and said, "I'll look in from time to time."

As he was leaving the room, Dr. Pasmantier turned his head, smiled broadly and said, "And Liz, try to live your life as you normally do. Don't let this slow you down." Liz nodded. She knew what he meant. If anything, she was determined to keep living, to keep moving, to keep her mind so busy and involved that there would be little time to dwell on the disease.

Bari set up the stand on which all of the pouches of medication were to hang and be transferred into Liz's body. And then the procedure began: the probing for a vein to carry the medication, the checking of the tubes, the release of stage-one medication.

Liz held a magazine on her lap. She looked up at me and said, "I'll be fine, darling. You don't have to sit here all day. I'd really like you to do whatever you would normally do: foundation work, office work. I'll probably nap."

As I left, I glanced down the hall. Mark was leading a threesome into his office: an agitated elderly woman, her agitated husband and a younger man, in all likelihood their son. He shut the door behind them. I was to witness scenes similar to this one for many years to come.

I confirmed Liz's next date with Myrna, told her I would be back to take Liz home. "She'll be fine," Myrna said. "And she'll be ready for anything you've planned for this evening."

I waited for the elevator, not at all reassured, not at all unconcerned. This was the beginning of the beginning.

• • •

I am looking at a photograph of Kim Brindel, née Baker. Kim sent it to us to make sure we hadn't forgotten her and Christophe, her husband. The inscription on the back reads, "Kim and Christophe, September 2001, Azay-le-Rideau, France." This is a small village in the Loire Valley where Kim, Christophe and their twelve-year-old son William now live. Kim, so central a figure in our lives for more than two decades, will never be forgotten.

The photograph is as true a representation of a lovely human being as any I've seen. Liz would agree. Here we see Kim, a beautiful, self-assured woman of forty-five. She wears small bronze earrings for balance, thin-rimmed spectacles, and her hair is gleaming chestnut, parted to one side. Behind her smile is the determination of a lioness. Kim is indomitable. She doesn't give up. And it was that intensity, saturated in loyalty, that got things done.

Extraordinary people, Kim for example, often spring from what seem like ordinary roots. Kim is Irish, born on the North Shore of Long Island of a solid middle-class family. She appeared at the company one day in the fall of 1981 just after we went public. We had advertised for an administrative assistant and here she was. But beyond her responsibilities to me at Liz Inc., she became essential in arranging our personal affairs so that we could move from here to there, from now to later, in a friction-free process.

Here's an example of how Kim managed an event in our lives that added zest and flavor to the way we were to live: in 1984, Liz was slated to make a number of personal appearances (PAs they were called). Neither she nor I relished her being away, but this was her way of listening to her customers. She was quite possibly the first well-known designer to meet her customers face-to-face on the selling floor. Liz had to been flown from one department store, Joseph Horne in Pittsburgh, to another, the Dayton Company store in Minneapolis. Because of time pressure, the Dayton Company chartered a Hawker 800 airplane. This is a relatively small six-seater, twin-engine jet. We both thought that was a dandy way to get about, so we decided to buy an airplane. We hired the pilots, and the pilots found the plane. Kim coordinated the work of attorneys, accountants and the negotiations on price and delivery. She made sure that the pilots handled the due diligence required. If the devil is in the details, he couldn't escape Kim. She is expert in handling the details.

On October 15, 1986, we became the happy, personal owners of a Hawker 800. Flying privately was our addiction; no reason our shareholders should satisfy that addiction. And they never did. The pilots were with us through all the years we owned airplanes, 1986 to 2000. We bought a Gulfstream III a year after the purchase of the Hawker (the Hawker's range was too short) and later a Gulfstream IV. We sold the GIV in 2000 and chartered thereafter. The Gulfstreams were larger, faster, longer-ranged and capable of flying at 45,000 feet, higher than any commercial plane in the air. This ownership of a plane and the later chartering made it possible to "live our normal lives" and for Liz to receive chemotherapy one day and fly to St. Barts or Montana the next day.

When we left the company, it was Kim who handled the details of the transition, sitting in space we had rented from the company while we flew around the world. She then arranged the physical move to our new office in Manhattan, where we rented space for both the foundation and the managing of our personal activities. To this day, the phone is answered, "Good morning (or good afternoon), Liz and Art's office."

Kim left us in January of 1991, not because she wanted to, she has often said, but because she needed to. She needed to find herself, she said. She needed to free herself of the mentors who loved her and whom she loved.

Liz had adopted Kim as a daughter, was always so openly appreciative of Kim's help, so that leaving was difficult, traumatic, but necessary. At first Kim found a business reason for leaving. She went to France to learn French to better manage our villa in St. Barts. Liz and I found this a bit mystifying since Liz spoke French and since English is quite workable in St. Barts.

It turned out that Kim actually wanted to live in France and become a baker's apprentice. Kim loved baking and has a distinctive approach to organic baking. She felt that once apprenticed, she would open her own shop. We actually believed that Kim desperately wanted to redirect her life. Her choice of baking, we felt, would do for starters. And that's how and why Kim stayed in France, and how and why she and Liz were in fax and e-mail communication from 1998 to the beginning of 2007.

Here is an excerpt from a fax that Liz sent Kim on July 31, 1998:

"Dear Kim, A long overdue explanation for the lack of communication. Since we left St. Barts—I have been very preoccupied with myself & the millions of tests I went through. But to make a very long, boring story short, it ended in a hysterectomy & now chemotherapy. It is cancer of the 'omentum,' which is part of the 'peritoneum,' both of which you will be acquainted with from your early 'scar' problems. But it was caught in its primary stage and the prognosis is GOOD*...But the chemo (so far anyway) isn't so bad except for the tiredness days four through seven."*

Another fax to Kim at the end of the year:

"Dear Kim and family—Happy Boxing Day...We both spent a quiet but lovely Christmas with many thoughtful, beautiful gifts from each other, remarkably alike. All for our 'edifice' to-be on the hill. But my best present was great results from my 'controle' (test): CA125 down to 14...Liz"

• • •

Mark had described Liz's physical reaction to the first chemotherapy go-round as "sailing through." She either deliberately downplayed her nausea and fatigue or he underplayed some of her comments. I think that's exactly what took place in the examining room. The short talks in his office that always took place after her examination and prior to that day's treatment were routine for the most part: a discussion of the latest CA125 and an assurance that thus far everything was on course. There was no reason for more than that. Bari remained the main attendant. Liz did what was required of her.

The conversation that played out in the treatment room after I was permitted reentry would sound like this. "How is she doing?" I would ask.

Liz, relaxed, confident, smiling broadly would break in, "Dr. Pasmantier says I'm doing just fine." Dr. Pasmantier, amused and pleased, would turn his graying head to me and affirm, "Yes, she's doing just fine."

"Great," I would say.

And then Liz would take on a more serious face and ask, "Dr. Pasmantier, is there anything else I should be doing?" This was asked, always, in a straightforward, businesslike tone of voice.

"No, Liz," Mark would answer. "You're doing all the right things."

I kept a daily record of how Liz was reacting to the treatment; Liz and I, as Mark had suggested, went about our business, except that we were both expending time and energy continually focused on how she felt. Not obsessive for her, by any means; more clinical, statistical. How Liz felt at any given moment became an essential part of my awareness of the world I lived in. Grasping the reality of being a living thing, accepting the paradox of life and death and joy and pain, is at best an uneasy, elusive sensibility. There was nothing elusive about this reality. The presence of Liz's cancer, the quantifying numbers, the qualifying sensations that newly intruded in her life, gave an unarguable center of reality to our lives.

The first entries in July of 1998, all transcribed from Liz's words, were intended to prepare us for the journey ahead, if that journey was to be extended over time, for what to expect and how to make the most of it.

Day 1—the 6th, "Feels good."
Day 2—the 7th, "Woke up feeling well but a little fatigued."
Day 3—the 8th, "A bit tired, but OK. Fair."
Day 4— "Slightly nauseous, poor/fair."
Day 5— "A bit nauseous, overzealous while exercising, thus slight head gash, poor to fair."
Day 6— "Good evening, feeling OK, somewhat tired, no nausea. Fair to good."
Day 7— "Woke up feeling better but still fatigued. Fair to good."
Day 8— "Very good today. Good walk—Good day."

• • •

A whaling station in 1653, a long salami-shaped sandbar a bit adrift in the Great South Bay of Long Island, New York, bearing a name that could have been derived in any of a number of ways, Fire Island is thirty miles in length and as narrow as two hundred yards in width. In its history, the island has known boat sinkings, as well as the wreck of large vessels that missed the inlet providing egress to the sea and crashed into the shore. Thus the Fire Island Lighthouse. The island is also known for its importance to the likes of W. H. Auden, the great English poet, and his friend Christopher Isherwood, not as famed perhaps as Auden, but long remembered as the author of *I Am a Camera*, wherein he created Sally Bowles, who enjoyed fame as an independent, talented woman. This intimidating duo caroused in a town called Cherry Grove. The carousing of others has not stopped since then. Indeed so many carousers had to be accommodated that another, less raucous community sprang up slightly to the east, Fire Island Pines.

But Fire Island attracted an assortment of people to its sixteen quite different communities. Liz and I came in 1960 and stayed on. We were year-rounders, coming to the beach in the drear of winter. We would have a late dinner at Captain Bill's restaurant on the bay, and were often motor-boated over by Tommy Sothern, beer in hand, and his wife, Marie, who was never without a martini. There were good nights and some terrifying nights, but Liz and I loved being on the island virtually all alone. "Tommy," Liz often said, "it looks like you missed the turn at Buoy 10." Tommy would pull back on the throttle and say, "But not by much."

Tom Moore, an Anthony Eden-like model for Ralph Lauren, designed our beachfront home in the community of Saltaire. Blind in one eye and heedless of his lack of depth and distance perception, Tom roamed everywhere over the rough framing of the house. That he could fall never occurred to him. It certainly did to us. The house is multilevel because the village of Saltaire's building restrictions were such that Tom couldn't cram all of the rooms we wanted into a traditional plan. Liz was to pay a heavy price for the ups and downs, but that would come much later. And so, over the years, cool to socializing, friendly to those who accepted our privateness, we became good citizens of Saltaire. We didn't consider it generous of us in 1983 when we made a grant to the Fire Island Preservation Society.

That was the first important substantial grant that made it possible to re-store the Fire Island Lighthouse. We considered ourselves privileged to be able to decorate the island with this very beautiful building.

Saltaire, Fire Island, was our safe haven during the first month of chemo-therapy. We lived that chemo month as routinely as in the past. Our week-ends at Fire Island were soul-refreshing. Liz would walk up our serpentine ramp, gazing to her left at the ocean. And once inside, we would both stand at the sliding glass doors that faced the dunes and look past them at the in-coming waves. I always stood to her right, put my arm around her and wrapped my fingers around her upper arm. We lived out most of the month in Fire Island or in New York City. My "Month-At-A-Glance" book does describe our whereabouts every day.

This is how we dealt with the month and the impending loss of hair. Two days after her first chemo treatment, Liz saw Ian Harrington, old friend and master hairstylist. Step one to baldness for Liz was cutting her hair short. She had already purchased her first two Ralph Lauren caps, one beige and one white. There was no way she would permit herself to look like her hair was falling out helter-skelter. The hair loss became very evident by the 20th of the month and by the end of the month, Liz asked Ian to shave her head. He came to the apartment to do so.

Ian Harrington, tall, master of small talk, client-pleasing, or large talk, normally about his wondrous blond son, Max, and handsome wife, Charsi, enjoyed a warm relationship with Liz. Together, they made the control of Liz's progressive baldness, when that was the case, or regrowth of hair when in remission, a major occupation.

Ian was working at Clive Summers' Salon on 57th Street. He supervised the hair-bleaching activity when Liz was in remission long enough for her hair to grow back. Even though bleaching can make one's hair more brittle, appearance was the thing. Liz would say, "My life is brittle. My hair might just as well be brittle, too."

"Most women," Ian recently told me, "deny hair loss out of shame. Liz prepared for it. We all worked so well together. You too, Art. You became a part of the color matching team."

We had dinner often in the early days of Liz's treatment with my sister, Gloria, and her husband, Hilliard Farber. They were regulars, so to speak, when we were in the city, much like Jon and Stephanie.

Gloria is nine years younger than I am, so our childhoods were much less mutually shared than siblings closer in age. I know that I most probably missed natural closeness. I'm not sure that a detached objectivity has served me any worthwhile purpose.

She is often described as "lovely," and that she is, soft and engaging. She is and always has been a pretty girl and is now a pretty woman. She engages in serious matters. She has a PhD in education and is a fervent Head Start director.

Gloria loved and admired Liz, and Liz, I truly believe, loved Gloria, loved her ingenuousness and loved her for her accomplishments.

Hill, her husband, a large man, once slim, tall and dark-haired, had grown wealthy in the investment banking business. Wealth, golf and a largely sedentary life takes its toll over the years, but Hill has run a successful business that was always open for employing needy relatives. We had had many dinners with them during our time at the company and throughout many of the years that followed.

We also took our first trip to Provence in May of 1992 with them. It was Liz's first introduction to St. Rémy, a Provence city she came to love. It was a trip full of delightful scenic revelations. I have memories of that trip that remain, for me, heart-tuggers.

I am grateful to the two of them for the care they gave my mother over the many years she outlived my father. She died in 1990. My father died in 1964. Many of those years were lived in Brooklyn Heights in an apartment about one block from the Farbers. We shared her rent payments; we shared her companions' salaries. There had even been a short period during which she lived with Gloria and Hill.

My mother adored Liz. Liz was a big booster of my mother's. She would tell me, "Don't sell your mother short. She's a smart woman. She has wonderful insight." And my mother reciprocated by loving and accepting Liz as true family. My mother would often tell us about her proud moments sitting on a bench at the Brooklyn Heights Promenade during one of her morning walks. The promenade is a gem of New York City; it is a pedestrian walk, perched above an intercity highway. From a bench at the promenade, my mother and the friends she made there had glorious views of the East River and the Manhattan skyline, and ample time to impress one another with family stories. Somehow my mother would lead the small talk to big talk about fashion, and then she'd spring. "Liz Claiborne?" She would say rather than ask. "Liz Claiborne, my daughter-in-law."

"Oh, come on Bertha, don't make silly stories up." And then my mother, smug in her rectitude, would say, "Make up a story? Liz Claiborne is my daughter-in-law. She's a lovely woman. She's my son Arthur's wife." And nod her head up and down. And then she was believed.

• • •

My mother's daughter-in-law had come upon more difficult times, eight years after my mother's death.

"I'm afraid this isn't a piece of cake," Liz told me. She was referring to a onetime production man at the company for whom everything was "a piece of cake," until we found him actually pilfering fabric from the company.

I said, "I know, darling. I wish I could fire your cancer just like we fired Mr. Piece of Cake."

"Me too," she said. "I'll be fine. This is just so new, this cancer business. I've lost my hair. I'm beginning to tire so easily. I'm beginning to become a different person. I can't allow that. I'm beginning to snap and get edgy."

"I know," I said. "It's OK."

Liz, despite her self-control and sanguine "play-them-as-they-lay" behavior, had become edgy, often easily irritated; "picky" was my description. Why not?

This could not be a stoic, solo fight. I had to understand that. I had to try to overcome my sensitivity to criticism. I had to be there in her corner during every round. I had to absorb and deflect some of her anxiety. But never once then and in all the years to follow did she speak of being victimized, never said or thought, "Why should I have been attacked by cancer?"

I've recently asked friends if they ever noticed tension or unpleasantness between the two of us at that time. "Never, all we saw was love and caring, Liz and Art, the way you always were."

Liz sent Kim a fax at the end of July in which she had written, "Art has been (and is) just wonderful. I can't tell you. He just can't help laughing when he looks at me because I am now the proverbial billiard ball."

As Mark had warned at the outset, one of Taxol's more benign gifts to the body in question is baldness.

July 1998, our first treatment month, we agreed, hadn't been too bad. We both somehow knew that we now inhabited a strange and unpredictable world. Our pre-cancer Liz had not been in unflawed health; she was prone to constipation and stabbing migraine headaches, infrequent, but difficult in both cases.

The second treatment was on July 28 and, true to trying to live out our normal routine, we flew to Tranquillity the following day.

My notes on Liz's general state indicate a quick bounce-back.

Yet on day four, the day she faxed Kim, I wrote, "Generally not too bad, but stomach upset and very tired."

Nonetheless, she improved rapidly and even rode her horse, Patches, on the seventh and eighth days after the treatment. Patches, at the time, was a stocky, highly agreeable, brown-and-white paint quarter horse who took to Liz at once. We trotted, Liz on Patches, me on Stormy, who was anything but stormy, a ten-year-old gelding, one year older than Patches. We walked, did a bit of trotting, a bit of easy loping, the soft side of a gallop, and later felt that the day was totally perfect. Liz grew to love Patches for his gentle, considerate ways. He was easy to mount, his ears always sprang forward as Liz approached. Horses, we are told, can be positive therapy for cancer patients. This was true of every horse Liz ever rode in the years to come.

Nevertheless, it was apparent to the two of us that these were now different times. Liz was weak-kneed for days, but other than that she did, as Mark would later say, "sail" through the next days. Much of August was spent at Tranquillity; guests arrived and guests left; no problems. We walked our morning trek on Lindbergh Lake Road. Liz would stop midway and sit on an off-road boulder, waiting for me to pick her up on the way back to the gate.

We flew back to New York on August 18 for treatment number three. Liz had not quite sailed through after treatment number two, but we both agreed she did well. We had dinner out that night with Jon and Stephanie. Liz remarked how wonderful it was for her to be with close friends. She would like to carry a huge photograph of the two of them, she said, and whenever she felt down or worse, she would look at their warm smiling faces and feel better. The following day was reserved for dentists. Liz was the victim of receding gums and was to be readied for implants for months to come.

Chemotherapy number three took place the morning of August 19. There followed a day of lawyers and dentists and then back to Tranquillity.

The ranch was the perfect hideaway Andrew Harper had claimed it to be.

The first number of days—day three through day five, post treatment—were uncomfortable. Liz suffered headaches and fatigue. We reasoned that an overdose of wine the night we had dinner in New York could be held responsible.

She began to feel more herself over the next few days, so we drove to Triple 8 where a busy schedule awaited us: the indispensable manicure and hair trim accounted for her first day and afternoon. Later in the treatment, we used the Windbag Saloon, Helena's most popular local hangout, as a final destination. This night we ate at the Windbag for the fun of it.

The Windbag has two huge plusses: it is located midway on Helena's lively pedestrian walking mall and it serves decent hamburgers. The mall is three blocks long, about sixty feet wide, plant and tree bedecked, and most importantly, full of appealing shops. There are art galleries, gift shops, a variety of shops for unique clothing, the Pan Handler—an upscale kitchenware store where Liz loved to shop, and then the Windbag. You enter the Windbag through swinging saloon doors and suddenly fall into a different, but congenial world.

The entry room is long and rectangular. The bar at your right is supervised by two collegiate young men. Thirty or forty paces into the room is the entry to the dining area. At about five of six, seating begins. We would descend a few steps and Jeannie, who we came to know well over the years, would escort us to our table, a table for four at the western end of the room. Important people, or rather big tippers, get to sit at larger tables. Kim, young working mother, or Eric, young post-grad student, working his way through school, would seat us, beam and ask, "How goes it," and we would beam and say, "Great," a double Chivas Regal for me and a martini, or ginger ale, depending, for Liz. It was ginger ale that day.

She said over her hamburger, "I'm getting there. Tired, but not too tired to eat a hamburger." The Windbag continued to be a familiar friend. It was the last destination point of our four-stop Helena day: the hospital; the manicure; the dishes at the Pan Handler; and the Windbag. For Liz, the dinner was perfection: a cheeseburger, a spinach salad, a baked potato, a decaffeinated coffee, and then home to the ranch.

• • •

The next day, we met with the Heritage Project executive committee at the Historical Society in downtown Helena. That year and all the years to follow until we withdrew from the program, we were the sole donors. We both wanted it that way. We did not want the concept diluted.

I'm going to tell the Montana Heritage Project story in one dose, because, in retrospect, I find it easier to follow that way and I feel you will also.

The program eventually had a life span of ten years. We had two executive committee meetings each year: one in the fall, attended by staff, the head of the Office of Public Instruction, a representative of the Library of Congress and the director of the Montana Historical Society; and one at the time of the Student Conference, generally around the end of March. Liz attended the fall meetings with me until 2006. By then the project had outgrown our ambitions and was largely being shaped by others: Michael Umphrey had added to staff and we at the foundation had hired the former director of the Montana Historical Society to oversee operations, but we

Clockwise: Montana Heritage Project Student Conference, 2000; with Governor Judy Martz, 2001; with Governor Marc Racicot and Nancy Keenan, 2001.

found that his attention had wavered. Over the years we had opened an office in Helena and had staffed it with a person who would serve as liaison between the Historical Society, the Heritage Program and the teachers in the field. The fruits of success were getting overly ripe. The program was growing increasingly costly as staff was added and as additional Montana schools were enrolled, and as Michael took on more authority.

Our first grant in 1995 had been for $100,000; our grants in 2004 and 2005 were over $400,000 each year. The breaking point was reached in 2005 when Michael and staff in collaboration with the Library of Congress produced a tenth-anniversary film, which seemed to us an advertisement for vastly expanding the program. Neither Liz nor I were aware of a film being made. Perhaps our focus on the disease had been responsible for our lack of involvement. Perhaps it was thought that a tenth-anniversary film would come as a happy surprise. Nevertheless, we felt that a line had been crossed that we could not accept. We, as sole and uninformed donors, were billed for the show. For Liz, pulling out of the program in mid-2006 was a bitter disappointment.

• • •

But we are now back in the summer of 1998 and Liz's first go-round in chemotherapy.

Again, as expected, Liz was feeling less fatigued, but for the first time her joints were beginning to ache, a new element to anticipate.

Consistent with her reaction to the first treatment, it was on August 28 that she felt "much better, almost normal." I was becoming an avid student with a major called "Liz." What became a given is that Liz, whatever the circumstances were, however she felt, always put herself together beautifully. Her smile was as enchanting, spontaneous and guileless as ever. Her silver bracelets, perhaps as many as two or three on each arm, made Liz-music as she walked. And then, of course, there were the impeccably manicured Liz Red nails.

She's always in front of my eyes. I have been writing my remembrances of things past these many months, often rewriting, rethinking to be sure I'm getting it right. Always, her smile and beauty energize the work.

When we bought Triple 8 it was with lifelong pleasure in mind. It would be a haven for us and our children, if they were so-minded, to be isolated from the rest of the world. Then, it never occurred to us that we wouldn't age together as a unit. It was to be our ranch for open-spaced riding, for breath-taking long-range views of a wilder, less-peopled landscape.

Threes and eights, or so it's believed in Hong Kong, are numbers that bring good fortune. Eddy Yao, short but not short on ambition, was the director of Star Freight Ltd., a company that handled a large volume of Liz Claiborne finished garments manufactured in Taiwan and Hong Kong. Eddy owned a light tan Rolls Royce limousine; however aged, it presented itself as a shining newborn vehicle: license plate number 888. He would pick us up at the airport as a business service, his automobile carrying the costliest license plate in all of Hong Kong. It brought him good luck. Eights, to begin with, are lucky, and threes are right behind eights as purveyors of good fortune. We agreed. Numbers are critically important in this life.

Triple 8, always identified as the ranch at the twenty-one-mile marker on Lincoln Road, is close enough to St. Peter's Hospital in Helena that we could drive from the ranch to the hospital in about forty minutes. St. Peter's Hospital is a two-story all-purpose hospital set on a low hill in the eastern, less dense part of Helena. The address is 2475 Broadway, but Broadway is a typical Montana misnomer. It's Broadway in so far as it's an east-west artery through town, for the most part residential. The homes are modest; immodest are the lovely variety of trees that shade the homes. But "broad" requires a non-New York eye for measurement.

The emergency entrance to the hospital is about one hundred friendly feet from the main entrance; both buildings are connected with access obvious and easy. The Cancer Care Center is in the main building on level one, down the stairs to the left of the entrance. We were to climb those stairs often in the years ahead.

That morning, September 3, the first year of the treatment, we met with Dr. Tom Weiner, the oncologist in charge of the Cancer Care Center at the hospital, then the only oncologist in Helena. Tom Weiner, a solid rock of a man, cheerfully youthful, robust, square-shouldered, handsome in a quiet way, emanated empathy. He struck us then—and the years only confirmed the first impression—as a thoroughly straightforward and decent man who enjoys nothing more than a difficult rappel on a sheer mountainside or a demanding soccer match. He always carried his cell phone. I don't think we've seen Tom when he was not wearing a button-down Polo oxford shirt and chinos. His assignment that morning was to have a member of his staff administer the Neupogen booster shot and to look us in the eye to establish a sense of one another, for future reference if needed. We glanced around the center, impressed by its spaciousness, so unlike the sardine can that Mark Pasmantier operated from. For now, Mary, the lead nurse, handled the injection.

We had dinner out that late afternoon, once more at the Windbag Saloon. The Windbag's hamburgers, virtually double-sized cheeseburgers, were for Liz a blissful ending to a productive day, cancer or not.

September weather in Helena can be insufferably hot. A temperature reading of one hundred degrees is not unusual. So it was each day for the following week. This was a disaster for Liz who was then beset with headaches and nausea. She had a stabbing headache the first night after the shot and was exhausted and felt headachy and fatigued the following day as well. The next day was easier and she was determined that, however she felt, she had work to do. We had bought four Icelandic ponies (how Liz hated to call them "ponies" but that's what they were) on our first trip to Iceland in 1995 and our rider had just moved off to Costa Rica. Iceland, known for its thermal underground vents, its clear and rapid rivers that are home to large, wild Atlantic salmon, is also known for its horses. It was perhaps a millennium ago when Iceland was first settled, when the first horses were brought with the settlers. For the next thousand years, the early herd developed to suit the large landholders. New horses were not permitted entry. Pony or horse, this is now a multi-gaited, distinctive-looking creature, accustomed to docility and herd living, and a delight to ride. They afford a fast walk, a trot, a gallop or a pace. Mainly we fast walked. The fast walk is called a tölt. Tölting became a passion of ours.

Three aspiring young women were due to be interviewed that day and that meant watching them ride each of the "ponies," saddle up, tölt around the outdoor arena and show off their gentle control of the horses. Thus, we came to hire the very special Hope Harper, sensitive in her handling of horses, as well as sensitive in her handling of people.

We returned to New York for the fourth treatment on September 9. We had now become better acquainted with what to expect: variation, for one thing, that often depended on Liz's food intake. She had to go easy on wine and probably forego martinis. She had to be on her guard as to how she ate:

quantity, length of chewing, foods that were easily digestible. Of secondary importance, but not to be forgotten, was her state of mind. Optimism and more optimism were essential, no matter what. We decided to spend a few days at the beach. The weather was brilliant and warm, far less oppressively sticky hot than Triple 8. They were restful days for Liz. But as well as she felt, new discomforts appeared: burping, mouth sores and a sour taste in her mouth. None of this eased our tensions. In small, distressing ways, the tension was relieved by her by snapping at me. I knew she had no other way of letting out steam. We made it work, nevertheless. There was no choice. As the "optimistic" doctors had said, "She knew there was nothing I would not do for her."

We flew back to Helena on the 16th. Liz was now less fatigued. We lived our normal life: dinner at Marysville, soon to be described more fully, usually with Kathy Orsello and her husband Marcus, and Irv Maudlin, manager of Triple 8.

We returned to New York on September 28. We hoped we were nearing the final turn of this learning lope around the track.

We had to postpone treatment five, a disappointment for the two of us. The blood test results showed that Liz had a minor infection. Mark assured us that this was quite normal.

Treatment number five was delayed until October 7. We flew back to Tranquillity the following day. Thus far, Mark was pleased with the course of the treatment. He could tell that Liz was edgy. He assured us that all was going as he had hoped. I don't think he was surprised at the strain that we both showed. So we continued to stay in motion throughout October.

We had divided time between Tranquillity and Triple 8. When at Triple 8, we had dinner out almost every evening. Helena offers a limited but highly differentiated assortment of restaurants. Often we returned to the Windbag, preferring its easy, congenial atmosphere and the attention paid us. We also enjoyed the Montana Club, catering or trying to cater to the upper crust of Helena: state legislators when they were in town, business dignitaries, Liz and me when we were at Triple 8. Its bar, at least one hundred years old, offers far and away the best seat in town.

And then, for those who either drink beer and are lusty serenaders or enjoy an historical setting, there is Marysville House, located in ancient Marysville. This is an old copper and later gold mining town, approached, once you drive to Exit 10 on Lincoln Road and turn south, over eight perilous miles of dust and gravel and barely negotiable curves. The road is heavily decorated, particularly on the drop-off bank side, with small crosses and occasional bouquets of flowers. Hearty people of less than hearty incomes make up a population of about one hundred in Marysville. Liz and I had been once-a-weekers. They treated us well, loved Liz and had no problem with me, a person with an uneasy self-image and thus a heavy tipper. The seafood skillet, served with a side order of vegetables, was my dish; chicken, crusty and cooked forever, served with a skillet of vegetables, was Liz's dish. She learned to chew slowly, carefully and generally emerged unscathed.

We tried to use our time to good purpose: a fund-raising meeting for what I consider the most appealing small library in the world, the Lewis and Clark Public Library in Helena. Tranquillity, on the other side of the Continental Divide, offered other worthwhile activities: getting a start-up conservation group off the ground (Northwest Connections), meeting with both the principal and the music teacher of a favorite rural school, the Swan Valley Elementary School, and all of this despite Liz's fatigue, restlessness, an uneven stomach and severe headaches. She forced herself to be up to it. She admired Bob Green, the music teacher. Many of Montana's rural schools lack the funds for music as a course, so we funded this talented and dedicated multi-instrumental and very musically sophisticated person. He's still in the valley and the foundation is still funding him.

October 26, chemotherapy number six, the cycle had been completed.

The following days were action-packed. The foundation's board meetings were always energizing for the two of us. Our colleagues are thoroughly knowledgeable conservationists. All had worked on the ground. We respected one another and, just as important, trusted one another's objectivity. That we loved being together was a bonus. There were times, though, that a full-day meeting, a ritual dinner for further discussion, often with an invited expert, demanded more fuel than Liz had. She was exhausted the following morning, but nonetheless force-marched herself to the continuation of the board agenda, left at noon and spent the next hour and a half in the hands of a restorative dentist.

She had inherited gum problems that required years of implant work. Her brilliant smile was not a gift. Genuine as it was, it was hard and painful work to own that smile. After the dentist's chair, it was dinner out.

It was now early November 1998. We were sustained by the optimistic prospect of remission, complete and lasting. But deep within ourselves, optimistic or not, we were uneasy, given to impatience and worry. It may be that human beings have evolved a hard-wired kernel of optimism tucked away in our gray matter, bathed occasionally by endorphins, but cancer is another matter. The disease itself is virulent. And the word itself is deathly ominous.

We lived each day submerged in our inner thoughts. Liz adjusted to the discomforts of the treatment. We saw Dr. Pasmantier on the 9th, white cell booster time. He appeared encouraged. We were happy to go along. We Thanksgivinged in St. Barts, came back to New York for a CT scan on the 15th of December and saw Dr. Buchman and Dr. Pasmantier the afternoon of the 17th. They had both seen the CT scan. The results were good. We felt we had had a pre-Christmas gift, the possibility of full remission.

We flew back to St. Barts for Christmas dinner at our favorite island restaurant, Maya's, and a celebratory New Year's Eve, just the two of us at our first villa in St. Barts. It had been bought ready-made many years ago, but had little of the emotional meaning to us of our new cliff-side complex. We stayed at the villa until the new cliff-side complex would be habitable. That house was still in process, a dwelling fraught with unfinished details. Despite the problems, the residence itself, a cantilevered dominance, concrete and brick exteriors, large sliding windows and doors visible from the road, was an architectural triumph. The magazine *Architectural Digest* agreed and featured it in their August 2004 issue.

• • •

My notes of the end of December are full of annoyance and resentment at Liz's impatience. I look back now at the last months of 1998 and wonder just what was causing the inner outbursts, usually at dinner with friends, that so ruffled me. And as I grope my way to the past, desperately aware of the craggy uphill climb that was ahead of us, I find if I could erase my notes, undo my earlier feelings, I would. She had become increasingly impatient of little things and I, annoyed and anxious, accused her of "pickiness." Her reply in a cheerful card to me a year later was, "That's why I picked you."

In rereading what follows, written a number of months ago, I am distressed at how I had reacted in those latter days of 1998. Perhaps that's what venting is all about: excess and self-indulgence.

Mark Pasmantier, during one of our discussions this past September, said that if we hadn't been anxious and worried, he would have considered us "loony."

We had to accept, individually accept, that our lives had moved from the victorious years, the golden years, to the cancer years. Despite the recent good news, she was not yet in the clear.

Both Dr. Buchman and Dr. Pasmantier had told me at the very beginning that Liz knew she was loved and that I would do anything for her. She never lost sight of that.

Her cards to me, not only cards of gratitude, but cards of love, were her way of saying "We are one, for all time." For my birthday in 1998, she sent a card with a photograph of *Punch*, a Deborah Butterfield sculpture we had bought that was now at Tranquillity. Inside she wrote, "8/13/98, My darling, I may be difficult at times, but I do love you and thank you from the bottom of my heart for all you have done for me…especially to make me feel good! I should only be able to enjoy being with you for a long time. HAPPY BIRTHDAY! From Punch and Liz (your loving wife)."

And here are two cards that she gave me on Christmas day in St. Barts: "12/25/98, I know I don't quite measure up…but I still am looking out for you in my own way. All love this very precious Christmas. Your wife, still devoted, Liz." The second read, "12/25/98, Windy hill & all, I hope to spend a few [crossed out] many years up there with you…all my love till the end— many years from now! Liz."

I had given her, as a Christmas card, a copy of a *New Yorker* cartoon. It showed a picture of a bar with a bartender behind the counter and a hedgehog sitting on a stool. The cartoon is based on a line among the fragments of an ancient Greek poet, Archilochus, that says, "The fox knows many things but the hedgehog knows one big thing." That's what the hedgehog says to the bartender, followed by, "Do you want to hear it?" I wrote below the cartoon, "Art loves Liz." That was the one big thing the hedgehog knew. That was also the "one big thing" that made life purposeful for me. She was not precisely a hedgehog and I was not precisely a fox. She lived her life with a central vision, integrated and as uncompromising as possible. Later she saw those few compromises as mistakes she would not repeat. I was considerably more flexible, willing to compromise the issue, not the principle, in order to keep the ball in play. The balance worked.

CHAPTER THREE, 1999

WE WELCOMED 1999 with fingers crossed. The cliff-side residence, still under construction, was guarded at the east end by a group of modest buildings designed in the mode of the original modern owner of St. Barts—Sweden. Like the early Swedish inhabitants, we had built brilliantly painted wood buildings: the home of the manager and his family, a utility building, a laundry building, a garage, each in boisterously different colors. The complex was not quite ready, and new and unamusing ways not to be ready kept popping up. Telephone lines were being laid and somehow they often were punctured in the process. Punch lists (a term to describe what a builder would call a misunderstanding and an owner would call a foul-up) designating things to be corrected never seemed to get any shorter. One thing was corrected, another fault was found. But, as always happens, in time the job was completed.

Understand that design and production and detail were Liz's forte. Architects who had worked with her were stunned by her mastery of detail and that throughout it all, she was, as Donato Savoie, friend and part of the team that designed the complex, said, "A pleasure to work with. You both were. We thought of you as one person." I take that as Donato's intention to placate me. I occasionally saw things differently than Liz did, but my difference of opinion was generally an unheard downwind sound. She knew what she wanted and she had the patience to send people back to the drawing board, the hammer and the saw, to produce what had been conceived and agreed on. Liz's French was Parisian fluent, which was a handicap in French-speaking St. Barts, since a hodgepodge of non-Parisian dialects were run of the mill. Eventually, a number of months into 1999, there we were in our cliff-side hermitage.

I wanted to name the complex "Wits' End," but Liz won the naming contest with "Terra Nova," after the ship that carried Robert Falcon Scott to the Antarctic in 1912. I went along largely to commemorate our 1989 trip to South America, which ended in Ushuaia. Why Ushuaia?

• • •

Patagonia covers a huge landmass at the southernmost part of South America. The name itself is ascribed to Ferdinand Magellan, who considered the natives of this land to be virtual giants. He called them patagons, or large-footed people. They seemed gigantic to Magellan because these natives were typically four inches or more taller than the average Spaniard.

Magellan, spurned by his Portuguese rulers, signed up with Spain. He was a master navigator who had a strong belief that by sailing west he would return to Spain with a cargo full of rich spices, gold and unimaginable exotica. And when his small fleet ran into the South American landmass, he sailed south until he found his avenue through this huge peninsula, later to be called the Straits of Magellan. This was in 1520. He named the landmass to his south Tierra del Fuego, Land of Fire, one large landmass surrounded by hundreds of tiny islands crossed through with inlets. The fires were those set by island natives for their ordinary purposes, cooking and the like.

Charles Darwin, on his world-altering trip in 1831, sailed along the southern coast of the main island of Tierra del Fuego. His was a voyage of discovery. He had been taken aboard as a naturalist. He was that as well as an anthropologist, fossil finder, surveyor, biologist and, in the long run, a man with a reverential view of life on earth. He was aboard a sailing vessel called the *Beagle*, the vessel that changed history. There is a long channel that flows to the south of Tierra del Fuego. Ushuaia was sited on its northwest bank. This most southerly of channels is fittingly named the Beagle Channel.

Liz and I were aware of the history of Tierra del Fuego and were entranced by the miraculous outcomes of the previous voyages. I, much more romantic, I believe, than she, just wanted to be there. We were both anxious to get the dour events of 1989 behind us.

We had flown from Lima in our Gulfstream III, the plane that had carried us to Lima and, as a gesture, had flown over Machu Picchu on our departure from Peru.

Flying over mountainous terrain and yo-yoing to the runway was another of our divinely guided adventures. No one in the air traffic control office spoke English, so a baggage man, somewhat acquainted with the language, talked us down and in. It took a heavy bank of the left wing, a jolting correction and there we were, safely on the ground at the Ushuaia local airport. For me, this was a dream come true. I had, as a boy growing up in a dismally grey section of Newark, New Jersey, a first-generation American, thirsted to go to Ushuaia. Such a poetic ringing name, "the most southerly city in the world." And now here I was, against all odds, with my beautiful wife. We both beamed as we checked into the "under construction" Hotel Ushuaia. Liz took a photograph of me behind the check-in counter grinning hugely with self-satisfaction. Then we found our "suite," a ten-foot-wide room with bath and shower, a cot just wide enough to hold two people who were accustomed to sleeping in close embrace, and one wire hanger. No matter. That absorbed, we strolled down Main Street, remarked that it looked surprisingly like Fort Lauderdale during spring break, and stocked up on film. We had a late afternoon lunch at the world-famous crab specialty restaurant, Tante Elvira. Neither of us had a care in the world other than one another.

Ushuaia, named by the Yamana natives hundreds of years ago for its location "at the back of the bay" is indeed on the bay. Every morning, a large ferry that holds over one hundred people would tour the area, go east in the channel, tour nearby islands and view the thousands upon thousands of birds and penguins. This was to be our first introduction to penguins and the bounteous life of the southern seas.

Our tour the following morning was the larger objective of our trip. We were mesmerized by the wild serenity and beauty of life we watched. We were both moved by the often bloody struggle of life to live. What could be more heartbreaking that watching a skua, a predatory gull, snatching up a penguin chick? We soon came to realize that nature is neither cruel or nurturing. It just is. We were beginning to accept this rhythm of life as creatures sought food and shelter, hunting alone as did many pelagic birds or by banding together, as did the various species of penguins we came upon. There were magellanics, gentoos, chinstraps, even a few kings, all viewing us from their safe island perches.

The city itself was somewhat like a pretty action painting because of its varied landscape of grass-covered hills leading to mountains in the near distance. There were dilapidated and charming little homes of faded color, and serious small churches to the north of the channel. The bay was peppered with skiffs, larger sailing vessels and boats of every style and age. The downtown area, ten blocks long, just to the north of the water, was replete with shops for all ages and tastes: camera buffs, T-shirt connoisseurs, jewelry collectors, wristwatch fanciers, whatever.

This, we knew at the time, was an unforgettable experience. It became the basis for our long devotion to conservation in Patagonia and the southern oceans. But it wasn't until we met Graham Harris, the Wildlife Conservation Society's biologist in the field, that we began serious funding for Patagonia.

• • •

Ten years later, the first number of months of 1999 went well. Alex joined us in St. Barts for Liz's seventieth birthday. Dinner was at Maya's, as happy a place to be as she could have wished.

"Maya's Restaurant" is somewhat of a misnomer because it excludes the significance of Randy Gurley, Maya's husband, business partner and the "outside" man. Randy runs the floor, handles all of the boring administrative chores, oversees inventory and pricing and all of the unglamorous work of making things happen. Randy, tall, thin with the thinness of overwork and overworry, but an expert at sitting on his haunches to chat with customers, sailed into St. Barts a few decades ago. He was a sharp-nosed sailor, a closet intellectual who preferred and prefers working things out to confrontation. He found the Betty Boop-cute Maya to be a sparklingly attractive and alive maiden from Martinique. She was from a family that expressed their love through cooking and eating together. Maya's Restaurant was the product of the liaison, put into place in 1984. An architect friend, Pierre Monsaingeon, introduced us to them. That was another key moment in our lives. Maya was to become Liz's best friend on the island and the restaurant was to become our nightly dinner table.

No person could have had, over the years, a more caring, more "I'll-be-right-there" friend than Maya was to Liz. Liz, many times, said, "I don't know what I would do down here without Maya." Then she would smile at me and say, "I mean the same for you, darling, but you lack Maya's connections. You lack her skills."

The restaurant had become over the years the most popular one on the island. The food was simply prepared, bought at market each morning by Maya herself. The menu was varied with a huge variety of appetizers and main courses. Vegetables were abundant. The staff was amiable and cozy to a point, but always deeply instructed in the ingredients of each dish. And Maya was in the kitchen. Nothing escaped her.

Shaped like an eyeglass case, the dining room is about seventy feet long and twenty-five feet wide. The south side of the dining room is somewhat protected from the elements by a three foot high wall. I say "somewhat" because on evenings when the wind hurtles across the bay, one no longer has a grand view of the bay. One has a grand wind in one's face. Randy and his crew would drop heavy plastic curtains to protect patrons, but often the wind lifted the curtains so that patrons were in severe danger of being spattered with food. Other than on such stormy evenings, we always sat at table six.

The night of Liz's seventieth birthday, Alex was forty-five years old, living in Los Angeles, a working blues and jazz guitar player. It was a supremely successful evening. Liz was happy, relaxed, sporting her genuine smile and her genuine straw-blonde bleached hair, her very own. She was, for the moment, in remission. She hadn't had treatment since the end of October, and here it was the end of March and she felt great. Her last CA125 reading, earlier that month, was 17. She was flying. No corrosive chemicals, no marauding seeds. And just at that moment Randy handed Liz the restaurant's cell phone. We all listened as our New York office staff blasted out a professional rendition of "Happy Birthday."

Here is a fax she sent Kim on the same day of our carefree, happy dinner. Feeling chatty, Liz had, tongue in cheek, explained the facts of life to Kim, particularly the mystic importance of having been born in the ninth year of any decade, in her case 1929.

Liz's seventieth birthday at Maya's in St. Barts, 1999.

"Remember 9 is divisible by 3 & 3 is my number! 3rd Month, 31st day etc!!! Remember the 3 sided triangle? You certainly did a lot of research and I love it! I was always aware while growing up of the dreadful 'crash' the year I was born but I must admit I never felt guilty, or that I caused it. (My father lost lots!) But most of all I love my Le Corbusier chairs: LC 4 the chair is called, designed in 1929, the best thing that happened that year.

"Yes," the fax continued, *"the hair is blond…about Art's length when his is long. One feels like celebrating—doing things one has always wanted to do. In any case it (the hair) is giving me more fun! How do you like our new fax paper? The 'Terra Nova' was Scott's ship name on his last and ill-fated assault on the South Pole. I think it fits the house, like Scott's trip, poorly planned. As you can tell, all's well in my world—numbers continue excellent. I've been given a 6 month span between CT scans! Hope all is well with you all. Thanks for the wonderful fax. Love to both boys. Liz."*

This fax expressing Liz's uncontained joy has become overwhelmingly painful to reread. But then I remind myself of Liz's determination to transcend the hurdles in her path. And the building of Terra Nova was proof that she would do so. Liz, Alex and I had celebrated her seventieth birthday.

106

I now marvel at her fortitude and at the pleasures we were able to share, despite the cancer.

All missions, or almost all missions, accomplished.

• • •

St. Barts turns humid in April. New house or not, we left for New York, went the rounds of doctors and dentists, attended the spring board meeting of the foundation, which was enjoyable, illuminating and, this time, much less of a drain on Liz. Weekends were spent at Fire Island, where being alone together always reset our clocks. Time ticked away. We read, walked on the beach, had dinner at home. It just occurs to me that I have not as yet mentioned what a superb cook Liz was. She loved the touch of food, the drudge of preparation, dinner by candlelight, now rationed to one glass of wine. But that was fine with her. Few people enjoyed the isolation. We loved it.

Mid-month we flew to Helena for two days to attend a Montana Heritage Project Student Conference. The mandatory photo op arrived and, as always, Liz was beautifully beaming, Governor Mark Racicot at her left, Nancy Keenan, the head of the Office of Public Instruction, at her right with a medley of supporting staff, including me, who had never been taught the spontaneous smile. It was nonetheless a grand success. This project, despite the inner tensions becoming more apparent, remained Liz's favorite. It gave her a great sense of gratification. She could see and hear from the students and teachers themselves and know that the project was working. The tact, poise and knowledge of the group were wonderfully rewarding. Whatever the future of the program, its past, as a single state effort, had been powerfully successful.

We returned to New York. Liz was feeling well. I was more relaxed. We were both ready to travel on when we received devastating news from Liz's middle brother, Louis (pronounced Lōō·ē′, as in French, stress on the second syllable). He was being treated for lung cancer.

The outlook was grim. Louis was now an English barrister, living in Wivenhoe, a small city in East Anglia. In the United States he was a lawyer of enormous prestige and skill who had argued more than sixty cases before the Supreme Court. He, too, had been born in Belgium, as had Omer, his older brother by one year, and his younger sister, younger by two years, Eliza, our Liz. They all returned to the United States at the outbreak of the war; all three of the Claiborne children had attended Mountain Lakes High School in New Jersey. Liz, of the three, did not graduate.

The war ended; Louis returned to Europe, where he graduated from the University of Louvain in Belgium and the Science Politique in France. He then returned to the United States and received his law degree at Tulane University.

Lincoln Caplan, a journalist with a sharp eye for the law, wrote a profile of Louis in 1985. It was titled *The Tenth Justice*, subtitled, *The Solicitor General and the Rule of Law*. He described Louis as returning to his ancestral home when he received his law degree. Ancestral home or not, there was much about the Claiborne name and its affiliations in Louisiana that Louis found distasteful.

"I regret to say," Louis was quoted in the tagline of his obituary that appeared in *The New York Times*, "Claiborne Parish is one of the worst. It was named after my great-great-great grandfather, who was the first American governor of Louisiana."

Louis was by far the most learned of the Claibornes. As Liz adored seeing, Louis adored knowing and making it clear that he not only knew, but accepted the posturing of humans, including himself, as good old-fashioned fun.

We loved and admired Louis. We loved his elegant and supremely haughty demeanor. We admired his devotion to justice for the underdogs of the world who most needed it. And I particularly admired his insistence on being armed with the facts in a case. Louis created an aura of drama around himself that forced attention.

• • •

Omer Villere Claiborne and his beautiful young wife married in 1924 and had their three children in rapid succession. Claiborne's earlier years had been spent in the military. During World War I, he had been sent to Europe to serve as an interpreter, since his French was fluent. His language fluency got him the job of secretary to an American general. He later expressed a desire to stay in Europe after the war ended and attend an English infantry school. He was permitted to do so. When the war ended, he stayed in Europe and entered the banking business. With a military background such as he had, he was a father who believed in discipline, and he disciplined all of his children. The discipline was measured and pointed, and, in his mind, necessary and controlled. And, in the long run, he and his wife shaped the character and talents of their extraordinary children.

• • •

Louis, who rarely spoke about his father, did more than practice law in New Orleans. He met and married a strikingly beautiful young woman, a visitor from Wales, who was working at his brother Omer's Café Lafitte in the French Quarter of New Orleans. Omer, at the time, was a young man, far from resolved as to career. But part-owning a café was as good a vocation as any while you pondered your future.

Louis, however, was married to the law. He was also soon married to Jackie. This was a conditional arrangement: Jackie would marry Louis. He would marry Jackie, and move to England, not immediately, but when he was sufficiently established in his work here. It didn't take very long; they were married in 1959. Jackie became the ideal Washington hostess: beautiful, witty, tireless and always supportive of Louis.

He boasted at one time after he had been appointed deputy solicitor general that he was the only member of the Solicitor General's office who hadn't been a graduate of an Ivy League school.

In the earlier years of his career, he had been noticed by Justice Felix Frankfurter. Louis had argued a losing case so brilliantly, or so Justice Frankfurter thought, that he was recommended to Judge Skelly Wright, who sat on the Court of Appeals for Washington, DC. That was the step up that launched Louis's brilliant career. It was Judge Wright, a strong believer in the strict enforcement of the *Brown v. Board of Education* Supreme Court ruling, who was largely responsible for the desegregation of public schools in the New Orleans area. Judge Wright was also regarded as the man who put the teeth into NEPA (National Environmental Policy Act) by applying the act forcefully.

It was on the strength of the work he did for Skelly Wright that Louis was promoted to the Solicitor General's office as deputy solicitor general. He remained in that office, on and off, from 1962 to 1985.

It wasn't until 1985 that they went off to East Anglia, to the charming and congenial village-town of Wivenhoe. Louis, unsurprisingly, worked hard to get his credentials to practice as an English barrister. Once he succeeded, Louis became one of a small group of lawyers who were both barristers in England and attorneys in the United States at the same time. He continued to argue cases in the United States, working for a West Coast law firm that specialized in environmental cases, cases that concerned the rights of indigenous people to land ownership, cases that might eventually be argued before the high court. An announcement of a case to be argued by Louis Claiborne could, in my mind, be likened to announcing the appearance of Maria Callas at La Scala.

He too loved beautiful things, and above all, affected a style that in the end was Louis himself. His arguments before the court have been archived and referred to often by the Solicitor General's office. He was admired for his brilliant, deeply learned briefs, often lyrical, always elegant. His arguments, like beautiful epic poems, were musical, often amusing, sometimes slyly irrelevant, but the irrelevance was known, it seems, only to Louis.

Louis and I had become close friends. We shared a love of irony, parody and black humor. Not Liz. She saw nothing amusing about the day Louis and I went shopping together. He was in New York on his way to the West Coast, and it seemed his wardrobe was deficient of serious clothes. "To Brooks Brothers we go," Louis said. "I'm an old client. Valued? We'll see."

So off to Brooks Brothers we went to "buy" (perhaps "select" is more appropriate) a serious suit for Louis. We found the "serious suit" floor, exited the elevator, and approached the only other breathing being on the floor. Not one other customer, fortunately. "Young man," Louis said, and, indeed, we had before us a thin, young man, dark-suited, canine-anxious to please.

"A suit for yourself, sir?"

"Yes, a suit for myself."

Many suits later, much fussing about and mirror-accosting, a suitable suit was found, alterations unnecessary. "I'll take it with me," Louis said.

"Who shall I charge it to? Do you have an account with us?" "Of course," Louis said. "Louis F. Claiborne, you probably have a number of addresses, charge it to my West Coast address."

"Of course." The young man took the suit, ducked behind a curtain and disappeared. Time went by and the young man remained disappeared. Lunch break, I wondered. Louis, unconcerned, just strolled about the floor.

Louis Claiborne, from Brooks Brothers to the Supreme Court, 1994.

I was impressed that he never once looked at his watch. Almost twenty minutes had gone by when the young man reappeared with the suit still unwrapped. He was flushed and uncertain. "Sir, your account seems to be overdrawn. Your last payment was three years ago." Louis frowned, scowled, curled a lip and responded in even, cutting tones. "Young man, you wrap that suit to go. My account may remain overdrawn for another three years.

That is no concern of yours. What is a concern of yours is that you are irritating me and there will be legal consequences if you continue to do so." Louis turned and continued strolling through the department.

The young man, possibly a bit less young now, appeared in five minutes with Louis's serious suit wrapped to go. "Please accept my apologies, sir," he said as he delivered the box to Louis.

• • •

It is now 1999, many years after the Brooks Brothers confrontation. Louis and Jackie were at their vacation home in Nerja, Spain, on the Mediterranean coast. Louis had insisted that we all turn the tour into a happy event, for his sake. He did not relish hand-wringing.

We asked Omer and Jeanette to fly to Europe with us. I planned a trip that would give Liz pleasure and memories. We included Omer and Jeanette both for the pleasure portion of the trip and the last stop in Nerja, where we would be with Louis and Jackie. Our first stop was the inn in Les Baux, discovered by Kim a number of years earlier, called La Riboto de Taven. La Riboto, elegant and lushly fresh at this time of the year, had been and would continue to be our first stop in Provence. Then to Granada and the Alhambra, which was a one-day affair. Tourist time seems to be the wrong time of the year to visit a well-known tourist stop. There were huge tour buses everywhere, waiting lines, debris underfoot, shrieking children (for me, a calamity).

Next, the drive south to Nerja. Despite his illness, we spent two lovely days with Louis. I admired him for his fertile, capacious mind, his encyclopedic knowledge of so many things unlikely to be of use, his haughtiness when plagued by a Brooks Brothers salesperson about a long unpaid bill, so effective that he left with a box of new merchandise and an earful of apologies.

The weather was perfect, clear, warm and dry. We strolled a good part of each afternoon, rested at an outdoor café in the village square, drank espresso, lunched. Liz took many snapshots of our group, most of which I still have. Everyone, Liz as well, looked healthy, she a bit thinner, but happy. We were so pleased to be with one another, fully aware that this would be our last visit together.

• • •

Omer, Liz and Louis in Nerja, Spain, 1999.

I've deliberated about breaking into the sequence of the story. You don't as yet know Bob and Ellen Knight, close friends from the time of the purchase of Tranquillity until and after Liz's death. And you haven't met Dr. Peter Raven, close friend then, close friend now, but a man with an army of friends, accomplishments and genealogical ties impressive in the extreme. But I've decided to do so. I want you to be aware of the special delight that Liz derived from these reciprocal friendships.

July and August were Montana months. All seemed well. We had seen the Knights at their ranch early in August. That was the late afternoon Ellen had snapped her to-be-famous photograph of Liz and me and Liz's revered Boxster. We had been feted at the Holter Museum in Helena the night of my birthday, a night we were joined by our delightful and famed friend, houseguest for the weekend, Dr. Peter Raven.

Bob Knight, a large man of deep convictions, our Montana attorney, was considered the best real estate attorney in the state. He was thorough, determinedly consistent and insistent on points that he considered uncompromisable. He took matters seriously, so seriously that he eventually retired from the practice of law. Ellen Knight is a lovely butterfly of a person, a pretty woman with a ready smile who finds life agreeable. She loves to study soft-bodied pond life. Give her a strainer and knee pads and a small pond, Ellen becomes happily busy for as long as you permit. I'm not sure anyone ever truly understood Ellen's love of invertebrate life, but that she found pond life fascinating is unarguable. Ellen Knight loves leeches among other wiggly things that flourish in ponds. We asked her once about her affection for those creatures. She smiled knowingly and answered, "I love these creatures. They have evolved to live simple, harmless lives. There's a lot to be learned from leeches and the world they live in."

They're both hovering on either side of sixty, are politically progressive and environmentally hard-nosed. Ellen makes the tastiest scrambled egg sandwich in Montana and Bob is a superlative man at the grill, an expert on barbecue and, incidentally, a head-over-heels lover of jazz music. However, as flexible and starlight strewn as Ellen may be, Bob found it difficult to let go of hard-held positions. He was always a gentle person during Liz's years, even though he gave up his law practice because the practice was held to be responsible for unsalvageable digestive problems.

They have a small cottage south of Ovando, Montana, about ten miles north of the juncture of Route 83 and Route 200. The cottage is almost midway between Tranquillity and Triple 8. It was here that we came early to dinner one late afternoon at the end of August and one of our favorite photographs was taken: Liz and me, my right arm around her shoulder, she bedecked in a bright yellow sweater, a white cap, a white shirt, blue jean and an overwhelmingly radiant smile. I'm in jeans wearing a darker jeans jacket over a chambray shirt. At Liz's right sits her "racing" yellow Porsche Boxster, purchased as a birthday present, but because of the special color, newly arrived. Sweater and Boxster were beautifully matched. Here was another nova outburst of the moment, captured forever by Ellen Knight.

• • •

August 13, 1999, my seventy-third birthday, was a Triple 8 required-attendance event. Liz and I were being honored by the Holter Museum, one of Helena's cultural reasons for being, the other being the Myrna Loy Center, named, of course, after the famous actress, once a native of Helena. The Holter Museum was erected in the memory of the Helenan Dr. Norman Holter, inventor of the Holter harness, a device one wears to monitor one's heart. I wore one a few years ago and can certify that clumsy and unfashionable as it may be, it is wearable.

Liz and her second love, her Porsche Boxster, in 1999.

The event was advertised as honoring the two of us because of our contributions to the arts, a contribution that involved a few years of contributing to this museum and the Yellowstone Art Museum. Fine enough.

Peter Raven had stopped by to refuel at Triple 8 and we were all prepared to shuttle to Tranquillity, where Peter's wife number four would be appearing. Dr. Peter Raven is the director of the Missouri Botanical Garden, possibly the premier garden in the world. Its home is St. Louis and Peter has been director for decades, it seems. His international fame, his background and foreground, as well as his intimidating knowledge, are softened by a sense of humor that delights him as much as the rest of us, possibly more so. Peter's loquacity demands an attentive audience. There is no choice. His sound box has no on-off knob, no volume-control switch. But the instrument always produces a delightful product.

He is a tall, bulky man with a round face, wisps of graying hair (remember, wives aplenty) and various physical ailments that keep him going at a slow pace: strained ankle, for instance. But nothing really keeps Peter going at a slow pace; he is a whirling dervish touring the world, generally with garden donors or trustees. His newest wife, one determined to remain his newest wife, is Patricia. Pat is an acknowledged horticulturalist who had spotted him as he wandered into the hotel bar one convention evening. He never escaped. I take it for granted that Peter is a happy detainee. He should be. Pat is a capable and caring wife, as well as a worthy colleague. That is perhaps why Peter is a man full of smiles. He is, whether the term pleases him or not, a jovial man.

Despite having a mind that recalls the most obscure Linnean plant descriptions, Peter is proudest of his family heritage. "You should be aware that I'm a direct descendant of Patrick Breen, who wrote the only diary of the ill-fated Donner-led trip to Oregon in 1846. He and his wife had met the Donners and all determined to go west. Unfortunately they got snowed in trying to navigate a pass through the Sierra Nevada mountains and then came their four months of ordeal. Of the original 87 pioneers, 39 died and 48 survived."

Liz pointed out to me that of those who survived, the majority were women and members of the same families. "You see, family counts. Women lead the herd." This was elephant talk, but Peter understood. He concurred.

• • •

The remaining days of August and the first three weeks of September, normal and natural, were spent in Montana. We had guests who came and went. We rode. We attended our regularly scheduled Montana Heritage Project fall executive committee meeting and dined with the group that evening at the Montana Club, a customary sequence. The project, at the time, seemed on track.

On September 20, we flew back to New York, where a routine check-up had been scheduled. The word routine no longer applied. Liz was beginning to tire more easily. She had been in remission for nearly one year, October 1998 to October 1999. It had been a wonderful but worrisome year. That Liz was sixty-nine when the disease was discovered, and that there was no guarantee that we could nip it in the bud, had been a given. We had been told that there was no valid reason to assume that the Pap test had uncovered a first-time appearance of the disease. We took nothing for granted.

Mark saw her on the 23rd and took a CA125 reading. It was 196. We knew the beast was back.

The sudden upward surge in a CA125 reading, seemingly without warning, is not unusual. Liz had being feeling well, all seemed under control, and suddenly the seeds broke out, very much like a small army, reassembling its forces.

Mark, in a later discussion, talked about what he called the "two-track" circumstance of this disease. I'm going to try to simplify the essence of that discussion.

I referred earlier to CA125 as a context-driven marker. The context is related to Mark's two-track description. First, let's remember that Liz's disease was atypical of an ordinary cancer; there was no tumor, as such, to contend with. There were tiny cancerous seeds. You can picture them as guerrilla warriors, hiding under the peritoneum, seeming to have been wiped out, but only seemingly so. When they reappeared and attacked Liz's digestive system, they left scar tissue on the surface of the digestive tract and throughout the bowel system. The residual scar tissue then further lessened Liz's ability to rhythmically move food through her system. Thus a number of painful, nausea-filled bouts followed. That was track one.

Track two describes the effect of the chemotherapy itself. The infusion of aggressive chemicals into the digestive system, on their own, produced side effects, such an innocent term full of bitter consequences. The drugs did attack the cancerous cells, but often at the price of exhaustion, diarrhea, and, over time, many other unpleasant, but described as perfectly natural, side effects.

A CA125 reading when Liz had not had chemotherapy for some period of time might be high, say 200 or more, but she might be feeling quite well. The same reading when Liz was absorbing chemotherapy would create a different physical circumstance, one usually more stressful. Nonetheless, low readings were always welcome. They indicated the possibility of some surcease in this ongoing battle.

The events of our lives seem to have been so arranged that even bad news had to be pushed aside until we honored whatever commitments we had previously made. So it was now. The Missouri Botanical Garden had institutionalized an annual award, the Henry Shaw Medal for conservation excellence. We were sure that Peter had been our chief booster, but nonetheless, we had been selected to receive the award on September 28 in St.

Louis. Henry Shaw, English financier and botanist, was the man responsible for endowing the Garden well over one century ago. It was considered a substantial honor to receive the award and so we took ourselves to St. Louis, living our lives as normally as possible as per Dr. Pasmantier's suggestion, and received the award.

I am holding a photograph taken that evening. Liz is receiving the medallion. We were there in full regalia, both of us in splendid tuxedos. Liz is smiling her radiant smile as if all was well with the world. I stand at her side, somewhat slumped, smiling feebly, worried. Liz had learned to compartmentalize her feelings. It was not apparent to anyone, excluding me, that she had stumbled in her long-distance run to win her race against her disease.

Chemotherapy 2—Taxol-Platinum 10/15/99 to 4/6/00

Liz was out of remission. Outwardly Liz was matter-of-fact with her doctor, but that was not how she truly felt. She was unnerved, deeply disappointed. We had spoken at length with Dr. Pasmantier. He was also disappointed, but his spirits were up and he was optimistic about the future.

"You handled the first go-round well," he said. "We all hoped for remission. We didn't get it. We're dealing with a subtle disease. It's hard to stamp out. But we have a full toolbox and we have a tough patient. Right?"

Liz did her best. She looked Mark in the eye and said, "Right. You know I'll do whatever I have to do."

I was in the room with her. I held her hand and I could feel the determination in her tightening grip. She added, "If that's the way it is, that's the way it is."

It was Mark's opinion that, all in all, Liz had tolerated the Taxol-platinum treatment well. The fatigue and nausea she experienced were expected from days three through days six or seven after the treatment. "You've done well, Liz. I know it's hard to accept the return to treatment. But you're resilient, much more than many much younger patients."

It would be Taxol-platinum again, a stronger dosage administered once every four weeks.

Liz and I performed our separate roles as actors in the script spoken in Dr. Pasmantier's office. She already had a chic supply of caps. It was time to start thinking about wigs. We readied ourselves for a longer journey. Ian had introduced her to Nicholas Piazza, a wig designer whose office was on the

Receiving the Henry Shaw Award from David Kemper of the Missouri Botanical Garden Board of Trustees, September 1999.

same floor as Clive's salon. We now had a standard to go by. Liz ordered three wigs to match the corn-yellow of her bleached hair, one synthetic in the event of dreaded rain, and two in hair. Wigs are not inexpensive, a bit over two thousand dollars each. If Liz was going to be a cancer patient, she would be a beautiful cancer patient.

Liz had few confidantes: there was Kim and there was, to a much lesser extent, Kathy Orsello, Triple 8 housekeeper, assistant chef, gardener and all-around cabin steward. Kathy Orsello is five feet nine inches tall, well formed, favored by Liz because she was an independent woman who had raised two sons alone and educated them while working at whatever job was available. Kathy, like Liz, never indulged in self-pity. Her long face, bracketed by black sleek hair parted down the middle to frame her Irish blue eyes, seemed to be an accurate rendering of the many strains of family background she carried in her blood.

She's not Italian, that's clear. Orsello was her father's adopted name, a name he inherited shortly after birth. He was Norwegian and Irish, mainly Norwegian. Her mother is Scottish and Welsh.

Kathy now proudly asserts that she's a third-generation Montanan and in Montana that's the equivalent of being a Cabot or Lodge in Massachusetts. She has flaunted an impulse to self-destruct but has always had the stamina and sense of responsibility to disarm the grenade. She was married at the age of nineteen, spurned a college education and bore a son three months later. And so the story went: another son five years later, a divorce eight years later, and so on. As a result of the on-and-off successive twists and turns of her life, Kathy admired the stability that Liz and I were able to bring to our now-threatened lives.

Liz called Kathy that October, a routine call about ranch matters. And then, according to Kathy, Liz suddenly blurted out, "I'm going to have to go back. I'm out of remission." And then, quite out of character, Liz said, "I'm frightened, Kathy. I hope my doctor is being straight with me."

Kathy, who has a number of widowed friends, then said, "Of course he is." She told Liz about a few of her friends who had cancer and lived many years after the discovery and treatment of the disease. "You can live a long time with cancer" was the message. For Liz, the message was positive.

She had lunch with my sister, Gloria, later in November. Gloria told me that Liz had repeated Dr. Pasmantier's words, "many tools in the toolbox."

Another battle with cancer was being lost a continent away. Louis was dying. Liz sent her sad news to Kim October 3:

"Dear Kim, If I've been off the radar screen again it's because all plans are on hold again! We came back here (Tranquillity) for the weekend leaving tomorrow AM for NY. Our week was the usual race—dentist, dermatologist, blood tests, CT scans, oncologist and slightly disappointing news. The numbers are not good. It looks like another round of chemo. But who knows.... With a little bit of luck? More depressing is Louis. He's dying, but working on a Supreme Court brief. It's gone so quickly with him. Jackie's great as is my devoted partner! Art's wonderful." She closed with *"Love from both of us to the three of you xxxx Liz."*

Louis died on October 6. He died at home, scribbling notes on a case his firm had been arguing in the United States. He thought he had found "the hook," the case in past law that would be the necessary precedent in this case. He was right.

We flew to England on November 5, a little window that Liz had between her booster and the next treatment. Omer was with us. Liz wrote Kim after we had returned to Fire Island that she thought the memorial service was dramatically moving, "a celebration of Louis!"

A few months ago I came across a file Liz had kept titled "Louis' Obituaries, Oct. 6, 1999." The enclosed documents were maintained as an ongoing tribute to Louis. Liz loved him, admired him and derived courage from him.

In her fax to Kim, Liz also referred to her treatment, the booster shots and the blood tests as a "damn nuisance!" Well, it was all a damned nuisance. But, being Liz, she mostly kept her anxieties to herself. It was enough if she acted them out from time to time.

She told Kim that this time it would be eight sessions, "so that by my birthday, I should be all finished, if still bald."

I often find that I must put my mind on pause and cease recounting, and, instead, think about what Liz's life and death taught me about the dualisms of life. The end of life, I thought, brought nothing but oblivion. I do not believe that any longer. I know that Liz is here, with me. She has made her presence palpable in ways that are, for me, undeniable. Does an essence outlive the material matter of human life? For me, my lifelong awareness of Liz's presence indicates that indeed that essence is real, that Liz's soul is within me.

A letter that I received a week after Liz's death from Mary Pearl suggested to me that Mary sensed that essence in Liz while Liz was still alive. Mary had been a trustee of our foundation and is now the director of Wildlife Trust, an effective field conservation group. The letter was dated July 5, 2007:

"Dear Art, I am heartbroken to think that Liz no longer graces the world with her beautiful presence. I was really proud to be able to spend so much time with her…I remember when she expressed sincere and enthusiastic pleasure enjoying the beauty of the numeral 8! She floored me with her grace when the only reference she made to her first recurrence of cancer was an expression of happiness that she had saved the many wonderful hats her friends had made to cover her chemo-induced bald head from the first time around."

I've thought about Mary's words often. I've also thought about Liz's "religious" love of beauty. It's become clear to me that Liz's love of beauty, her love of absorbing the world through all her senses led to her insistence that the things she surrounded herself with be "pretty" as well as functional. It's been made clear to me that her love of "seeing" is of major importance for all life: creatures of the wild who "see" and fulfill their roles, and creatures, such as us, of the "civilized" world. She gave us, through her living of her life, as she saw and sensed and felt what it is "to be," a compelling justification of human life itself.

"Seeing," for Liz had the broadest of meanings: intuitively feeling oneself a part of all things, a fragment of the great sensibility that gives life and awareness their deepest meaning. And the beauty of what we are privileged to see assured her that beauty was the essence of life; that in beauty, was the soul of life.

• • •

By October, it was evident that more treatment was needed. Liz was not finished, perhaps far from finished. The two of us were aware that she was now under siege. Mark Pasmantier's quiet optimism, his assurance that there were many chemicals available, many roads to travel, helped sustain us. We believed him and he was right. So she marched forward, appearing matter-of-fact to all the world except me. She was under attack. Her opponent was subtle and tricky. But Liz was a person of unsinkable determination and courage. She would stretch the outer limits of endurance.

November 24 was our first test of the schedule for the return of chemotherapy. The treatment was in New York, and then we were off to St. Barts the next day and then back to New York for the booster and a layover in New York awaiting the next round. The first cycle put us back in St. Barts on December 17. Liz was paying a price for this scurrying about. Nausea, headaches and fatigue plagued the first few days after each treatment. Some dinners were canceled. Soup became her evening comfort. But, as with the first cycle, as the days passed, she slowly recovered. It was hard on her, painful to watch, and at times so frustrating for her that she leaned even harder on me.

There was no thought of canceling the holiday arrangements. Alex was due in St. Barts on the 23rd and was to stay through Christmas and leave on the 29th. Neil, my son, a few years older than Alex, was coming to St. Barts with a friend to spend New Year's Eve. Nancy, my daughter, a year older than Alex, would be spending the holidays at home with her mother in Oak Park, Illinois. Neil and Nancy had grown up in Oak Park. Their mother had moved there after our divorce became final in 1957. Her parents lived in Chicago and Illinois was where she wanted the children. That's how it worked out. Liz and I took my children every summer. Liz encouraged that. She was kind, fair and always supportive. Neil and Nancy responded to her, sometimes defiantly testing her, but never losing her affection.

Neil is good-looking, dark-haired, tall, with a body developed through weightlifting, kept in use through many hours on his treadmill. Liz had always liked Neil. She very much liked a certain gentleness that was a Neil trademark.

We had seen little of Neil over the months and less of Nancy. Neil was then and still is working on a documentary film that absorbs much of his time. Nancy, living in Oak Park near her mother, had found fulfillment in photography. She is blessed with a loving nature, had taught preschool children earlier in life, strummed her guitar and sang lovely songs for the children. They adored her. Now her photography is of great importance to her. She's had a number of shows in Oak Park. Liz and Nancy hit it off as photographers. Nancy welcomed Liz's critiques.

Neil and Nancy both admired Liz. As I think a bit more about it, I would say they loved her.

• • •

It is the holiday season of a disappointing year-end: Christmas and the beginning of the New Year. Alex is with us for a short while; Neil for New Year's Eve. Liz, her determination once more in total repair, has just a handful of family with her. She, despite having no true family in New York once Alex had moved to Los Angeles, never felt that it was she, the personal she, who had been quarantined. Omer's four children, from a prior marriage, had become isolated through distance and some mistaken sense that Liz lacked interest in them. I now find this loss of connection distressing.

I have a packet of photographs taken in 1984, fifteen years before the time I now describe. The photographs were taken at Tita's wedding. Tita, nickname for Elizabeth, is Omer's only daughter. Louis and Jackie were there, as were Omer and Boofie, Omer's first wife and mother of his four children. Liz was at the peak of her powers, beautifully draped in white silk, and so obviously fond of Tita and happy for her that I am virtually capable of time travel and we are all once again at this endlessly gay wedding. We danced en masse as a loving family.

Now, Alex, even in Los Angeles, had to fulfill Liz's need for family.

Alex, as I have earlier described, is the son of Ben Schultz, Liz's first husband. After her father and mother had left her on a street corner in New York, one piece of luggage beside her, a fifty-dollar bill in her hand, she got on with her life. She found a job through *Harper's Bazaar*, met Ben Schultz, then art director at Bonwit Teller, showed him her portfolio and was denied a job, but asked out on a date. Ben was Jewish, more than ten years older than Liz, and seemed a most imperfect beau to bring home to her father. So she married him. For Omer Villere Claiborne, a man of tradition, a man of a background who carried the blood of the first and second governors of Louisiana, that broke it. He didn't talk to Liz for the next seven years, not until she brought her second Jewish husband to Pass Christian, Mississippi, in 1957, the day Liz and I were married.

Liz was never fully able to square her divorce, when Alex was a baby, with her obligation to be a traditional American mother. It wasn't the norm, back in 1954, for a working woman to continue working after having a child. Liz continued working. She had divorced Alex's father, later married me and given over a major part of her life and time to her career.

She had to accommodate herself to supporting Alex, having trustworthy help to care for him while she worked. She lived in a five-story walk-up and had hired a loving and capable mother's helper, Yvonne Stephens, to take care of Alex while she worked. The years of going through her apprenticeship, raising Alex and determinedly waiting for me to dissolve my marriage were years that only a person of Liz's determination could have navigated. I have a portfolio of sketches of Alex as an infant that Liz drew when time permitted. I found them in her files after her death.

Liz's mother had managed to secretly send her a monthly cash allowance by mail, never more than one hundred dollars. Her father not only had ceased talking to her, but he had forbidden his wife to help Liz or be in communication with her. Thus each letter Liz received, and they were infrequent, was headed in huge letters "OFF THE RECORD!!!!" The letters were secretly mailed and no response was required.

In an interview in the early 1990s, Liz told Gene Landrum, a student working on a PhD thesis, "I worked to the last day of my pregnancy and came back to the office two weeks later. In retrospect it's not such a smart thing to do."

Landrum went on to say, "Liz was ahead of her time in juggling a career with family and her son paid the price for having an often absent mother. She was an adequate mother and an eminent entrepreneur. Her creative genius was realized only after her son was grown, so she was unobstructed when faced with starting Liz Claiborne."

Despite the turns in the road, here we were, Liz and me, Alex and Shar, Alex's girlfriend of the moment, and Neil. It was far from a full house, but we managed a number of unusually warm family days together. We had a three-foot-high Christmas tree which Liz tinseled, wrapped in a rainbow-colored string of lights and made a Christmas as festive as if for a village. We hung a wreath on the front gate of the residence and a wreath atop the glass entrance sliders to our living room. Stocking stuffers were matted around the base of our little tree. We had a wonderful Christmas, dinners out, smiles everywhere, and best of all, Liz felt well. She had given me three small gifts. I don't remember now what they were except for a "feel calm" thin bracelet.

I have a file drawer in my study in which I have placed a file of all the cards we have exchanged over the years. These cards are beyond priceless. One reads as follows: "12/25/99, To my partner, my supporter, my friend, Merry Christmas 1999. May the year 2000 be less 'trying' (perhaps I should wear the bracelet) YOUR ADMIRER, as always, Love Liz."

We celebrated the new millennium by sending "good wishes" cards to our closest friends. We used Ellen Knight's joyful photograph, taken in early August at Bob and Ellen's cabin. We had considered the snapshot so appealing—Liz with her cap snugly on her bald head, grinning with such radiance, exuding joy and optimism, delighted to be showing her Boxster and husband to the world—that we used it as our first and last New Year's card. Even though Liz was back in chemotherapy, she refused to be other than joyful.

Our message: "May the new millennium bring us all kindness, openness and all good things. Liz & Art."

CHAPTER FOUR, 2000

LIZ HAD TWO chemo treatments in January, one in February, one in March. Her CA125 was now down to 41, not quite there. She told Mark in April that it was now taking her longer to feel well, four to six days. Despite her discomfort, at times more than discomfort, we continued our schedule of going to St. Barts the day after a treatment. There was Terra Nova to be considered and detailed. Day one after treatment was generally the easiest day. That was travel day. The following days, as Dr. Pasmantier had advised, difficult as they might be, Liz was to try to live as a normal, healthy person.

I considered myself a privileged person in a theater, where the only act on stage was Liz, puzzling over a drawing of the angle of a sliding door, the dimensions of a closet, the shelving arrangement for dishware in "la cuisine." If in pain, she might even take a Fioricet headache pill, or lie down for fifteen minutes. But then she was back on her feet, and the work continued. Work was an ongoing antidote.

I believe that this involvement in living for future gratifications was essential for the two of us. We never stopped building to accommodate our future together.

Eight hundred sixty Fifth Avenue is a twenty-story prewar building, well maintained, between 67th and 68th Street in Manhattan, facing Central Park. For me, living on Fifth Avenue facing the park was another childhood dream, like going to Ushuaia, now attainable. Once we stepped into apartment 18H, it had to be ours. We passed the board and, cancer or not, Liz and I looked forward with pleasure to the fun of design, really a renovation of what seemed to be a Turkish seraglio, heavy maroon velvet draperies and cornices, deep pile Kurdistan rugs, brass and faux gold adornments everywhere. That all went, to be replaced by poured cement floors, large sliding glass doors, leather furniture in brilliant colors—i.e., a nine-foot red leather sofa backed by a mirrored wall that extends the space forever—plants everywhere, an indoor free-form planter, plants on the front terrace and a seasonal garden on the south terrace. Liz was immersed in designing again. Her focus could be so supremely intense that all else was forgotten. The work she did amazed our architects. She designed an entire bedroom wall that contains well over fifty compartments: shelves, hanging space, bottom drawers, top storage space, all behind white enameled facings. Liz measured each space to the nanometer, submitted her drawings to the architects and supervised the work. The apartment is full of Liz design and therefore gaspingly beautiful to the eye and to the mind. I insist that she lives here now with me. I will rarely make an important decision without asking her.

I am told that talking to oneself is either an affliction or a solace for people who suddenly find themselves living alone. It is neither. For me, it's perfectly normal.

We shared St. Barts that year with time at Fire Island. Liz loved being at the beach. Alex visited in April, spent time at the island with us. We walked the beach together, speculated on Alex's future as a musician. Was his development as a musician satisfactory to him? Time was passing. When would he settle down? Liz very much wanted to see Alex married. She wanted to be sure that he had someone to take care of him. As was generally the case with Alex, no conclusions were reached. "We'll see." We were all accustomed to this scenario. Merely airing it again was sufficient for Liz. Open-ended or not, for Liz it was a happy time.

The Le Corbusier chaises still sit where Liz put them, one in the living space of Cabin B at Triple 8. There's a white shag rug with long tassels tossed across the bottom of the chaise. Liz would pull the rug over herself. As time went on she became increasingly vulnerable to cold. The other chaise sits in the observatoire in Terra Nova in St. Barts. This is indeed an observatory, a small library with a semi-circular white pillowed couch and our trademark sliding glass doors opening to a round terrace overlooking St. Jean Bay. Liz's Le Corbusier lounge chair, heavy white canvas bordered head and foot in rich tan leather, perched on a wrought-iron black frame, sits across the room from the sofa. What an eternally cheerful space. There is a round cube of stone about eighteen inches high on which stands a Deborah Butterfield metal horse. It's a thirty-inch-long collage of brilliantly painted pieces. The horse is called *Cosmo*. He looks toward one small shelf on which rests a small driftwood sculpture of a seabird, a Louis Claiborne sculpture. This was Louis's hobby in his last years at Nerja. He sculpted birds out of driftwood. This was a present from Louis to his sister, Liza. That was her family name: Liza, stress on the second syllable.

Chemotherapy 3—Topotecan 5/11/00 to 9/18/00
Administered five consecutive days, once monthly

Mark Pasmantier could see that determined as she was, Liz was having a more exhausting time handling the side effects of the treatment. Even though eight months of Taxol-platinum had been scheduled, he felt that the side effects of the treatment were overly taxing. Thus far, the Taxol treatment had reduced Liz's CA125 to a bit over 40—good, but not remission. She seemed to have stabilized, but we were targeting better than that, remission.

So Dr. Pasmantier introduced a new chemical cocktail and a new schedule: He explained the drug as a chemical mix, just like the other chemotherapy drugs. "I think we've gone as far as we should with the Taxol. I don't want it to lose its long-term effectiveness. And I don't want you to have to undergo tough side effects. We call topotecan a consolidator. Its use will consolidate, or retain the effect of the Taxol."

Liz was happy to escape Taxol treatment.

"I'm going to administer this drug five consecutive days, one week each month. They'll be short treatments, and because of the frequency, less toxic."

On May 15 the new treatment began.

There was still work to be done in St. Barts, topotecan or not. We had so poorly planned our breakfast nook, secreted in the most gale-receptive part of our outside walking terrace that, despite heavy plastic hangings, despite pulleys and tie-down cleats, breakfast was normally eaten in the teeth of a gale. That's the way the wind blows in St. Barts. It relieves the mind of other oppressions. Terra Nova, indeed, was a planning of space worthy of Scott. The only answer was to punch a doorway through the west end of the kitchen and construct a dining turret. And so it came to be, a circular room about fifteen feet in diameter accommodating a round stone table on a round stone centerpiece. All of this was enclosed by about sixteen feet of sliding glass curved windows. And thus we had a windless dining room and a magnificent view of St. Barts. Work on the turret had begun on day one of topotecan.

We had learned how to keep our lives arranged so that disorder was rarely apparent. We created separate compartments to accommodate a broad variety of activities. There was a dimensionless compartment for our reconstruction in St. Barts. There was a time and space for any event we felt important.

• • •

The Council of Fashion Designers of America had chosen Liz to receive their Humanitarian Award that year. The work of the foundation was well-known as was Liz's personal involvement. She was interviewed by Eric Wilson, then of *Women's Wear Daily*, during the first week of June. The two-page spread appeared on June 14, 2000. A banner headline stretched across the

Left to right: Liz in Antigua, 1964; in the late 1960s; at the Youth Guild, 1971.

pages. It read "Liz's Wildlife Lessons." There were six photographs under the headlines showing Liz at certain times in her career, from 1962 to 1999. I've excerpted parts of the interview.

"Claiborne is seventy-one and looks nearly the same as she did when she re-tired. She is tan and wears a black T-shirt and pants, a white Liz Claiborne jeans jacket and big red Liz Claiborne glasses, all of them kept from her days at the helm of the company. The only thing not Liz Claiborne about her is a white Polo Sport cap, which she wears to mask the result of chemotherapy treatments for a rare cancer that affects the lining between the abdomen and the reproductive organs, with which she was diagnosed three years ago."

Toward the end of the interview Eric asked Liz, "How are you doing with your treatments?" Liz responded, "I'm at just about the end of it. But they still want me to have a few more treatments, and it gets more difficult as you get to the end, because your body has had so much, and it takes a little longer to recuperate. But I feel great and when I first heard I was going to have to go through chemo I thought, 'Oh my God, this is terrible.' But it's not that bad. I'd like to be able to tell everybody that. So you spend a bad day or two or three bad days a month. Anybody can do that."

She appeared at the awards presentation at Lincoln Center in a black tuxedo, wearing a black fedora with a colorful feather tucked in a four-inch

Left to right: The Beginning, 1976; in 1978; in the 1980s.

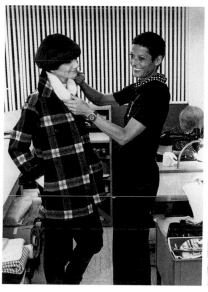

white satin band. She looked smashing. As Dr. Pasmantier always reminded me, that was her specialty, looking smashing.

The July treatments took place at St. Peter's Hospital, which for Liz became a pleasure jaunt. She felt thoroughly unpressured. The room was large, space for treatment always available. The nurses were always on the floor, attentive and unhurried. I sat in a small chair next to her a good part of the time. Dr. Weiner, all smiles, blue oxford and bright assurance, had little but good news for us. But best of all, Liz drove her Boxster the twenty miles to town for every treatment. And better yet, the treatment seemed effective. Her CA125 was down to 35 in July. We saw Dr. Pasmantier for a general examination at the beginning of August and he delivered the good news. Her CA125 was now 30. We flew back to Montana and celebrated my birthday on the 13th with Bob and Ellen Knight. All was well with the world.

The year 2000, new millennium or not, had thus far brought a whirlwind of action. We had been to Washington, DC, at the end of April for an overnight trip. Georgetown University, led by Dr. Richard Lazarus, who had written a classic profile of Louis's work at the bar, had staged the afternoon.

Liz opens our Singapore office, 1987.

Top: Liz at Lindbergh Lake, Montana, 2002. Below: Corporate portraits from the 1980s.

Glamour magazine named Liz Claiborne among the best dressed women of the year, 1985.

Liz looking smashing—and determined in Alaska, 1986.

Former members of the Solicitor General's office attended. It was more than a memorial. It was a poignant goodbye to a man, but a sadder goodbye, they knew, to a fully civilized life. We had flown up from St. Barts and returned the next day. Liz's June was packed: the new treatment, the interview, the humanitarian award. During all of this activity, topotecan was at work.

• • •

Red Lodge Workshop—July 18, 2000—The Concept Meeting

Before Tom Moore came on the scene, the dining room at Tranquillity was an interior space, the eastern façade of the building a solid mass of logs, vented to release cooking odors. There against the log wall, extending about thirty feet north and south, sat the kitchen. Tom had it all flipped, cut huge holes in the eastern log façade, and voilà, a lovely dining room with glorious views of the Swan Mountains.

On July 18, 2000, eight of us sat around an antique dining room table: an environmental educator and magazine publisher; the dean of the School of Forestry; his subordinate; the dean of the Bolle Center; Jonah Western, now the foundation's expert impresario on workshop planning; Liz, me and Jim Murtaugh. We were there to lay out a plan for a workshop that would stress the emerging importance of cooperation among stakeholders in addressing resource-use conflicts. It was to be called Collaborative Resource Management in the Interior West, an area extending from the Sierra Nevada, curse of the Donner party, eastward to North Dakota.

The impulse for this ambitious undertaking derived from Liz's strong belief that it was critically important to focus on our own country's conservation needs. At a 1990 self-examination board meeting, ten years earlier, Liz had particularly emphasized this belief. Jonah's notes were detailed:

"We should use Montana as a prototype of the problems our country is facing now and will be facing in the future. Habitat for wildlife is decreasing and competition for resources such as timber and water is on the increase. We will be faced with new global competition for resources. What effect will these pressures have on local peoples and on the natural resources they depend on, not only for jobs, but for recreation and for spiritual sustenance?"

136

Back at Tranquillity, now in 2000, I looked across the table and considered the past events that had brought us all together. I knew that Liz and I had always been thankful for our past relationship with the former dean of the School of Forestry, Arnie Bolle. He had inspired much of our thinking about the national commons: forests, waterways and the public's need to find gratification in their use.

My mind drifted back to St. Valentine's Day, February 14, 1994, six years earlier. We had similarly gathered in a small auditorium at the University of Montana. There would be four speakers and people from the press. At a table on the dais sat Arnie Bolle, Liz and me. The speakers, all admirers of Arnie, were Governor Racicot; Senator Max Baucus, senior senator from Montana; Jim Lyons, Under Secretary for Natural Resources and Environment and thereby head of the Forest Service; and George Frampton, director of The Wilderness Society.

Arnold Bolle had been the dean of the School of Forestry from 1962 to 1972, when bone cancer forced him to retire. However, the mark that he left on our national forest management policies became indelible. As a forest economist, as well as a seasoned resource manager, he introduced the concept of balanced multiple use in forest management. He set standards for the way work would be done on the ground in our national forests. He taught that what you left on the ground was as important, if not more so, than what you reaped. He set standards for water management, for monitoring wildlife, and for local citizen involvement in decision-making with the Forest Service that are relevant today. And he was always proud to be called a conservationist.

Perhaps, to his conservation public, he was best known for the Bolle Report, a work he produced in response to Senator Lee Metcalf's request that Arnie appoint a task force to work under his, Arnie's, direction. The public, or enough of the public to get attention, was objecting to Forest Service practices: clear-cutting, terracing mountainsides, forest-road design and unnecessary construction. The Bolle Report caused a furor. One hundred thousand copies were printed and distributed. The final product was the National Forest Management Act. To this day, the act is central to national forest management.

The event was reported with touching accuracy by a local newspaper:

"On St. Valentine's Day, 1994, Liz Claiborne and Art Ortenberg donated a major gift to the University of Montana Foundation to enable the formation of the Bolle Center for People and Forests. The gift was a valentine to their beloved friend, Arnie Bolle, and is its own legacy to The University of Montana, and a challenge to the College of Forestry and Conservation to continue the Bolle legacy of excellence in conservation."

We were there to dedicate the Bolle Center, a center that would encourage the teaching and learning of forestry conservation principles.

There we sat on the podium on this long-ago Valentine's Day. Arnie was now a close friend, a colleague who had been on the governing board of The Wilderness Society and who sat next to me at our biannual meetings. His hair was noticeably thinning. His lean intense face was bent close to the top of the table, intent on the notes he was taking. The effort was unbalancing his spectacles. His left sleeve was empty, pinned under his armpit. Arnie had cancer. His arm had been amputated.

We sat together now, Arnie, somewhat shaky, not completely in control, dressed in a suit, sleeve pinned. He was uncomfortable, but deeply pleased.

The speeches were short and to the point. Arnie was a man deeply admired by all.

He died within a few days. He had begun to lose bodily control. He no longer recognized his friends. His valentine gift continued his work for him.

• • •

The meeting at Tranquillity was the beginning of the planning for a workshop that would emphasize the principle of collaboration among stakeholders in the use of our national resources. A little over a year later, on the morning of October 21, 2001, we dedicated the Red Lodge Workshop to the memory of Dr. Arnold Bolle. The workshop, which I will describe shortly, was another high point in Liz's life.

The year had also brought its share of disappointments. Liz's closest friend, Elly Maggiore, fashion stylist and Fire Island buddy, full of good cheer and vitality, had been found to have cancer and was dead within months. She died in February.

138

In a fax early in the year, Liz had mentioned the discomfort of "rashes, diarrhea and other unmentionables."

In her fax to Kim about Elly's death, she wrote, "My treatment goes on and on. Numbers going down but not normal yet, but I'm lucky—it's treatable & I seem to tolerate OK."

In April she had faxed Kim:

"Thank you for the birthday wishes. I've had better birthdays but Art did some wonderful things prior to the chemo (the 30th of March) and even at the doctor's, they gave me a huge and delicious cake!!! & the beat goes on…numbers improving."

She had commented on the topotecan treatment:

"We will probably be in NY July 10 thru July 14 if all goes well with the new treatment. It kind of lays you low with very low white blood counts & platelets (& red also) so he (the Dr.) cannot guarantee that all will go on schedule. Art is getting worn down by these changes. This new schedule is so unpredictable & then what??? But he's wonderful—never pushing, always supportive. Lots of love from wonderful Fire Island. Liz."

The year was ending, nonetheless, on a hopeful note. There had been no treatment for three months. Alex had visited again in November and we continued speculating on his future. We made some light-hearted banter about his indecisiveness, but for Liz it was becoming more and more worrisome. She wanted to see him married.

Liz's fax to Kim at that time was consistent with so many in the past, a blend of frustration and hope:

"The summer seems to have whizzed by. We go back to N.Y. Sept. 7 for tests and regrouping, as my oncologist puts it! Schedule and plans will have to wait. I've no idea if more or different treatments will be in store…I do not allow myself to think it's finished! But I continue to feel well, so let's see."

Her CA125 was 40, a little disappointing. Another reading at the end of the month was more encouraging; the number was 30. There was no treatment scheduled for October, but Dr. Pasmantier felt that a laparoscopy was in order. The procedure took place at the end of the month.

She faxed Kim a few days later:

"Am sitting up in bed recouping (resting actually) from minor surgery yesterday. A 'laparoscopy'—holes in one's tummy to look-see, the biopsies etc. This is the last & final defining test. It's minor but uncomfortable. So far the look-see was good. Will know more next week…"

Her next fax to Kim was sent from St. Barts November 21. The handwriting is large, emphatic and angry:

"Hi Kim—Well it's still not over! And with me also—Good results but not perfect—Radiation treatments are now on the menu, so will have to leave St. Barts for about two months—except long weekends—Xmas, New Year maybe—Anyway…Everyone optimistic and I gather this is much more easily tolerated. Enfin! A very Happy Thanksgiving to you all. Back to NY Dec. 1—Much love—Liz."

Radiation—Daily for six weeks 12/6/00 to 1/8/01

Liz's radiation was to be supervised by Dr. Dattatretydu Nori, professor and chairman of New York-Presbyterian Hospital–New York Cornell Campus, Cornell Radiation Oncology Associates. The process began with two consecutive days of measurements of her abdomen area. Think of this as pinpointing finely placed targets for the radiation beam to penetrate. Precision is critical. The actual radiation began on December 6. She was not at all happy about any of this. This was an impersonal, uncomfortable process. But as the month progressed, she began to feel better, then much better and then, by the end of the month, just great. How wonderful! We had dinner out every evening, more often than not at an upscale restaurant. We were at Fire Island for both Christmas and the New Year. I still have the photograph of our Fire Island Christmas tree, the one and only time we had one there.

Liz's radiation treatments continued until January 8, 2001. There would be no further treatments for the near future. Dr. Nori would examine Liz in the spring and issue a report on her condition mid-May.

Liz's CA125 had plummeted, followed by a number of quiet months, dentists and implants, dinners with friends every evening, and weekends at Fire Island. We held our breath. She was feeling well, implants or no. She was considerably less active than during the early golden years. St. Barts was our winter haven. Liz treadmilled, less vigorously than in the past, but she insisted on a daily workout. I swam and treadmilled occasionally. We read for hours at a time. We had dinners, as in the past, at Maya's.

A special bonus emerged from the radiation treatments—no loss of hair. What a delightful time we had at Clive's salon, as the hair-bleaching process took place. The color had been established, all that remained was careful application. The wigs and caps were retired.

Despite the curves in the road, the loss of Elly, the ongoing discomforts, the year 2000 had ended on an upswing. Liz had little time for cards and gifts, but I do have some cards that she wrote during the year.

On July 5, our 43rd anniversary:

"I may be 'picky' but that's why I picked you in the first place—I wish we could have forty three more! I love you—your wife Liz."

For my birthday she had sent a card with a picture of Marilyn Monroe on the cover. The script in bold capitals read, "Forget Diamonds, you're the best friend a girl could have. Thanks for every thing!" Below the printed message, Liz wrote, "That's true! I'm no Marilyn (God knows!) but you make me feel like I'm as good as her & that's pretty neat! All my love, Liz, your wife."

CHAPTER FIVE, 2001

LIZ HAD JUST finished her radiation treatments in early January of 2001. She was feeling up, perhaps less energetic, but optimistic and glad to be Liz again, the Liz who had just left her company and found meaning in her new life and our foundation. I was quick to recall the fantastic recognition both she and I had received just ten years past.

And what a past—1990 and 1991 had been years that neither of us would ever forget! How proud we were of the recognition we received for the work we had done in building a great company. But very specifically, how proud I was of Liz and the honoraria she received.

Looking backward had become a necessary therapy for the two of us. We had saved photographs and documents, moving mementos of the extraordinary life we had shared. We shared the best of times, as we shared all times together.

There is a stunning photograph of the two of us, relaxed, all dressed up in evening wear, standing side by side and holding hands. We are at the Ritz-Carlton Hotel in St. Louis, Missouri. We have just descended from a luxury suite and are being readied to be honored. We are chatting with Dave Farrell, chairman of the evening's events, chairman and CEO of May Department

Stores, husband of Betty Farrell and an active board member of the Missouri Botanical Garden. Dave was the lead figure in this evening's event. It was April 11, 1990. Dave, a friend of ours, was known as a tough retailer, but also as an active and productive educator. He was the chairman of the Junior Achievement's 1990 U.S. Business Leadership Conference.

Junior Achievement Worldwide, formed in 1919, had been partnering with *Fortune* magazine since 1975 to introduce young people to the world of business. Junior Achievement Worldwide is, in its words, "a partnership between the business community, educators and volunteers—all working together to inspire young people to dream big and reach their potential."

The conference taking place that evening was, according to the program, to introduce to young people, to the business community and the world "eight business executives who will be inducted into the U.S. Business Hall of Fame. These laureates have attained the highest level of achievement in their industries and have made a tremendous impact on our free enterprise system. They serve as examples and role models and business executives throughout the country. Tonight we recognize the remarkable accomplishments of these laureates and showcase their remarkable experiences."

The selections had been made by *Fortune*'s board of editors with input and recommendations from business leaders, business reporters and educators throughout the country.

I have a group photograph taken that evening: a resplendent Dinah Shore

At Junior Achievement's 1990 U.S. Business Leadership Conference.

The entrants into the U.S. Business Hall of Fame, 1990.

sits center front, beaming happily. On her right is Charles Brown, CEO of AT&T. Liz sits at her left, wearing a short black tuxedo jacket over swishy white silk pants and a white silk high-necked T-shirt. Next to Liz sits a somewhat dour Thomas Watson, the founder of IBM. He is the only non-smiler in the seated row. Standing behind this group are six men, uniformly swathed in single-breasted tuxedos. Left to right, they are Jim Burke, CEO of Johnson & Johnson, the man who personally assumed responsibility for the Tylenol packaging fiasco; the son of Juan Trippe, the founder of Pan American Airlines; the sons of Louis B. Mayer and Samuel Goldwyn, legendary men of film; me, as tall and pleasant looking as the rest; and, to my left, James Hayes, the publisher of *Fortune*.

Fortune wrote, "Whether style makes the woman or the woman makes the style is now a settled question. Liz Claiborne has forever solved the conundrum. She is the woman who made the style that made the company bearing her name." As to Art Ortenberg, "He supplied the managerial talent to match Claiborne's creative brilliance."

The Waldorf-Astoria in New York City, March 26, 1991, was the venue of the next event in which Liz and I participated as honorees. Here we actually were at the Waldorf and we and eight others were to be inducted into the Marketing Hall of Fame. Barbara Walters was the mistress of ceremonies; Tony Bennett, the entertainer. Liz was dressed in a white silk pantsuit. That was her way of being noticed in a group photograph. She was right, of course. The group was photographed onstage fanning out from the central figures of Ronald and Nancy Reagan. Liz stood at the President's left. We had the extraordinary honor of not only being on stage with President and Nancy Reagan, but also with Katharine Graham of *The Washington Post*, and Sam Walton, the founder of Wal-Mart. Bob Hope was to have been honored as well, but he was too ill to attend. President Reagan accepted on his behalf.

Liz accepted her award and made a short speech, as did I. I may have been as eloquent as Liz, but all eyes were glued to her. Her earnestness and elegance were bewitching.

The Marketing Hall of Fame ceremony, attended by President and Nancy Reagan, 1991.

"I stand at this podium awestruck that my one modest ambition has brought me here…the ambition to create clothes for a broad range of American women…for our Nancy Everywoman…who come in all configurations…to our own, slim, elegant Nancy Reagan. To give them access to an honest, valid product…a product that in its clarity of design, its functionality, its durability and its lack of pretension would express the spirited optimism of the American experience. I thank you all. I thank my partner, and I particularly thank the designers and engineers, the marketers and merchants, every member of our Liz Claiborne family for permitting me some small success in that effort."

But the highest point of Liz's professional life, without qualification, came a few months later. She received an honorary doctorate degree from the Rhode Island School of Design, a prestigious, highly respected institution and a producer of extraordinarily gifted architects, designers and artists.

June 1, 1991. There stands Liz, her face aglow with pride as the medallion is placed around her neck.

She is ready to give the commencement address. She inhales deeply, clutches the podium and begins:

"This moment in my life is my scaling of Mount Everest, humbling and exhilarating, receiving this honor bestowed by peers, colleagues and fellow designers.

"I have tried very hard during my working years to shape my defining career decisions as a designer, true to the demands of good design as I saw them.

"We founded a company driven by the primacy of design and engineering and I resigned from the board of directors of that company fifteen years later because I could

Receiving an honorary doctorate from the Rhode Island School of Design, 1991.

no longer enforce that principle and because I felt at the time that scale and the compulsions of the world of dollars and cents, the apparent hostility of commerce and design in pursuit of ever-growing market share, made that principle unenforceable.

"After months of reflection, attempting to recapture and reevaluate the sources of my professional beliefs, I remain convinced that my resignation from the board was both proper and inevitable."

I sat in the audience in a seat that would permit me to look about without disturbing anyone. The silence in the room was overpowering. Liz was speaking slowly and I could feel her intensity as she grasped the podium. She would look up occasionally. I could feel her emotions, as I'm sure the audience did as well.

She continued:

"I was born in Brussels. My father was a compulsive buyer of paintings, my mother, a miraculously nimble and fearlessly inventive sewer, the first great technician from whom I learned to respect the mutual dependence of creative concepts and the skills needed to actualize those concepts."

This, for Liz, was a towering theme. She was to repeat it often.

"And then, I had the good fortune to have an extraordinarily sensitive teacher of painting at the academy in Nice who took me out of the classroom to the countryside, but before permitting me to begin sketching, said in the gravest of tones, 'And now I will teach you to see.' Quelle surprise! I, who had been exposed to fine art and lofty architecture all my life, who had been painting for years, who had perfectly functional eyes and knew how to use them, or so I thought. But slowly, under his tutelage, I learned the difference between seeing and truly seeing. I have never looked at things quite the same way since. The visual quality of everything around me became illuminated and intensified.

"My apprenticeship in seeing began as a small child. I was focused by my parents, by my teacher, by that special world they directed my attention to, to respond, almost viscerally to the graceful utility in my surroundings: the arrangement of flowers, table settings, napery and flatware, the lines of furniture, the rugs underfoot, wall hangings, the house one lives in, the way one wears one's hair, carries one's body. My entire life seemed to be immersed in things visual."

I was no longer aware of her audience. I knew so well what she was saying and how central to our lives was her sensitivity to the physical world she created for the two of us. My eyes were flooded with tears, then as they are now.

"I loved to draw. I loved to sew. Nothing seemed more natural than to combine the two. My prescribed classical art studies concluded, and being a full twenty-one-years-old, I headed for the fashion industry. My apprenticeship was to continue. I was determinedly a designer-to-be.

"My first job was with Tina Leser, a name now forgotten in our industry. But in 1950, when American sportswear was becoming a marketplace reality, Tina Leser was a sportswear designer with a point of view about clothes. How lucky I was, at the outset, to work for such a designer. The construction of the clothes was uniquely Tina Leser and deviation was not permitted. She believed that clothes should be fun to wear and that bright colors were essential. She believed this so fervently that no product line was ever without soaring color. I've never forgotten that principle. I learned many other valuable things from Tina Leser: that being a designer meant hard, long, interminably long hours of work, that no aspect was unimportant, from learning proper telephone speech as the trim buyer to illustrating clothes in someone else's style and doing it quickly. I learned how to model in the showroom so as to get the feel of the clothes, how one consciously reacts to the movement of fabric on one's body and knowing when the feeling is right."

We often spoke about Tina Leser and how valuable those days were for Liz. Tina Leser was highborn, much traveled and an avid connoisseur of the costumes and fabrics of the exotic places she visited. She nourished herself on riotously colored textiles and unexpected color combinations. Liz had built her company on the foundation of gay, happy colors.

Liz continued. I riveted my eyes on her, as did everyone in the audience.

"As rewarding as this initial experience was, I was convinced that my apprenticeship required familiarity with a much greater range of approaches to design. So I embarked on a planned program of working for a variety of designers, from very expensive Seventh Avenue couture (highly constructed) to classic, New England, preppy sportswear and eventually to action-packed junior sportswear and my introduction to the world of mass marketing. I discovered designing sportswear for a large audience was what I really wanted to do.

"Here I was given my first so-called design room, even though I was the lowly second designer, a room that could barely contain a cutting table, a sewing machine and two bodies, me the designer and her sample hand. Occasionally, the door to the room was flung open and fabric appeared, waiting for me to transform it into a salable product, well priced, constructed for manufacturability, exciting to look at, acceptable to every possible consumer, and to every house salesperson. No one had prepared me for serious draping, pattern making and cutting my own garments. But starting with what I had learned in my early apprenticeship and with a little help from my friends, I muddled through and made it to the number one design room—with a pattern maker and an assistant—and all the trappings of the house designer. This was my continuing beginning. This was the room that led me many years later to another room that closed the final door of my apprentice's journey."

And what a journey, I thought. She had built a company that in 1985 was named the second most admired Fortune 500 company in the country—and fifth most admired the following year. She had built a company that had the highest return on investment over a ten-year period, 1978 to 1988, of any Fortune 500 company in the country. She was the first woman chairperson of any Fortune 500 company in history. But those distinctions were not nearly as important to Liz, I knew, as being true to her craft.

"What did I learn during that journey that may be of some lasting value to you, as my colleagues? I believe that my most important lesson and the one whose implementation required the most courage was discovering who I was as a professional person: what did I truly, truly believe and would fight for—in terms of taste level and style—and what was visually and technically consistent with my standards of good design?

"I learned the qualifiers that must overlay any designer's work:

"A. Who is your audience? Who are you dressing? What does she do? Is she a suburban housewife, a school teacher, an assistant in a corporate setting? What is her income level? What age range are you trying to reach?

"B. And how do I communicate with her through the clothes? How can you grab her attention in a crowded, not so neat retail environment? Even more basic…how do you get the clothes in the store at all? What does the company you are with 'stand for' in the eyes of the buyers? How do you sell your own sales force?

"C. And to appreciate the fine line that often exists between design and engineering, clothes that truly fit are engineered by designers and by knowledgeable production personnel, not only to fit, but to flatter. Professional designers know that fit, con-

struction, manufacturability and quality are all vital parts of a compelling aesthetic. You simply must become expert in the details of your work.

"These principles, values, techniques, this respect for my consumer and this confidence in her ultimate good judgment formed the bedrock of our company.

"Early in 1976, with little capital, with a handful of investors who believed in us, with a third partner who had wonderful manufacturing skills, we invented Liz Claiborne Inc. I was the sole designer. It was my name, my company, everything a designer could ask for. My husband, my partner, claimed his role was to carry the banner and lead the charge. He surely did!"

Now I knew where Liz was headed. It was time to sit quietly, as did everyone else in the room, and absorb Liz's thoughts about her journey.

"It is now fifteen years later, fifteen years during which the company's volume went from zero to more than one billion dollars when we retired in 1989. I had long ago ceased designing. I counseled. I sat in on fittings. I stressed the fundamentals. I worked in the showroom to maintain my sense of continuity with the marketplace. I participated in planning meetings. I sat on the board of directors and, in 'The Little Prince's' term, concerned myself with 'matters of consequence.' I saw my name moved from clothes to shoes to scarves to fragrance to belts and hats and bracelets and more. And with each added factor of growth and of product, the job of identity maintenance grew that much more difficult. If identity became vague, if taste-level consistency diminished, I now know, having reflected much, that the responsibility is mine.

"As a designer, the further one removes oneself from the actual work, the less value one adds to that work. Perhaps my interests had changed with time and perhaps such unexpected success had dulled my younger zeal. But after retiring from the company, sitting on the company's board of directors only removed me further from the process that had been my responsibility.

"The forty designers now designing product at Liz Claiborne must become their own champions through their work. I believe there is no inherent conflict between good design and good business at any level of scale. Look at the great automobile companies, the great appliance companies, and yes, some great apparel companies. And if in my more despairing moments I find myself conceding the issue, that at one point the marketplace requires unacceptable compromise, I know it is my obligation, just as it will be yours, to insist on reclaiming the field.

"We human creatures, swept along through space and time, have been driven to impose purpose on that process by designing and redesigning the world we live in.

Design is an ennobling human invention, an enlarging human capacity.

"If no commencement address is complete without exhortation, here is mine: the gift of being taught the wonder of seeing brings with it the imperative to find your tongue, your uniqueness as a designer, and to dedicate your work to the society that produced you."

Liz assumed the burden of guilt for the swift decline in our company's dedication to quality and taste. She rued the day that we, or more precisely, I, had agreed at the insistence of the original investors that the company own the name, her name. From their standpoint, from any investor's standpoint, it made little sense to invest in a company that did not legally own the brand. I couldn't convince prospective shareholders that they accept our ownership of the name. I think, in the long run, Liz understood. Nevertheless, it was painful for her to shop the stores where she would see the new Liz Claiborne merchandise: cheaper fabrics, a frumpier look and fit, a product that carried her name and label, a product that she would never have endorsed.

Liz and I rarely talked about the different company that emerged after we left. The Liz Claiborne flagship division became a foundling, surrounded by new labels: lower-tier sportswear companies, clothes made for other stores' house labels and special offerings to be distributed throughout the mass market.

Liz could never heal this open wound, this burden of betrayal. Those dedicated Liz Claiborne fans who had waited for hours years ago in a shopping mall in Detroit, who rose to applaud her when she appeared, had been deserted.

• • •

We hadn't retired quietly and gone off to sunny climates and golf links. Free of the company, we spread our wings and gave our energy to nonbusiness pursuits. It seemed we had followed a recommended *National Geographic* travel plan. That was far from the case; we planned to please ourselves.

Toward the end of October 1990, after our first exploratory trip to Moab and Arches National Park in Utah, captivated by the wondrous beauty that time had sculpted through eons of driving rain, we vowed to return the following year. But first, Liz, in her zeal to experience as broadly as time and our Gulfstream IV would permit, and fearless as always, lobbied for a one-month trip that would, with the grace of her gods of good fortune, get us home for Christmas in St. Barts.

October 20, lift-off time from Teterboro, New Jersey, to Hilo, Hawaii, for a fuel stop. We were soon aloft and on our way to a glamorous evening in Fiji. We stayed at an oceanfront inn with a view that was endless and service that was every bit the equivalent of that on the French Mediterranean coast.

The next morning we were off to Auckland, New Zealand. Auckland fascinated us. It sits on the north island of New Zealand, the largest urban population in the country. It's difficult to describe precisely where Auckland is, difficult because it lies on and around an isthmus, has two harbors and opens to the Tasman Sea and the Tamaki River. Bridges span both harbors. Ancient volcanoes dominate inland.

We were paying guests at a lovely home overlooking the Tasman Sea. All meals were served at the inn along with lovely stories of the early days of the settling of Auckland, so water bound that it was called "The Sailing City." Auckland kept us for four days, exploring, walking and stopping often to photograph or chat with local Aucklanders. They speak English, but New Zealand English requires intense attention.

We had hired driver and car, an embarrassingly long white Ford limousine, driven by a man who was a knowledgeable student of New Zealand and spoke careful English. He drove us north. Our destination was the Bay of Islands where we spent two evenings on a houseboat in fabled Whangaroa Harbour, one of New Zealand's most beautiful harbors. We explored the sea caves, grottos and tiny but navigable inlets. All of these lovely natural wonders were ringed by towering rock formations and long-dormant volcanoes.

Neither of us had considered the possible joys of spelunking. The word itself was a bit scary, but the act turned out to be the equivalent of exploring a living museum, rich in the fresh odors of greenery renewing itself on the cave walls, changing colors and fragrances the deeper one rowed within the cave.

For Liz, this was a bountiful feast. We planned all of our trips together, but this was a trip Liz particularly wanted to make. Comfort was required, but captivating scenery was always essential.

We drove south on October 28 to Rotorua, a city on the eastern coast of the North Island, famous for its geothermal activity. There are a number of geysers, one active but approachable, atop a huge crater. People of zeal, like

Liz, for instance, with camera in hand, could hire a helicopter to land about fifty feet from a mist of thermal steam atop a lofty hill called the Isle of White and peer over the crater which plunged at least fifty feet downward. And then with an incomprehensible (for me) sense of satisfaction, she could board the helicopter and fly away.

We spent two days at a charming small hotel, the Solitaire Lodge, chatting away with the owners and other guests, drinking and barbecuing at nightfall, completely unaware of who was saying what and what it meant. Smiling and drinking were the common languages. During the days we adventured and Liz photographed.

And then we flew to Wellington, the capital of New Zealand. It bears a distinction somewhat like that of Ushuaia. This is the southernmost capital in the world. It sits on the southern tip of the North Island. We had been booked into a sheep farm just across the bay. Its unpronounceable name is Wharekauhau; *wh* pronounced *ph*, we were told. Liz, always fascinated by local cultures and the way a family made its living as part of those cultures, had strongly suggested this stop.

The farm raised and sold about two hundred sheep every year. The family that owned the farm ran it as a tourist stop as well. Horses were available and so we rode for a few hours each day. Small bungalows were lined up outside of the main house. We stayed in the bungalow nearest the main house. All meals were family style. The farm experience delivered precisely what we had wanted: lovely scenery, simple delicious meals and pleasant, undemanding company.

The family that owned the farm had come upon hard times. The sheep market was soft and they were looking for partners who would help them develop a more robust tourist trade. I look back now and wonder whatever beset us to consider such an impractical investment. But we did consider it, charmed as we were. The more we delved into the particulars, the less charmed we became. We never invested in the sheep farm and soon forgot the travails of sheep farmers.

We were ready for the next stop. Off we went on November 1 to New Zealand's South Island, home of Christchurch and its beautiful gardens. It was also the place where we rented a helicopter for an adventuresome trip down the west coast and through what are known as the Southern Alps of New Zealand.

Liz, camera in hand, hopped aboard. I followed, already apprehensive at the sight of the rotors in motion, but nonetheless ready for a trip to remember. Why not? We were scheduled to fly through the snow-packed mountain range, swoop down over numerous inlets and sounds, fly along the western coast, called Fjordland, and put down at a handful of desolate beach spots. Indeed, one was named "Desolate Sound," but the sun was bright and it was anything but desolate. And best of all, we were able to land atop Mount Cook and have the photographs to prove it. It was now time to head back to Christchurch and, as fate would have it, a blizzard accompanied us. Once more, as in Alaska, we were piloted through mountain ravines in blizzard weather by a pilot perhaps even more casual than Andy. We snaked through mountain pass after mountain pass. Liz had assumed her helicopter-in-danger face, teeth clenched, eyes shut. As we flew toward Christchurch, our pilot chatted distractedly with his wife over his phone while his white-knuckled clients were barely breathing. And, as in a recurrent dream, we broke into the clear. The helicopter landed gently in garden-filled Christchurch.

The rest of this trip took us first to Sydney, Australia, on November 5. Then to Adelaide on the south central coast of Australia where we boarded a small single-engine plane to fly south and to spend a day on Kangaroo Island, the third-largest island of Australia. Because of its isolation from the mainland, situated about ten miles off shore, it had been largely undeveloped. Given the chance, I believe Liz and I would have gladly returned. There are five reserves for animals and thus a variety of creatures from seals to wallabies to echidnas to koala bears to bandicoots (large-tailed rats). Rabbits and foxes have been barred from the island. We needed a permit, a wise requirement on the part of the government to control the number and behavior of tourists.

The next day took us back to the mainland and then north to the dead center of Australia, where sits the imposing Ayers Rock. This huge sandstone monolith is about 1,200 feet high and about three and one half miles in depth underground. At the time of our visit, Ayers Rock was being used largely as a tourists' challenge climb. The heat and the zeal to climb quickly killed many Asian tourists. The local hotels consequently demanded prepayment from arriving guests. We did not climb.

On November 13, we flew to Darwin, on the northern coast of Australia. We spent a day at Kakadu, the home of crocodiles, moving walls of mosquitoes and birds of every size and color and capability; the Jesus bird, for instance, that walked on water. It was also the home of ancient petroglyphs, still magical and untranslatable. And then we returned to our sumptuous hotel in Darwin.

We left Darwin the morning of the 18th, refueled in Hong Kong and set out, exhausted, but satisfied, for the last legs home: first to Anchorage, Alaska, to clear customs, then on to Missoula, and then to Tranquillity.

We had had our fill of adventure. We certainly did not anticipate nor desire any more, particularly at three o'clock in the morning on American soil. The flight was pleasant and the landing was easy and comfortable. The weather was frigid. We were exhausted after nine hours of flying. We dozed but had little sleep.

Hong Kong to Anchorage, our first stop clearing customs: the posse was there, three in the morning or not. A woman was in charge and she wanted us to know that she had come down to the airport herself specifically to meet Liz Claiborne. And so she did. To extend celebrity time, or maybe because zeal conquered all, she questioned a wristwatch that Liz had bought years ago, probably in Hong Kong, and had declared a while back. That cut little ice in Anchorage. Liz stepped back to watch my performance. I paid no duty and said, "Let's keep moving."

Missoula, Montana, was our next stop. Jerry Mamuzich, owner of Minute Man Aviation, was awaiting to helicopter us to Tranquillity and the happy end of a marathon trip. It was now November 19, and the fun time, for me certainly, was over. The next fun would be sleeping in our own beds at Tranquillity.

Anchorage to Missoula was easy, except that, unsurprisingly, a blizzard greeted us as we landed.

"Well, we'll just wait it out," Liz said. "Sure," I agreed, "we'll sit in the lounge until we can see our hand in front of our eyes."

Liz's later fabled calmness under pressure had everything to do with what she or we could control or manage. We could not control or manage the undauntable Jerry Mamuzich, a man with whom we had flown many times before.

"Jerry," I said, "let's wait this out for a while. We're probably going to run into a slashing blizzard over the Rattlesnake Range or over the mountain ridges and probably over the valleys as well."

"No need to wait," said Jerry. Jerry is tightly wired and always ready to go. He was over fifty, now married to a much younger woman. Jerry was tough and determined. He boarded the plane. We followed. And off we went. Liz shut her eyes. Fifteen minutes later, I called out to Jerry, "Take us back to Missoula. We'll pay double for the trip." Liz had my arm and shoulder in a vise-lock, her eyes glued closed. She said nothing.

This is about a twenty-minute flight on any day that has an element of visibility, but not this morning.

Jerry was no longer a "no problem" person. He was now an "I don't know" person. And then, miraculously (it must have been fate intervening on Liz's behalf), the clouds parted for a moment and down below we saw a large, snow-blanketed field, and Jerry, invitation or not, put the machine down. He kept the rotors spinning, just in case. A brute of an unhappy dog came bounding out and snarling at us, followed by a hobbled octogenarian carrying a rifle pointed straight at us.

The rotors were shut down. Jerry opened the door. Liz stepped out and said, "Good morning. I'm Liz Ortenberg. We're lost. We're trying to find Tranquillity Lodge." And then she smiled her Liz smile. (We in the plane had banked on a woman not being shot at and Liz volunteered to clear the path. She was right.)

"Well, howdy, I'm Joe Clark and you're on my farm and you're welcome." The gun was lowered, the surly dog unsurled and wagged his tail. "We're sort of neighbors. Come on in and have a cup of coffee. I'll see if my wife and sister can join us. They'll probably be in robes. They won't mind." The tail was wagged even more happily as we drank coffee with the Clarks. We called Tranquillity on the phone and Roger came and got us. We drove to Tranquillity and were soon in bed.

Fearless Jerry Mamuzich had overshot by about thirty miles. A voyage that had started on October 20, via Hawaii, was now over.

True to our original schedule, here we were on November 19, 1990, at Tranquillity. Our first year free of the company was now ending. We had more or less pogo-sticked all over the world.

· · ·

Nineteen ninety-nine, the year of awards and adventure, was also the year we made good on our resolve to return to the beautifully sculptured landscape of eastern Utah. We had read and had been entranced by Eliot Porter's brilliant book of photographs, *The Place No One Knew*. That land had been erased from the earth, washed over and buried by the reservoir created as a result of the construction of Glen Canyon Dam. We had read Mark Reisner's book, *Cadillac Desert*, written in 1986 on the American West and "its disappearing water."

I had also read Edward Abbey's *The Monkey Wrench Gang*. I liked it, noisy and bellicose as it was. I knew Liz would find it irritating. She saw nothing hilarious about violence and this was certainly a violent bunch Abbey had created. The setting was the saving grace, Canyonlands and Arches National Park.

Ken Sleight, owner with his wife, Jane, of the Pack Creek Ranch outside of Moab, had been the model for one of Abbey's more sanguinary characters, a man of numerous wives, all geographically separated. His name in the book is Seldom Seen Smith. We drew no inferences. The ranch, more aptly a "pleasant country inn," sits in the foothills of the La Sal Mountains. Liz had been looking forward to returning to Utah, especially Arches National Park. There was much to photograph. It promised to be an easy trip. Her brother Omer and his wife, Jeanette, were eager to return to Utah. We were all enthusiastic about staying at Pack Creek. Its reputation was excellent. That's where we would start. Glen Canyon would follow.

The four of us arrived mid-afternoon and were pleasantly surprised at the readiness of our rooms, which were large enough, pretty enough, and, for me an essential, had a bathroom with a private john. Good. Would we like a short ride? Sure. A troop of docile horses were led out. Riders and horses assumed doleful countenances and we strolled along. We were all relieved, horses and riders, when the jaunt came to end. We showered and then all had a potato and beef, Utah-style dinner with Ken and Jane at our table. We were feeling pretty up about the Pack Creek Ranch. We slept well, looking forward to Arches National Park, Canyonlands and whatever else time could make available.

The next morning, well fed and now about to take off, Ken told us that they had a very special treat in store for us. We were sent off on a trip to Arches with their daughter Katie, a fifteen-year-old whom everyone seemed delighted to send off for the day. Katie, impish, wearing a small, knowing smile, was to be our guide. It was surmised, I guess, that Katie would be a helpful guide. I'm pretty sure that was the intention. It didn't work out that way.

Once we had hiked our way well into Arches, Katie took over. It was a little past one o'clock. The weather was heating up. Perspiration was forming on all brows, precisely what Liz really disliked. We trudged on and on, following Katie.

"And now you're going to experience the Fiery Furnace," she eventually said. There ahead of us were two huge boulders, so huge and sheer that they were unclimbable. The boulders sat in a nest of larger boulders that somehow we had blundered into. Only Katie knew whether we had blundered into this fix or perhaps had been led into it. The only way forward was through a narrow slit, perhaps eight inches wide at its widest point and about twenty feet long from one end to the other. I know that sounds unlikely. And now, as I sit comfortably in a wide leather chair as I write, it seems impossible. But it didn't seem so at the time.

I still have no idea how she worked that out and how we fell into that trap, but there it was. It now seems unimaginable that the only way back was by squeezing ourselves, one at a time, through that narrow opening, but explore as much as we did there was no other answer.

Katie had slid through the opening as soon as we were all in the "furnace." And then we heard her voice, cheerful and unconcerned, "So long, see you later." Then we heard her laugh. Katie was playing a trick on us, it appeared. So long, indeed! We decided to explore further, frankly uncertain that we could all make it through the escape route that Katie had used. It looked narrower and narrower the longer we stared at it. The temperature climbed with each passing minute.

"I'm going through," Liz said. "Sometimes it pays to be flat-chested. If I make it and you all are stuck, I'll get help." Slender and courageous, she inched her way through. Omer went next. Fortunately he was far from stout and far from long. After what seemed like an hour, he was through. It was now Jeanette's turn. Jeanette was not at all flat-chested. Being pretty, blondish, well maintained and full figured was suddenly a potential problem. We were all fearful that she might get stuck between the boulders, but she was game. She slowly entered the passageway. It was hair-raising, and had she not managed to slip her belt off and hold her breath for what seemed like many minutes, she might very well have spent eternity in the Fiery Furnace. But she finally made it. I followed.

Katie had disappeared. We had been working our way through the Fiery Furnace for three hours.

When we arrived back at the ranch it was about five thirty in the late afternoon.

Our luggage had been neatly stashed in one bedroom. We were told that an error, innocently perpetrated, had caused an overbooking, and thus new people were in our room and nothing remained but for all four of us to spend the night in the one room left to us. That didn't happen. Ken and Jane eventually gave up their room to Liz and me. Liz and I were not scene makers. But we were very stubborn and unmovable. The reasoning behind the Sleights' surrender of their bedroom for the evening had as much to do with Liz's name as their embarrassment for having mishandled an important first-time guest.

Katie hadn't returned, but no one seemed distressed. "How did it go?" Ken asked. "Fine," I said. I had no stomach for any comment other than that.

We departed the following morning. It was not a terribly warm and cheerful departure. The eggs were not quite as hot as scrambled eggs should be, the bacon not as crisp as bacon should be. Too bad, I thought. This is such a beautiful layout, run by really good, progressive people. But, as I'm often told, "stuff happens." We were glad to be alive. We were upset, but alive.

The trek through Utah continued, back into Canyonlands, on to Glen Canyon. We rented a motorboat and drifted about the reservoir. We noted the downward movement of the waterline indented in the shoreline rocks. Liz was so moved she refused to raise her camera. "Lost," she said. What had been a river full of vigor and life was now a sinkhole, a waste puddle.

We exited Utah two days later. But first we drove through St. George and Zion National Park, further on to Bryce National Park, back to St. George and then were homeward bound.

• • •

160

And now ten years later, we awaited Dr. Nori's report. It was due in May. It was very favorable. Radiation had given Liz a number of months free of treatment.

The early months of 2001 had gone by smoothly. Dental treatment continued. The implant work seemed interminable.

Other discomforts became more emphasized; the numbing pain of arthritis was becoming more frequent. Her knees were beginning to ache when she tried to maintain her active, free-swinging walk. Time on the treadmill was becoming more wearying. We set up her first appointment with Dr. Steve Magid at the New York Hospital of Special Surgery, a section of the New York-Presbyterian Hospital.

Dr. Magid, an open, amiable and involved physician, is listed as "Professor of Clinical Medicine—Specialty, Rheumatology." Liz first saw him on July 25, 2001.

She had been given a form to fill out headed REVIEW OF SYSTEMS. Here are some of her responses to questions on the form: She circled ANEMIA and added the word "slight." Under GI she circled CONSTIPATION and added in pencil "chronic" and under URINARY she circled WAKING AT NIGHT TO URINATE. She was still drinking her martini at night, when in remission, followed by a glass of wine.

I spoke with Dr. Magid on October 4, 2007. This is what he told me: "She came to see me with lower back pains. She had spinal stenosis, all spine nerves pinching her spinal cord. This is painful and disabling and progresses inexorably as women grow older." She initiated ongoing appointments. He was to see Liz nine more times from 2002 to her last appointment on November 22, 2006.

As Dr. Magid explained, spinal stenosis is a fancy name for the narrowing of the opening that holds the spine. The rubbing of the spine against its container can cause weakness in one's arms and legs. It can occur in a variety of ways in the spine, but however it happens, it irritates the surrounding nerves. It causes pain in your lower back. It causes discomfort in the nerves that run along the back of the leg.

Dr. Magid continued, "Her condition was not unusual for a person her age. Many women become wheelchair bound and spend their lives watching TV. The disconnect was how she handled it: exercise, weights. She was indomitable, tougher than nails. She continued to live her life as she wanted to."

She did initiate a series of spinal cortisone injections at the later suggestion of Dr. Magid. Her knees had begun to ache so that she desperately needed relief. The injections helped. They began in 2004 and continued biannually until December of 2005.

It was evident to Liz, in this, her third year of adjusting to living as a chronic cancer patient, that unalterable changes had to be accepted. The two-track description of the disease made that clear. So to say that other than the spinal stenosis, 2001 was a good, active year may sound callous. Nevertheless the year had been positive. Liz was in remission, we lived our lives as normal, active people. There were the mandated number of visits to Dr. Buchman and Dr. Pasmantier, visits to East River Medical for CT scans and other imaging, but all was well. We had both celebrated our birthdays in Montana, she at the end of March, me in mid-August at the Hungry Bear, about five miles north of Tranquillity.

The Hungry Bear served us in Montana as did Le Bernardin in New York. Le Bernardin is a four-star restaurant in Manhattan. We had known the owners in earlier times, sent flowers on the day the restaurant opened and had become preferred clients. We always had a favorite corner table, available at short notice.

The Hungry Bear is located on Highway 83 at the thirty-eight-mile marker about a twenty-minute drive from Tranquillity. That's a long way from 51st Street in New York, but a lot closer to the Windbag Saloon, just over the divide. As tony as is Le Bernardin, that's about as rustic as is the Hungry Bear. One can easily say the same for Maguy Le Coze and Eric Ripert, chief owners of the New York restaurant, tony but not seriously so. They exude style.

To the left of the dining room at the Bear is an immense barroom, with at least twenty people slouching at the bar guzzling beer, watching the TV set, and a layer of blue-jean clad, cowboy hat-wearing men and women, hip to hip, a half of a pace behind the front row. The bar crowd usually spent the entire evening at the bar. The dining room served only those who actually preferred food with their drink.

Further to the left of the bar was a function room. Most of the time the room accommodated a large pool table and a strictly amateur pool match. But when there was to be an actual function, the table was removed. A ping-pong table was set up, a checkered tablecloth draped over it, wooden chairs lining the perimeter. Serious talk often took place. Liz and I sponsored a number of "let's-talk-this-through-rather-than-waste-energy-at-shouting" meetings there.

The owners of the Hungry Bear are Mike and Sue Holmes, people in their sixties, longtime local people, parents of three sterling children, all overachievers at Seeley Swan High School. Mike and Sue could have been twins, they looked that much alike: medium in height, stocky in build, prairie-open faces, too accustomed to hard ranching work to dissemble. In their own different but authentic way, they also exude style. They had been overseeing a livestock ranch for a Missoula landowner. The work was such that they had time on their hands and a need to provide for their later years. Because of their amiability, their generous relationship with their staff, their ability to do everything that needed to be done on their own if it came to that, Mike and Sue Holmes had become the first financially successful owners of the Hungry Bear in years. Like Maya's, like Le Bernardin, the Hungry Bear was our dining room away from our dining room.

My sister, Gloria, and her husband, Hilliard, had joined us at the Hungry Bear for my seventy-fifth birthday. Brian Kahn, now a close friend as a result of time spent together preparing for the Red Lodge Workshop, and his tall, lean, blondish, huntress, artist wife, Sandra Dal Poggetto, completed the group at our dining table. It was an up evening for all. Liz was in remission. She chanced a martini and it sat well.

The next day, Liz, Brian and I got together again. We continued the work of preparing for the workshop.

The workshop had been scheduled for October 18–21, 2001, in Red Lodge, Montana. The venue was the Rock Creek Resort, cradled in a canyon just below Beartooth Pass, anchored in the foothills of the Absaroka Mountain Range, about sixty miles west of Billings.

• • •

It was now almost seven years since that Valentine's Day in Missoula when Liz and Arnie and I shared the podium. It was now more than a year since our Tranquillity preparation meeting. Now the platform belonged to Liz. She had been the true believer in the collaborative process. It was her time to be on stage.

The gavel came down the first morning of October 21, 2001, a number of weeks after 9/11. Liz was in top form, despite the discovery of spinal stenosis and despite the arthritic aches that she had been experiencing. Despite all of that, her corn-yellow hair was her own. Nothing troubled her as she stood alone at the podium. Her CA125 was 18. She gloried in the turnout, more than one hundred people, practitioners, public policymakers, agency people, conservationists, members of our own foundation who would be sitting in on breakout sessions taking notes, journalists and other foundation leaders.

And then she said, as she had said years ago at the Airlie workshop, "We're here to learn from you, to learn what you feel your needs are, and how we who have assumed the task of supporting your efforts at accommodation and problem solving can best be helpful. Just as at that workshop, held almost seven years ago, we will be examining a number of case studies. The Airlie workshop, held in the warmth of Virginia, concerned itself and its attendees with community-based conservation in perspective. It signaled a breakthrough in a new approach to conservation. This workshop, we hope, will signal a breakthrough in the collaborative process. The process here will be very much like that at Airlie—case study based. You've already received this workshop's case studies and an analysis of the issues involved. Welcome."

And then she smiled again. "Plenary sessions, breakout sessions, and more plenary, and then drinks and dinner."

She next introduced Brian Kahn, master of ceremonies, but much more than that. Here is what I wrote about Brian in the summary document:

"In retrospect, a recounting of the dynamics of the Red Lodge Workshop would greatly miss the mark without special comment about Brian Kahn. He was more than a moderator and discussion leader; in actuality he was the central presence of the days to follow. If you had to conjure up in your mind's eye a picture of 'The Westerner,' you'd probably conjure up someone exactly like Brian Kahn. He is consummately skilled in the art of neighborly talk. It doesn't matter who the neighbor is, fifth-generation rancher educated by the seasons and the needs of his stock, obsessive hunter or angler, Harvard PhD, economist, philosopher, historian, ten-year-old, or a ninety-year-old, Kahn relates and speaks their tongue."

The workshop was a huge success. We know that the seeds planted there flowered throughout the West. The Red Lodge Workshop gave birth to the

Red Lodge Clearinghouse, with its web site, www.rlch.org, which kept collaborators abreast of important events affecting their work. It provided funding and face-to-face assistance for startup collaborative groups. At the outset, late in 2002, its office was in Helena, Montana. It is now a program of the Liz Claiborne Art Ortenberg Foundation, managed by the Natural Resources Law Center at the University of Colorado Law School.

The clearinghouse was just what Liz had in mind the day of the luncheon meeting at Tranquillity. She participated in the web site design, and, with me, reviewed our monthly home page updates. When Dr. Pasmantier advised her to go about her business as usual, this was one important way of doing just that. Liz and three trustees of our foundation, Alison Richard, Bob Dewar and David Quammen, joined Jim Murtaugh and I in taking notes at breakout sessions. We were each assigned a room and acted as scribes.

Collaboration in natural resource management has become a reality. We had created a new way of doing business, not only in the West, but throughout the country.

The foundation's fall board meeting took place at our office in New York City three weeks after the Red Lodge workshop ended. The dates of the meeting were the 14th and 15th of November. At that time our trustees were Jonah Western, whom you've met and will spend more time with; David Quammen, who had been with us at the workshop; Alison Richard; Bob Dewar and Mary Pearl.

There are two photographs of Alison Richard and Bob Dewar mounted in my wall collage. They were taken at the same time, in 1998, a month before Liz and I became aware of Liz's cancer. One picture is of the two of them, seated on horseback, sitting calmly in front of a barn at Triple 8. The other is of the four of us standing on the deck of Cabin A. We are boy, girl, boy, girl; I am the lucky man with a woman on each side. On the back of this picture, Liz had written "888 ranch, '98—Bob, Liz, Alyson [she never got it right], Art." Liz and I are wearing T-shirts brought to us by Alison at the request of the people of Beza Mahafly, a village in Madagascar.

We had been supporting Alison's work in that community since 1993. Alison and the young Malagasy team she recruited had been concentrating on the health and fertility of both the village and the forest reserve that bordered it. The objective was to help the community develop farming, chicken raising and fishing practices that would not be harmful to the wildlife in the reserve. Another objective was to help the villagers develop a participatory political system whereby women had a policy role, as well as a maternal role. In the process, young Malagasy students were being taught important skills. The reserve contains large numbers of sifaka lemurs. The research done and the conservation work done over a number of generations of lemurs has been impressive. Alison, provost at Yale, was on the ground in Madagascar at least one full month each year. She was responsible for the professional training of a number of Malagasy conservationists. The foundation continues to support Beza Mahafly. I still have the T-shirts.

Bob was the head of the archaeology department at the University of Connecticut. Liz and I not only adored Bob and Alison, we had unlimited respect for them.

And there we all are in our wall photograph. Alison's striking dark hair crowns her head, sits over a face of amazing mobility. Even in a photograph, you are entranced by her expressive face. I define Alison, as did Liz, as supremely huggable. Bob is taller, leaner, his grey hair wispy and thinning, his face often set in a deep ponder or a deep smile and, when in dress-up clothes, his head is firmly held to his shoulders and neck by one of his hundred bowties. Bob is too pleasant looking to be called handsome, but attractive would not be far off the mark. They are both overwhelmingly attractive. And they were both knowledgeable and fair and thoughtful trustees of our foundation.

You already have met Jonah and David, but here's a bit on board member Mary Pearl. Mary was also a Yale graduate, also had her doctorate in anthropology. We met Mary when she was with the Wildlife Conservation Society. She directed the international grants program, and at the time, she directed the Society's Asia-Pacific programs. She was a colleague of Jonah's. They worked well together.

Board meeting agendas follow a fixed sequence. We start at nine o'clock the first morning with a review of operating costs versus budget and any other relevant financial information. We follow with a review of all ongoing programs. Often we have reports from the field to discuss. From time to time we have a guest appear during the latter part of the first morning who will exchange thoughts and information with our board members. It isn't until the latter part of day one that we discuss new programs. That's when we talked about Red Lodge and its implications in terms of future funding. By then it's usually time for our sumptuous dinner. Often these dinners were used as a platform for an invited guest, a member of the fraternity of field biologists who might have a special story to tell. Such took place one evening with a prestigious guest, Iain Douglas-Hamilton, and his daughter Dudu.

The story begins with reference to a memorable photograph that Liz took on the 1995 trip to Africa. It shows Alex and I, arm in arm, standing at a road sign that reads, "Lake Manyara Corridor, donated by the Liz Claiborne Art Ortenberg Foundation." The funds for the corridor had been passed through to Iain Douglas-Hamilton, elephant conservationist in Tanzania, who had arranged for the purchase of the corridor from the Tanzanian government. Iain was the first biologist to spend consecutive years studying elephant behavior. He had raised his family on the shores of Lake Manyara.

Iain told us the story of the matriarch elephant that he had been studying for years, Boadicea, ferocious in her willingness to give her life for her herd. She had been named after a first-century East Anglian tribal queen who had been denied leadership of her tribe when her husband, then leader, died. The Roman occupiers had other ideas. She led an uprising which was cruelly defeated; she was flogged as history tells it, and her daughters raped and killed.

"Yes, in the long run she lost," Iain said, "but my elephant won't lose. When she gets too old or sick to fight, there will be another Boadicea ready to carry on, to follow her example."

These meetings always left us all intoxicated by the gladness of being together, the richness of the new knowledge acquired and the programs that we had funded.

In December, we returned to St. Barts. Christmas and New Year's were happy times. Alex was down for the Christmas holiday and Liz and I spent New Year's Eve at home, where we watched the fireworks exploding from the water barge hired by the Eden Rock Hotel for that purpose. Later, we saw dimmer offshoots from downtown Gustavia, and even later from across the waters in St. Maarten. Despite spinal stenosis and new aches in her joints and bones, Liz felt that 2001 had been a year of pleasures and good work done, love and hope.

CHAPTER SIX, 2002

THERE SEEMED NO reason to anticipate anything other than a continuing smooth ride throughout the year. The post-radiation CA125 readings had all been excellent: February, CA125—22; March, CA125—18; June, CA125—19; October, CA125—18. CT scans, taken periodically, also showed good results. The low readings were all very real: no antigenic activity, no chemical infusions; both tracks had been shut down.

So we started 2002 with great hope that we were in the clear. Liz felt cancer-free, applied herself to strenuous physical workouts and dealing with spinal stenosis.

The early months were routine with one large exception: We met Christina Miram in February. Alex and Christina, his newest young lady friend, arrived in St. Barts on Valentine's Day and stayed through carnival time, February 17.

I'm amused by the entries in my daily date book during that period. I refer to the couple as "Alex and friend."

Alex had met Christina one evening in Stuttgart, where he and his jazz group had performed. The couple hadn't separated since. She was a fine-looking, intelligent young woman from southwest Germany, south of Stuttgart, north of Munich. She is tall and handsome in a soft, rounded way. Her figure is well molded. She is athletic and moves with vigor; perfect for Alex. Christina appeared mature, came with no baggage and was a tenured teacher who found physical activity rewarding. She shared Alex's enthusiasm for hiking and, as important, loved his cooking. Alex had become a master chef and was ready for domestication. That was our first introduction. Liz was pleased. We hoped Alex was on the way to settling down.

March was routine. We were in St. Barts. All was well.

Or all seemed well. It was time to fly back to New York for Liz to have blood drawn to check her CA125 and for the two of us to attend to teeth, conservation work and working with our office. We had a routine weekend at Fire Island, dined with Nevio Maggiore, Elly's widower, one evening, when Liz ordered her usual cheeseburger and a glass of wine. As I thought about it later, she ate more slowly, if possible, than was her custom.

We were back in the city the following Monday and had dinner out as usual. Despite the fact that her general sense of well-being seemed not to have diminished, both of us were apprehensive.

We met with Dr. Pasmantier at noon on the 18th. I was stunned. Liz's CA125 reading was 323.6! She received the news more calmly.

This was more of a major disappointment than a shock. It was the second time during the course of the disease that remission had suddenly come to a startlingly swift halt. Back in November of 1999, the numbers were high, but not this high. Then Liz had been in remission twelve months. The radiation remission was closer to sixteen months. In both cases, one can liken this surge to a stream of seeds spurting forth from a heretofore clogged hose.

Dr. Pasmantier was calm and apparently satisfied with the length of Liz's radiation-induced remission. The next chemotherapy session was scheduled for May 16, a return to Taxol-platinum, administered once every three weeks. We had planned a trip to Provence and Dr. Pasmantier gave us his OK to go. We were all willing to chance more antigenic activity without, as yet, bombarding Liz's digestive system with chemicals.

"Remember, darling," she said, "one way of dealing with these disappointments is to remember the wonderful times in the past. I'm well enough to go to Provence this year and well enough to appreciate our exciting lives. I doubt," she said, "if I could handle a replay of that excitement, but I enjoy remembering. Did those things really happen? I ask myself," she said.

170

"Yes, darling, they all really happened," I said.

It was a sober dinner that evening. We, who loved to travel, reflected on the excitement of past travels. In this case it was a trip just one decade past, an instant in time, that we talked about that evening. We had planned the year as a celebration of Liz's honorary doctorate, received at the Rhode Island School of Design in 1991. Liz loved absorbing the beauty of new places, the beauty of peoples of differing behavior and costume and certainly of differing circumstances.

· · ·

In January 1992 we had joined John Sawhill, then director of the Nature Conservancy, at the Chin Chin Resort in Belize. This was a modestly lovely hidden resort. Our days were filled by trekking to ruins or horseback riding the back roads, easy time at the bar in the evening or an overflight of the brilliant reefs offshore. We left John and his cohorts and went on with a guide to the ancient, once earthquake-prone capital of Guatemala, Antigua, still recovering and rebuilding. Then we went on to Chichicastenango, a village fixed in time, with gay costumes and marketplaces brimming with local handicrafts. Another stop was Panachel, a mournful, poor village sitting parallel with the shoreline of Lake Atitlán, a magnificent swath of water rimmed with symmetrical hills. We were lucky to find a small suite available for a few days overlooking the lake and within walking distance of the village. The women villagers, Maya Indian descendants, wore lushly colored wrapped clothes. They were poor, unclean and looked upon outsiders as legitimate prey. We almost adopted two young girls, adopted in the sense that we would finance them through grade school, but this was of little interest. Money was of interest. So money it was. The rites of the village, seemingly reflective through ageless repetition, continued. We were able to view a funeral procession, its soft assonant music and soft assonant moaning meandering at a snail's pace through the streets, and then, when that was finished, we returned to the marketplace, buying, selling, haranguing. Liz took picture after picture, stunned by the color-drenched beauty of this scene. Here was a traditional society, poor in things material, but rich in a tradition that had become programmed in its spontaneity. The entire society, small enough in numbers so that everyone knew everyone, had shaped a centuries-old stability.

We barely had time to develop the film before flying off to historic Eilat in Israel. Eilat lies at the southerly tip of Israel, the anchor city of the Negev Desert, and the gateway city to the Red Sea. Why Eilat? There was the desert, where horses were available, and we had contacted a noted Israeli biologist as a guide. Two days later, we were to fly to Kenya to pick up Shirley and Jonah and then fly off to the Seychelle Islands. Liz's enthusiasm for the Seychelles was low-keyed. She never was much of a birder, particularly not for small birds. Eagles and herons, squawky, aggressive birds, were more her style, although in Africa she did become a fan of the ibis, the crane and the kori bustard.

That was the plan, in this case, more my plan than hers. All of this taxiing about would be done in our Gulfstream IV, blessed with speed and the ability to fly at 45,000 feet. Our pilots were young, daring and skilled. Here we were in Israel, planning to fly over Egypt's airspace, then over Sudan's airspace and then on to Kenya. That's not the way things were done in those days.

We never made it to Nairobi and the tale is another one that convinced me that Liz's life was charmed. The usual Eilat to Nairobi flight plan required a convoluted itinerary constructed to respect border sensitivities. The plane was to leave Israeli skies, fly north to Cyprus, wheel about and then head south. We had been assured in Eilat by the Egyptian Air Force that this would not be necessary. That's what our pilots reported. We could fly directly south to Kenya, we were told. The script for that morning was as follows: the Egyptian observers on the ground were to ask our pilots where the plane was coming from, the pilots were to say "Cyprus" and then they would be told to proceed. But the script had been torn up. We had been deliberately baited. Our pilots may have been fearless, but they were also naïve. Egypt demanded that we descend and put our plane on the ground in Cairo. Our pilots refused, knowing full well that the plane would be seized and forever lost. There we were, climbing to 45,000 feet, nothing but sand and sea below and silence in the plane. Liz grimaced. "At least we're not flying in a blizzard," she said. "Just wait and see," I answered.

We continued flying south into Sudanese airspace, a perilous place today, a perilous place then. We looked down and below us, climbing at what seemed to us the speed of light, were six Sudanese fighter planes. "Land or get shot down," we heard a voice say over the radio in good enough English so that there was no misunderstanding.

172

I looked over at Liz and was surprised at her calm demeanor. It was as though she was watching a movie in slow motion. Our pilots climbed once more to 45,000 feet, about our limit, wheeled about, headed north, banked to the left and flew on, banked to the right and flew on. We were too high and too fast to be intercepted.

Suddenly we were alone in the air. "See," Liz said, "no problem when you've got a good product." I'm sure that what really pleased her was that we would have to cancel the Seychelles.

The return trip took us north over Cyprus and when the air control crew on the ground in Eilat asked us where we were coming from, the answer "Cyprus" was on the mark.

To this day I find it amusing that we might have been victims of a complicated con game. Our original hotel room was waiting for us. When we made it to the bar there was a Tanqueray martini and a single malt scotch in attendance. Probably coincidence. That took care of the Seychelles. We went to Barcelona instead. Liz really preferred the wonders of Gaudí to peering through binoculars at smallish, multicolored birds.

• • •

Nineteen ninety-two, benign and exciting year that it was, afforded us two trips to Provence, the first one in May, the second one in October. How Liz loved Provence! The landscape, so packed with rich, arable soil, so modestly sensual in its hills and valleys, and the people—such in-your-face provincials—delighted her. The first trip in May was with Gloria and Hilly. That trip has already been described. What I haven't yet described was the immediate attachment that Liz and I, particularly Liz, formed for Provence. The second trip, in October, was with Kim and Christophe and introduced us to the old fortress town of Les Baux, now a tourist center, and an elegant country inn, La Riboto de Taven. It sits at the foot of the old fortress city. Our visits to La Riboto became an annual ritual until our last trip with Randy and Maya in 2003.

It remains alive and well. Alison and Bob have become devoted patrons. I actually flew commercial this past May to join Bob and Alison there for a four-day weekend. I invited Andrew, Louis's son, and his wife, Corinne, to join me. I have no doubt, nor do any of the others, that Liz was with us.

But back to 1992. Early in April of that year we had initiated the planning for what was to be as defining a voyage as our 1987 trip to Africa. This journey was primarily structured as a follow-up to our earlier time in Ushuaia, but would include new spectacle, adventure and a meeting up with Graham Harris, the Wildlife Conservation Society biologist responsible for leading the organization's programs in southern Argentina. We were also to be guided on a good part of our tour by Maurice Rumboll or, as he was known, the legendary Maurice Rumboll.

Maurice is a large, burly man, an Argentine of transplanted English stock. He wears a full white beard, perhaps to compensate for his thinning hair. He is jovial and handsome. His candor, tact and impish sense of humor are all integral to his appearance. And he is rarely seen without his binoculars swinging on his chest as he walks. We surmised that he never was without them. Maurice is probably the greatest ornithologist and naturalist that Argentina has ever produced. We couldn't walk ten feet through a forest without Maurice turning pebbles over and explaining, in the softest of baritone voices, the vast variety of life that lived under that pebble. He is a brilliant songster and an equally brilliant punster.

Maurice has since led many tours, most aboard ship, including as many as sixty trips to the Antarctic.

Bill Conway, who had devoted a good part of his conservation fieldwork to Patagonia, is an old friend and ardent fan of Maurice. Bill had written a four-page journey agenda. He copied Maurice. And then more correspondence followed: Maurice to me, me to Maurice and a note from Graham.

I have before me a mound of documents pertaining to that late November trip. I also have Liz's daily notes identifying each roll of film and where the pictures were taken. I know what remained with Liz and me when we flew from Chile to Gulfport almost four weeks later. I know also what we found amusing, what we found overwhelmingly beautiful, what we found frightening and, in the long run, what we knew was important.

Graham Harris, born in Argentina of British parents, as fluent in British ways as he is in Spanish ways, was the most important person we met. Graham, Guillermo, as he is called, is also the society's link to Fundación Patagonia Natural, the largest nonprofit conservation organization in southern Argentina. He lives in Puerto Madryn, a thriving coastal city and jump-off point to the Valdes Peninsula, Punto Tombo and other coastal viewing areas.

We visited them all and saw our fill of penguins, seals, jumping whales and a staggering variety of seabirds. Graham is now a man in his early fifties, serenely fine looking, tall, slender of build and gentle of voice. He is a first-class artist and has published a number of books. His subject matter, like that of Bill Conway and Maurice, is most often birds. Liz was again stuck with birders, but as long as we included penguins in birdlife, she was happy to view birds.

Iguazu Falls in Brazil was our first stop. We were again accompanied by Omer and Jeanette.

The falls, a two-mile-wide stretch of numerous cataracts, each about 200 feet above the Alto Paraná River, are dizzying to absorb. Their energy and sound are such that one never forgets. And, as elsewhere, like begging vervets in Amboseli, langurs in India who have made temples their homes as they have learned to beg from humans, the coatis—raccoon-like, long-snouted, weasel-size beggars of the falls—crowded around tourists, pawing for handouts.

Then we went south to Buenos Aires, the Los Angeles of South America. But unlike Los Angeles, Buenos Aires is noted for the tango and for its beef. We ate at the Carnivore, a restaurant renowned for the gluttony of its clients and the beef to satisfy that gluttony. There were only two women customers in the restaurant, Liz and Jeanette. Liz, whose enthusiasm for food matched her other enthusiasms in intensity, had pulled out all stops. Perhaps, in later years, her inability to eat as she pleased caused her as much misery as other disabilities. But in Buenos Aires there were no such concerns. She gorged herself on Argentine steak and later that evening and the following morning, she paid the price. She lay in bed that day as Omer, Jeanette and I, with guide, toured Buenos Aires and had our first run-in with the Argentine police, escaping with some heavy finger-wagging. We had crossed a stop line by no more than two inches. The Argentine police, as was later confirmed, take their work seriously.

November 28, we arrived in Puerto Madryn and had our first meeting with Graham. We had come to see Patagonian coastal life, and that's what we did for the next four days. We came back to Puerto Madryn each evening, had dinner as a group, always with Graham's lovely, soft-spoken wife, Patricia, and were introduced to the large family of mice who lived under the hood of their nonfunctioning ancient Ford car.

The foundation still works in all these beach fronts: Península Valdés, Punto Tombo and Playa Escondida.

Maurice was waiting for us at the airport in El Calafate. Bill Conway had described El Calafate as a city so situated that the scenery is spectacular. He had not overstated. El Calafate, pleasant as the town is, is blessed with its views of Lago Argentina to the west and the Andes to the north. It is in the westernmost part of Argentina, at the Chilean border, and affords access to the beautiful lake, Lago Argentina. Condors soar above the mountains and glacier lakes surrounding El Calafate. We were there in good weather and were taken by boat to view the famous glacier on the lake, the Perito Moreno. If you haven't seen or heard the immense rending, ripping sound of a glacier calving, it's hard to be aware of the power of nature as it goes about its business of building up and tearing down.

December 3, we were on our way to the Estancia Cristina via a boat ride across the lake, through waters dotted with small icebergs, to be deposited on a sandy beach, luggage with us and no one in sight. This short visit had been recommended by John Sawhill, good friend and director of the Nature Conservancy. We later wondered just what John had in mind, how he and his group had found this estancia, reminiscent, for us, of the sort of ghost house found on a ghost island in an Agatha Christie mystery. But there we were, alone and uneasy. Maurice began to whistle. So this is what a wild surmise is all about, I thought, but not for long. Out of nowhere, a tall, nonchalant man, swinging a stick, followed by a dog that looked alarmingly like a Doberman pinscher, strolled into sight. "Welcome to the Estancia Cristina," he said. "Follow me." He made no effort to help us with our bags. There was nothing for it but to follow him.

The stay at the Estancia was more bad theater than real life. We had dinner that evening with our putative hostess, a wooden woman who spoke no English and sat at the head of the table, occasionally speaking with Maurice. I was certain that she had been hired for a one-evening performance. There was no ice available for our drinks so Maurice and I walked back to the beach, commandeered a small boat, found an accessible iceberg, chipped ice and returned.

The sleeping quarters were as shabby as the ramshackle main house. The only item in the estancia that seemed in good repair was the guest book. And yes, there was the name of John Sawhill.

176

We did some glacier viewing the following morning and then waved goodbye to the Estancia Cristina. Liz took no photographs.

December 5, we flew to Ushuaia. We spent the next four days there, actually stayed at the Hotel Ushuaia, somewhat more complete than it had been three years earlier but still with only one so-called suite. We strolled about the city, boated once more through the Beagle Channel, drove through the national park, drove inland through the forests and all in all, with Maurice as tour guide, came away with a more intimate understanding of the area.

I'm afraid that a day-by-day account of the next number of days, spectacular as the scenery was, impressive as were the towns we either flew to or drove through, would be excessive. Chile, long and slender as a dagger, sheathed by the Andes to the east and the ocean to the west, is full of staggering sights: the Torres del Paine National Park chief among them, and the San Rafael Glacier, viewed from a motorized sailing vessel that we spent three dismally uncomfortable days aboard. Liz and I were motored by the young captain of our vessel, the *Australis*, to a safe distance from an immense glacial front and again recoiled at the sight and sound of a glacier calving. With it all, Liz was cheerful and undaunted, more so than I. Maurice set the pace for us all, sleeping in the most cramped bunk, never failing to point this out or that out, so that tired or not, we were informed.

December 16, we flew into Calama, an unmemorable city that would be our takeoff base for our must visit to the Atacama Desert. All arrangements had been made by our tourist connection in Buenos Aires. We were to be picked up at three o'clock in the morning, driven to the fuming geysers on the Atacama Plateau, the equivalent of Yellowstone on the other side of the hemisphere. Maurice, much more sophisticated about arrangements made in Argentina to be executed in Chile, wished us all a pleasant early good night. I had been assured, via fax, that all was well arranged. No need for concern.

We were up, warmly dressed at three o'clock in the morning, as were Omer, Jeanette and Maurice. There, at the hotel entrance, waited an unidentifiable automobile, at least ten years old, and an unshaven driver. We all gulped simultaneously and boarded the car. The plateau is at about twelve thousand feet and our driver let us know that it would be colder than frigid when we arrived. We would drive south for about three hours, we were told. We would park on a plateau where the geysers were. We would walk about and see the geysers. After we had our sufficiency of geysers, we would leave the plateau and breakfast in the town of San Pedro de Atacama, followed by a leisurely seventy-mile drive back to Calama and our hotel. We were scheduled to fly to Lake Titicaca in Peru the following day.

The drive was a rattlingly shaky experience, more like being dice in a shaking container than passengers in a car. For Liz, extreme temperatures, cold or hot, were unbearable. We finally arrived at the plateau. Liz and Jeanette remained wrapped in blankets in the car. Omer, Maurice and I joined a small group of young European tourists dressed in lederhosen and sandals and walked about for a short while, breathing in, without gusto, the heavy sulfuric fumes. It was obviously time to retreat. We awakened our driver and discovered that our touring car needed a great deal of coaxing and pushing to fire up. It finally did. It will take a miracle, I thought, to see us safely back in Calama.

We drove through the village of San Pedro, following a bus bringing people to market with chickens squawking and children screaming.

The bus was brought to a groaning halt by a slick, tall, brilliantly uniformed police officer. He stood imperiously in front of the bus and glared at the driver. Then he waved the bus through and raised his hand again to bring us to a stop.

There was a surreal quality to all of this: this elegant officer, black leather-booted, in black lacquered mustache and riding whip that he flexed impatiently against a boot. He wore huge, super-black sunglasses, as black as his boots. We were mystified that he could see through them.

He approached our driver, demanded papers, read them and sneered. He paid no attention to any of us, only the driver. He was far from satisfied with the papers as he read them. "You are wearing improper glasses," he said. (Maurice translated for us.) "Your vision record requires much stronger glasses. I can either jail you or fine you." Maurice entered the discussion and it all eventuated in a fine or a charge of some sort and we drove off.

We found an open café, had coffee and pastry, began to shed much of our clothing. The driver went off to a repair shop. He was worried about one of his tires. He would have it patched.

The car soon rattled to a stop in front of the café. We were assured that the tire had been repaired. And now for the drive back to Calama, a drive that would take us once more through the Atacama Desert. We had driven this road the night before. We had dozed through much of the drive. Now, in daylight, the barrenness of the landscape was frighteningly evident. There would not be one building, not one rest stop, not one phone, not one anything between San Pedro and Calama.

"Maurice," Liz said, "please ask him if he has a phone. Suppose we run into a problem." Maurice asked. He was assured that, yes, the driver had a phone. He could call for help if necessary.

I reflected on past events. It would be the pinnacle of irony if we all perished in the desert. But off we went, and then, almost two hours later, with the sun reaching its zenith, the repaired tire blew. Our driver showed some concern at this point. He retrieved another tire from the trunk of the car. And then, to his amazement and our fury, he discovered that the tire didn't fit our automobile. It seemed to have been stored in our trunk for storage sake, not for use. And next, we discovered that the car radio phone was broken. And all the while, not a car or truck was seen.

We had little water. We all knew what the evening temperature in the desert would be. We would either succumb to thirst or to cold. Liz smiled ruefully and then said to the group, "Well, if we die it won't be in a blizzard."

Maurice, cheerful as always, said, "I can sing my gnu song if you'd like."

It goes like this: "Don't you wish you knew a gnu?" He began to hum. "It's a good luck song," he said.

Time seemed to creep by. The road remained untraveled. And then, from far off to the south, we saw a pickup truck heading our way. We jumped in front of it as it neared us and the driver stopped, curious as to why a number of people would dance about the desert in a glaring sun.

We convinced him, at a sufficient price, to ferry all of us except our driver, who wished to stay with his vehicle, into Calama and our hotel. I'm sure we would have strangled him if he had tried to drive off without us.

Liz and Jeanette sat up front with the driver and Maurice, Omer and I sat on the merchandise being transported to town: six-foot-long, thirty-inch-high, razor-edged oil-well drilling bits. Everything was stacked on top of everything else. We didn't quite sit, as contact with any of the seating surfaces might well have produced severe gashes. Well, we all lived to tell the story. Somehow, Liz's gods of good fortune had reached down and put a pickup truck on the road to Calama.

We never made it to Lake Titicaca; we received a call at the hotel in Calama that Liz's mother was not well. We flew to Gulfport the next morning.

We had said our farewells to Maurice and, as close as we had become, that was the last we saw of him. During the intervening years, I've tried to keep a tenuous hold on our relationship. Liz and I admired Maurice, probably as much for his human gentle qualities as his professional stature. "One of the most renowned naturalists and ornithologists in South America," says one short bio. Maurice, as Antarctic-traveled as anyone, can describe the Shackleton trip from Elephant Island to South Georgia virtually wave by wave. He can point out the birds that flew over the dinghy. He sent me a short note after Liz's death that I treasure. I hope to see him again and will lean on Bill Conway to make it happen. It's a long hop in time from the Atacama Desert and I'm sure Maurice has slowed down. But not enough, I'm afraid, to have talked him into investigating Provence with us.

And so began our program's dedication to Patagonia. We started by funding Graham Harris's administrative costs, Graham being in charge of the entire Patagonian program for the Wildlife Conservation Society. Graham, as an Argentine, had already established excellent relations with policymakers and with other non-governmental groups in the field. He supervised well over twenty biologists working on various programs. Over time, we funded a broad variety of field programs through Graham. The breadth of the work, still ongoing, covers the Patagonian Coastal Zone Management Plan, which was designed to research and then implement the conditions under which a broad variety of coastal species are monitored, and then to strategize their conservation—southern elephant seal, southern right whale, bottlenose dolphin, a variety of penguins, black-browed albatross, three species of cormorants and a large assortment of more varied birdlife. Península Valdés, Punto Tombo, Playa Escondido and other key coastal zones were closely monitored. A new program broadening the area to be covered and hoping to establish a marine reserve in the southern ocean has been in play now for three years. It's called Sea and Sky and is headed by Claudio Campagna, an impassioned marine biologist. We encouraged the development of the program and contributed the initial seed money.

Our investment in those programs is now over two million dollars. I was not as enthusiastic about rangeland programs in Patagonia, but Liz asked, "Why not? I like guanacos." So guanacos, vicuñas, maras (small, deer-like ungulates), pumas, flamingos, swans and other inland creatures expanded our Patagonia portfolio. Our investment in that program is close to $400,000.

Bill Conway, seventy-eight years old now, though retired from his former responsibilities at the zoo, is far from retired in his passion for Patagonia.

Chemotherapy 4—Taxol-Platinum 5/16/02 to 8/26/03

Liz was to once more resort to poisonous chemicals to extend her life, which had become an ongoing battle with a disease that would not be conquered. I'm sure that was no surprise to her. I'm sure now that her comforting talk with Kathy Orsello, after it had become clear that she was no longer in remission, had readied her for a long battle with the disease. And I'm convinced that her faith in Dr. Pasmantier's toolbox metaphor was accepted as just that. Toolboxes eventually become empty of tools.

Despite the leap in the numbers, Liz felt well. We had planned a refresher trip through Provence, a trip to satisfy the eyes and senses, a trip to reawaken the memories of lovely, soft places and fine food. Liz, almost above all else, loved food, sensitive cooking and easy eating. We were determined to live as we had lived. And as earlier discussed, Mark had no problem with that. We put off the first treatment of the new cycle for one month.

Now Liz and I had to accept that she had joined the ranks of chronic cancer patients. She had prepared earlier for a long-distance run with her first purchase of wigs. She bought two more off the shelf.

I spoke to Dr. Pasmantier recently about his patients' general reaction to hair loss. "Horror," he said. "Most women find it hard to accept. But Liz always looked so good it was hard to tell if her hair was natural or not."

We asked Brian Kahn and Sandra to join us. Liz had no interest in driving and I had little interest in being the only driver in the south of France. We knew them both well. We considered them congenial and intelligent. They are as close friends as any we had.

The itinerary was Liz-selected—a stop for the evening in the Azores, then off the following morning to Aix-en-Provence, where we stayed at the most elegant of secluded villas, the Villa Gallici Hotel. It remains so secluded and special that the bar is tucked away in the basement, tastefully so, I should add, and the only requirements for entry are that the gentlemen wear a double-breasted navy blazer and the women be beautiful. The villa's famed restaurant sits in the next room and serves only twelve. In the most hushed of tones, dinner is ordered. What a splendid evening.

Aix is a students' town, with architecture that bridges the ages, a vibrant marketplace, curbside cafés where an espresso and some good talk are sufficient to satisfy the owners and waiters and waitresses who often will sit with you and assist in bemoaning the savage conditions under which we all live. Liz adored Aix. She adored any place, it seems, where people were not in a hurry.

It was in Aix that Brian snapped Liz and I walking ahead, so typically "Liz and Art" that I can barely look at the photograph without tears coming to my eyes. We are walking hand in hand, Liz's head turned to the right, glancing at a shop window. I am looking ahead. Her hair is her very own, beautifully bleached to just the right corn-yellow color. We had both agreed that the color was beautiful. Clyde had approved the color. Ian had approved. And now Brian had made the color timeless.

We sampled favorite villas for the remainder of our visit: La Riboto de Taven in Les Baux and Le Vieux Castillon in Castillon du Gard, a favored resting place for cyclists on their westward, high-altitude endurance performance. The villa sits a few meters from the ancient Roman aqueduct spanning the Gard River, the Pont du Gard. I often thought that its sole reason for being was so that Liz and I could be photographed, alone or together, leaning against the west wall, the river gushing below. And then on to Michel Bras, as famous a chef as Woody Allen is a comedian, this mentioned because in size and lack of heft and facial appearance, Michel Bras is a dead ringer for Woody Allen. His hotel is perched on a high ledge about three miles from Laguiole, famed for the unmatchable knives for all uses produced by the artisans of the area. The dining experience was all that Liz could have asked for. Her appetite was strong and she loved every moment. The guests were invited in judicious procession to "experience" the kitchen, which was the size of a basketball court, full of blinking and twitching and snorting and steaming equipment and large computer control panels registering activities being performed throughout the room. The maestro himself, perhaps a mere five feet tall, sporting on his head a chef's hat at least as tall, ran about the room pointing and snapping and adjusting whatever demanded adjustment. There was no way dinner could be anything other than delicious, engineered to be perfection.

Our rooms were so thoroughly Japanese in décor and attitude that one felt a strong inclination to sleep in the hallway and not encumber the room with human presence. We beat back the impulse to slink about the room and in due course settled in.

Sated after two days of the wonders of Michel Bras, we boarded our vehicles and drove south to the airport at Rodez, there to enplane for Paris. But first, another Liz-protected adventure.

I was in the lead car on a two-lane highway, pursued by Brian and a lengthy string of high-speed automobiles, an unbroken chain of cars along the road speeding north when suddenly—believe me, so suddenly I didn't fathom what had happened until it had actually happened—a car heading north had veered off the road into a tree, bounced high off the tree and came hurtling across the road, virtually horizontally, grazing my hood and windshield, leaving no marks, and implanting itself into a tree on our side of the road. It then burst into flames. Both Brian and I had passed through untouched. Liz was once more spared. She, as always, was calm. "Close," she said. "Shouldn't we go back and see if we can help?" By then the scene was densely packed with helpers. We continued on to Rodez, to Paris and the Hotel de Crillon.

The Crillon is the hotel where Colonel Omer Villere Claiborne had been quartered during World War II. He had been in charge of finding the artwork and gold bars and all articles of value stolen by the occupying, then retreating, German army.

His days in Belgium and in Paris had fortified his love of France and the French language. He had lived in the tiny penthouse atop the hotel. We booked it so that Liz could experience a long-forgotten corner of her father's life. We came back to New York on May 15. That was our last trip to Paris.

· · ·

The new treatment began the following day: Taxol-platinum, administered once every three weeks. June was a routine month, but routine was no longer as comfortable as it was in the past. Liz was slowing down. She had chemotherapy on June 6th and then again on the 27th. We went off to Montana on the 28th, but first stopped in Chicago to spend a day with my daughter, Nancy. That evening at our hotel, Liz had one of her very first painful nights, experiencing nausea, vomiting and exhaustion. We managed to sleep a bit. Then I called for a wheelchair to take her to the lobby, where we were met by a car that got us off to Midway and from there to Missoula. It's a short enough flight, but Liz was beginning to feel restless and uncomfortable. We landed in Missoula and took off for the emergency room at St. Patrick's Hospital. The physician on duty diagnosed Liz with an early stage of shingles, early enough so that with proper medication it could be headed off before it fully developed. Instructions were followed and that was the end of the shingles concern.

Liz rested at Tranquillity until it was time to head east to Triple 8. Treatment number three, July 3rd, was to be absorbed at St. Peter's in Helena under the supervision of Dr. Tom Weiner. This time around was more difficult for Liz. She experienced greater nausea and was more exhausted and headachy than earlier. She suffered her first really bad reaction.

Liz's veins, narrow and by now overused, had become difficult to access. It was decided that she needed a port that would serve as an entry access for chemotherapy treatment as well as hydration fluids. Performed with a local anesthetic, the port placement took place on the 12th. The procedure was simple, painless and went off without a problem. The port was located about two inches above her left breast, and about the size of a pacemaker. It was put to use often during the years ahead.

The booster shot ten days later added to her discomfort. She was having difficulty swallowing. It became painful to eat or drink. We went back to the hospital. Dr. Weiner assured us that this was not an uncommon reaction to chemotherapy. The lining of the esophagus becomes raw. The patient is hooked up to the IV stand to be hydrated. Morphine and medication are applied and in due course the patient finds relief. Run-of-the-mill stuff, he assured us. It might be a common byproduct of chemotherapy, but we knew without dwelling on it that common byproducts would become more and more a part of the world Liz would be forced to adjust to. Her weight began to fall off more noticeably.

She left the hospital on the 17th. She was back in the game, not aggressively, but for the moment well enough to drive to Tranquillity. Alex and Christina were visiting, stopping for a few days while touring the great American West. Liz continued to feel unsteady.

It's a long way from our bedroom at Tranquillity to the bathroom. To make it even more difficult, there are a number of steps between the dressing room and the bathroom that had to be negotiated. And to add to the complexity of those days, I had arranged a tour of Section 24, a square mile of former Forest Service land situated next to Tranquillity.

The Homestead Act of 1862 was passed by a Congress that wanted to encourage the new railroad industry to make the capital investments necessary to help settle the American West. Alternate sections of land, a section being 640 acres or one square mile, were checker-boarded in parts of the northern and central west. The railroad industry had free access to every other section; the rest was open for individual ownership and development or turned over to a federal agency, such as the Forest Service. A private piece of land had become available at the southwest corner of Glacier National Park that the Forest Service wanted. We bought that land and traded it to the Forest Service. That's how we came to own Section 24, 640 acres of forested land abutting Tranquillity.

A group of noteworthy conservation leaders, Carl Pope of the Sierra Club, Bill Meadows of The Wilderness Society and Rodger Schlickeisen of Defenders of Wildlife, plus members of their staff, agency people and foresters were to walk the land and evaluate the restoration work that Liz and I had put into motion years earlier.

Liz never made it. She slept little and vomited much the night before. We called Dr. Weiner, arranged for a plane to pick Liz up in the morning, fly her to Helena and then take her to the hospital for hydration and rest.

I led the walk and played out our role as enlightened stewards of the land. I led the group for a visit to the Clearwater Stewardship Project and the Swan Ecosystem Center and then hosted a getting-to-know-you dinner at the Hungry Bear. Liz missed the dinner.

The previous day, I had insisted on canceling the walk-around. Liz wouldn't hear of it. She threatened to refuse to fly to Helena, but fly she did and walk around the group did. The dinner included a diverse cast of characters from Seeley Lake and the Swan Valley area along with the visiting conservation leaders. I believe to this day that the lingering impressions formed that day and night have been valuable. I believe that Carl Pope, Bill Meadows and Rodger Schlickeisen, all directors of large conservation organizations, now understood the inextricable nature of the bond between people and the resources upon which they depend.

All of this was of no comfort then. Liz was due for chemo again on July 31. Dr. Weiner reduced the dosage. The good news was that Liz's CA125 had been reduced to 133 in July. That was positive news but indicated what we had already assumed would be the case; the chemicals were activating a retreat on the part of the cancer cells.

Alex and Christina passed through again for a number of days. We had entertained other visitors. We seemed to have leveled off. We saw Dr. Weiner again on August 9. He found Liz in need of a booster for her reds (anemia, at one level or another, bedeviled Liz throughout). It was becoming more and more apparent that continued weight loss was now a major concern.

We flew back to New York on August 21. Dr. Pasmantier's office drew their usual quantity of blood to assess Liz's condition. She had a CT scan the following day. The weekend of the 24th was lighthearted and fun. We went to Fire Island. My son Neil introduced us to his new girlfriend, Karen, a beautiful, young person of Taiwanese origin, schooled in America, who came packaged with an ineradicable smile, no matter what the circumstances. Alex joined us. We had dinner at the only restaurant in town, but old subscribers that we were, we had our prime table. Everybody was up for it. It was a grand evening. Looking at a photograph of the six of us at dinner that night, you would not believe that Liz was anything but a beautiful, healthy woman.

The meeting at Dr. Pasmantier's office on August 28 was more sobering. Liz's CA125 was now 96.9. The indicator showed slow, continuing progress in the retreat of the cancerous cells, but at a cost. Liz had suffered the expected side effects of the chemicals. And, as usual, these side effects were the norm. I waited for Liz outside of the examining room.

Mark and I met on September 6, 2007. We spoke about that morning at the end of August in 2002. He first wanted me to know that Liz had been calm and low-keyed throughout the meeting.

"Is this the way it's going to be from now on?" Liz had asked. "Not necessarily," Mark had answered. "You'll possibly have some rough days or nights, but you're remarkably resilient. You're a very together person. Sure, you're down right now. Who wouldn't be?"

My meeting with Mark that day helped me regain my perspective as to what we had been up against the five years from 2002 to 2007. My instinctive reaction to all dire news was what can I do now to make her better? I had begun to lose my peripheral vision. I never thought to ask, what can I do to make things easier for Liz?

Mark went on. "She was beginning to show signs of depression. We talked for a while and I could see her squaring her shoulders, snapping back. I remarked to her that she was an extraordinarily adaptable person."

Mark was startled, and he now admits, somewhat awestruck by what followed. "She told me her story: her first marriage, living alone, bringing up a child alone until she married you. She wanted me to know that she had to manage her life, to control and shape events. She had become accustomed to struggle for what she wanted. She told me all of this only because I had brought it up. She told me her story calmly, quietly, undramatically. She was not complaining. She just wanted me to know that she had been through hard times and hard work."

My notes of September 6, 2007 continue. Mark clarified the two-track road that Liz was then straddling. "There are two things happening with a patient like Liz. On the one hand she has suffered the irreversible physical effects of the chemotherapy. And on the other hand she has to deal with the discomfort of absorbing the chemicals. You can alleviate discomfort or operational misfiring through certain medications, but what's done is done. We're dealing with the equivalent of gang warfare. Not with tumors that can be shrunk, but with invaders who disappear and then later, may well reappear."

It was not news to me that Liz's years as a cancer patient had been an ongoing struggle to ease the pain of blockage in her digestive system. She had suffered severe cramps and many of the other discomforts caused by constipation. Recall that she added the word "chronic" to Dr. Magid's questionnaire, which included the word "constipation."

She had told Mark that day in late August of 2002 that her constipation was getting more troublesome, thus more difficult to balance her intake and outgo. He was not at all surprised and told me, this past September, why he wasn't.

"That was track one, the functional track. There was also track two, the ongoing chemotherapy, the searching out and trying to kill, once and for all, the lurking cancer cells. These were corrosive chemicals. They always left a calling card. Whatever success we had, and we had periods of extraordinary success, her CA125 continued to fluctuate."

I was not depressed by Mark's recounting of that day in 2002. I, too, believed then that the toolbox was far from empty, even though 2002, with its good times, was proving to be a year with ups and downs and sideways and some painful evenings.

At the end of August, we flew back to Montana and spent the entire month there, shuttling between Triple 8 and Tranquillity. The month was uneventful. We were active that September, dinners out—Liz's appetite reasonably good, her spirits reasonably high. She had her next chemotherapy session on September 25 without problems. Tom prescribed Zometa to help her bone density problem. He saw Liz again on October 4 and had a Procrit shot administered once more to reduce anemia. Her CA125 was now down to 65. We were once more going in the right direction.

We flew back to New York on October 15. Liz had been troubled by vision problems and had arranged to see Dr. Eric Zweifach, our ophthalmologist. He was to see Liz a number of times until he performed a routine cataract procedure in late May of 2006.

I spoke with him at the end of September of 2007 about his meetings with Liz, her spirits and her general demeanor. "She was generally optimistic," he said. "It was cyclical. At times she was frustrated. It looked like she was going to beat this thing, then back to zero again. But never self-pity. She squared her shoulders and went from there. She never doubted that she would beat the disease. That was the impression she gave."

Dr. Pasmantier saw Liz again on October 22 for another chemo session. All went well. A booster followed on the 25th.

We had our biannual board meetings October 30 and 31. Liz and I loved the work our foundation does. We had the good fortune of Bill Conway accepting a seat on our board. We, who had put such emphasis on the purposeful work that a team of professionals can produce, loved and respected our fellow board members. There was little time for depression and every reason to soldier on.

The October board meetings that year were gate-openers. We made our first contribution to an ambitious jaguar conservation program that would involve continued research on the ground from Belize to Mexico to assess numbers of jaguars through the use of camera traps. The program would plot jaguar movement, assess the prey base, spell out the threats to jaguar survival and engage local politicians and agency people in jaguar protection. When Liz died, we had invested over one million dollars in jaguar conservation. We felt we had played an important role in helping jaguars to hold their own. The population was truly a meta-population throughout jaguar range, meaning that no subspecies had developed as a result of groups of animals becoming isolated one from the other. The work continues, from northern Argentina to the key area of the Pantanal in Brazil, through Central America and to the northern border of Mexico.

We also participated in a program in the Congo that protects a reserve, Nouabale-Ndoki National Park, rich in elephants and home to a diversity of animals that is a rarity, even in the wild. The program was originally funded at over $100,000, seed money to add to the Wildlife Conservation Society's own investment, and continues now, even under many threats from growing human populations, poaching and disease, threats that are common to much of Africa's wildlife. At the time of Liz's death, we had invested more than one million dollars in the program. We have invested as much in many other programs.

This was Liz's other important life, the life that ignored cancer, the life that fought larger, more important battles.

And now there is new news from the Congo; more than 125,000 lowland gorillas have been discovered, a significant number of them living in areas our funds have protected. Our losses may be permanent, but our victories, small or otherwise, would never have happened without Liz and others like her.

The chemo schedule continued routinely: November 19 and December 17. And then, the following day, we flew off to St. Barts. The year ended quietly, a Christmas Eve dinner that reminded us, once more, how fortunate we were to be alive, together, and to know that nothing could diminish the love we had for one another.

I close the year by quoting from a card Liz had sent me on my birthday, back in August. We had both read the David McCullough *John Adams* biography, and she quoted from a letter written by Thomas Jefferson to Adams toward the end of their lives.

Liz wrote to me:

"My dearest friend, though I am old and worn, here a pivot, there a wheel, now a pinion, next a spring will give way, but there are times when the heart is peculiarly awake to tender impressions, when philosophy slumbers, or is overpowered by sentiments... it is then that you lend me an assisting hand through the difficulties... and I bless the hand from which my comforts flow.

I remain, despite the lost 'pinions,' your loving wife. Liz."

CHAPTER SEVEN, 2003

THE DEATH OF Liz's mother, Louise Fenner Claiborne, in 1993, was a key event in Liz's life. But the fullness of their relationship and the devotion each had for the other continued through their lifetimes.

We had started the year quietly. We had planned no lengthy trips. St. Barts was to be our pleasure dome and it truly was. Liz's mother had not been well. Liz, devoted daughter that she always was, had been visiting her at least three times a year in her home in Pass Christian, Mississippi. Mrs. Claiborne had been living there ever since her return from Europe many years ago and after her husband, crusty Omer Villere Claiborne, had decided he had enough of all of us, ceased eating and died quietly at the age of ninety-five.

In the early 1990s, we would often bring Liz's mother with us to St. Barts or to Montana with her loyal and helpful companion Lorna Daniels. We loved Louise and enjoyed being with her. After her death, her ashes were buried in a low hillside at Tranquillity, looking toward the Swan Mountain Range. Now that I've sold Tranquillity, her ashes have been moved to Triple 8, where they will be buried not too far from Liz.

Louise, while alive and in her last years, had made her home into a sanc-

Portraits of Louise Fenner Claiborne.

tuary for stray cats. It was this compulsion, we all agreed, that shortened her life. She had tripped over her beloved black, ill-tempered cat, Speck, fell and broke her hip. She was ambulanced to the Gulfport General Hospital, where she remained until, not too long after the fall, she died. Liz and I visited in February. Liz visited again in March and April, and then in May, after her mother had died. Omer and Louis were there to handle the final arrangements; Louis to plow through his mother's renewed but unread abundance of subscriptions, her bank books and the rest of the tiresome matters that accompany a person's death.

Liz wrote the obituary that would appear in the *New Orleans Times-Picayune*:

"Carol Louise Fenner Claiborne was born November 20, 1903, in New Orleans, Louisiana. Married at twenty-one to Omer V. Claiborne, she immediately went off to Europe, where she spent most of her adult life, returning to New Orleans only for visits to the family and occasionally to Pass Christian to spend the summer with her three children.

"When her husband retired as the Director of the Brussels' branch of the Guaranty Trust Company in 1950, the family came back to the Gulf Coast, where they lived until 'Camille' washed their house and all their belongings away. This was an excuse to return to Europe, where they settled in France for about five years. But the

Louise Fenner Claiborne in Pass Christian, Mississippi, 1990; and with her cat "Speck," 1992.

pull of the Gulf Coast brought them back to Pass Christian."

"It was then that she started her love affair with cats, having as many as a dozen at one time. She realized that she could not properly care for that many and as time went on she reduced the brood to one terribly spoiled cat, 'Speck' by name.

"She always loved animals and had a soft heart for any homeless dog or cat and could not be discouraged from feeding them, and to everyone's distress, inviting them in as boarders.

"She remained, stray cats and all, in Pass Christian until her death in May of 1993."

The dynamics of Liz's relationship with her mother strike more deeply than this tender remembrance. In 1991 Liz had described her mother as a "miraculously nimble and fearlessly inventive sewer—the first great technician from whom I learned to respect the mutual dependence of creative concepts and the skills needed to actualize those concepts."

True enough, a utilitarian view of one's mother. Louise Fenner Claiborne, married at twenty-one, as fragile, vulnerable and beautiful as a gossamer wing, had married a dashingly handsome man, a man of solid blue-blooded credentials, ten years older than she was. He was military in bearing, assertive, charming, but sadly flawed. His father, Liz's grandfather, a man she never knew, had gone fishing and left "dear mère" to bring up three children.

Henry, the first son, never married and became a naval officer. Omer Villere, the second son, as noted, became a military man. And Clarisse, always in pink, coyly pretty, later married well and hid the cupboard keys from the help.

They had little money and could afford few of the trappings that New Orleans required of high society members. This always troubled Omer Villere. He insisted on financial independence, though he had to work for every penny he had. He inherited nothing. Liz's mother understood her husband's insistence on dominating his family. She did not put her body between him and the children. He ruled, and she accepted.

"Dear mère" knew her second son well, his inflexible demands of his family. She knew he was a proud and sensitive man. She knew that a time would come when Liza, stress on the second syllable, our Liz, would have to stand on her own. When that time came, fortunately "dear mère" was in New York.

And Louise, intimidated as she was, tiptoed around him to send a loving letter to Liz and a handful of money, all surreptitiously, every now and then.

I have a letter addressed to Liz written in 1970. It is addressed "Dearest Angel," as were all her letters to Liz, and the final remarks, written in huge letters, "OFF THE RECORD." Louise writes from Pau in the southwest of France, a letter to "Mrs. Arthur Ortenberg at 72 Bank Street in NYC." She has just turned sixty-seven. DeGaulle had just died. Louise chats about this and then, full of complaints about the cold, about the lack of a "permanent" residence, about past winters in France, about Omer Sr.'s frugality. His answer to the cold had little to do with turning up the heat, everything to do with walking about outside to work up some body heat.

But in 1970, there had been some bend in our relationship. Liz's parents had visited us in New York. A frosty relationship was rekindled. Louise's letter really amounted to instructions to Liz in the event of her (Louise's) death. It may very well have been her heart's desire to get out from under Omer and to put an end to the cold and disarrangement.

Omer Sr. died in 1988. Louise lived on for more than fifteen years. She ended her days in warm Mississippi. Her daughter visited her often. I grew to love Louise and I arranged for her to visit us accompanied by Lorna as often and comfortably as she had the time and strength. She had failed as matriarch, though her failure was not of the heart, but one owing to overwhelming circumstances. Liz forgave her this failing.

One late afternoon in July of 1993, Liz and I walked about one hundred paces west of our gate at Tranquillity, past a boulder marking the uphill line of the horse trail leading away from the ranch. There we found a sloping area that we all had agreed was just where Louise would be happy, reaching out to the Swan Mountain Range to the east. Liz carried her mother's ashes in a small urn. I carried a pint bottle of single malt scotch and a tablespoon for Louise's portion. We put her urn into a prepared burial spot and I shoveled a few spadefuls of soil over it, and then asked Louise if she would like a farewell drink. I thought I heard her say, as she always had said in the past, "Yes, but just a little one." I spooned out a small amount of liquid, and scattered it on the soil.

We all sat at the Tranquillity bar a bit later. I knew, that as she often did, Liz was reliving that dramatic moment in 1950, when she had declared her determination to strike out on her own. I have often looked at the photographs of the precipitating events: Liz's winning the *Harper's Bazaar* design award, much to the displeasure of her father; Liz and the sketch of the winning design; and Liz and her mother photographed on the platform of the train taking them to New York, prior to boarding the boat for France. The two of them, mother and daughter, look enormously pleased with one another. They are grinning, arm around arm, smiling and waving rapturously with their free arms. And now my thoughts take me back to that moment in 1950. The Claiborne trio, father, mother and daughter, have disembarked from the boat that has brought them to New York's harbor. Their automobile has been brought to boat side for their immediate use.

Liz has re-created the event over and over again. They drive off, headed for New Orleans. The car stops at a light. We are somewhere in New York City. Liz announces she's getting out. She is twenty-one and she will stay in New York and find work. Her father calmly gives Liz her suitcase and a fifty-dollar bill and says, "Good luck." Her mother does nothing. I imagine now that that must be a partial telling of the story, but that's how Liz remembered it. Her mother and father drive off, Louise at the wheel.

And here the elephant matriarch analogy, so meaningful to Liz, falls apart. Louise, in the living out of her life, demonstrated the many faces of self-sacrifice.

Liz and I supported a spay/neuter clinic at the Humane Society in Gulfport, Mississippi, for many years, the Louise Fenner Claiborne Clinic. The area had become overrun by homeless cats and dogs that were reproducing exponentially. The clinic was in business, successfully so, to sterilize these animals. But the clinic was washed away by Hurricane Katrina in 2005. A new building has since replaced it. An aggressive capital campaign has largely rebuilt the many buildings of the institution. I have purchased the naming rights for the new clinic, the Louise Fenner Claiborne Spay/Neuter Clinic. It continues the work we were doing prior to Katrina's wiping out the earlier facility. The new clinic is much larger, much better equipped and managed. The program is more aggressive. Liz would approve.

• • •

It was 2003 and the treatment continued. We were now using the efficient St. Barts clinic for blood tests. All was satisfactory at the beginning of January. We flew back to New York for chemotherapy on January 14, and Liz's general routine remained unchanged: the mandatory post-chemotherapy manicure, dinner out, a few quiet days at our new apartment and back to St. Barts by the end of the week. February was much like the previous month: chemotherapy on the 11th, the blood report from the St. Barts clinic. March continued as routinely, chemotherapy on the 11th and back to St. Barts on the 13th. So far the year had started well; Liz's CA125 was slowly falling. She felt well. A good part of the month was once again spent in St. Barts. We were not taking anything for granted. What often seems like stability is really a period of cancer consolidation. And the full effect of the chemotherapy had not yet become evident. We knew this was a razor's edge existence, best to keep moving and doing. We ended the month in Helena at the spring Student Conference of the Montana Heritage Project.

April was a different matter. Liz had chemotherapy on the 8th. We returned to St. Barts on the 10th. But this time Liz's reaction was severe. She spent an evening throwing up, shaking and trembling, barely getting any sleep. Her CA125 may have been improving but at a heavy physical cost. Once more it became clear that fighting guerrilla warfare was very much like throwing bombs—in this case, the chemicals, in the direction of the invader and all too often striking one's own troops. We were back in New York on the 11th and went directly to the hospital.

196

She was hydrated and given four units of blood. She spent three days in the hospital. The infusion of blood, as anticipated, reenergized her.

So back to St. Barts we went on the 15th and attempted to resume a normal life by having a bland dinner at Maya's Restaurant. It didn't work. Liz had two more tough nights. We had now become more expert at coping. Medications to control the spasmodic nature of the esophagus were taken as prescribed; Liz's trusty Fioricet, her major weapon to soften the hammering of a migraine, was always on hand.

By the evening of the 17th, she felt well enough to go out to dinner and the next number of days went well.

As Dr. Pasmantier pointed out on May 6th at the next chemo session, these events were the normal cyclical ups and downs common to the disease. Liz had had a PET scan at the end of April. The results were encouraging. Her CA125 was 35 despite the sturm und drang of April. Uncomfortable events were normal, Dr. Pasmantier had reminded us. We gambled a bit and decided to skip June treatment.

In early June, Liz was the honored cancer patient at a Cancer Care event arranged by her good friend—to Liz, virtually a daughter—Dana Buchman. Dana had been one of Liz's early hires, a wispily lovely sweater designer, a Brown graduate, a person we felt had the possibilities of becoming a full designer, capable of carrying a brand. We had her trained in designing, fitting and draping woven fabrics so that Dana would become a complete designer. She would no longer be solely a knitwear designer. It worked out. The company was able to build a higher-priced product line around Dana. We were delighted to be able to appear on her behalf. It was black tie and black tuxedo time again for Liz. She loved it and breezed through the evening, while I was once more her somewhat frazzled chaperone.

On June 14, we enplaned for another Provence trip, this time escorting Maya and Randy. We had become close friends. Maya and Liz had formed an understanding over the years. Both were creative artists. Both selected the implements with which they worked. Both supervised the products they created. We were one generation removed, and our backgrounds were dissimilar. Maya had been born in Martinique, one of many children, a member of a happy, financially comfortable family. Meal time was ritual time. It was at her home table that Maya had become a superb chef. In that sense, she, like Liz, had started her education at home. Her relationship with Randy, evident from our earlier experiences at the restaurant, was low-keyed and supportive. They would be ideal traveling companions.

This was to be another delightful trip, with lush scenery, beautiful lodgings and superb dinners. And once more we stayed at the Japanese-Hollywood setting of Michel Bras outside of Laguiole.

On June 22, Randy and Maya took off on their own and Liz and I flew to Poitiers. Poitiers is an ancient city famous for two great battles fought in the fields outside of the city. During one, Charles Martel, leader of the Franks, stopped the advance of the Muslims in 732. The next great historical Poitiers event was the mighty battle of 1356, when the French, with a substantial numerical advantage, managed to lose to the English, and King John of France was taken prisoner.

But circumstances and time, as is generally the case, have readjusted the balance of power and Poitiers is now a peaceful resort city. It's fairly close to Tours so Kim and Christophe were able to join us for dinner at the Chateau. This was the famous summer of 2003 when Paris was smothered in heat and indoors was the place to be, especially for the aged and infirm. I'm afraid we qualified on both counts, but Poitiers was southerly enough to be bearable. So we ventured to the swimming pool. As I write, my mind's eye is fixed on Liz as she stepped on the diving board at the pool. Other hotel guests lounging around the pool were struck by this slender figure, poised in a one-piece swimsuit, arms outstretched, her back erect. It was too hot for a bathing cap. She was bald. Her body entered the water almost soundlessly. She swam with such obvious delight, loving the coolness of the water. Her Australian crawl was flawless. I swam afterward, far from as graceful and deft, but bursting with pride.

We had dinner later with Kim and Christophe, the perfect ending of a beautiful day.

Our penultimate stop on this tour was to be a visit to Mont-Saint-Michel on the Normandy coast. I had glamorized St. Michael, defending the faithful against all heathens invading from the west. We had booked into the famous Les Terrasses Poulard Hotel on the island. Andrew Claiborne, Louis's son, and his wife, Corinne, were to meet us there. They were to arrive from England at Dinard, the local airport, pick up their luggage, meet at the hotel, and we would then dine and have a marvelous next day guided about the wonders of Mont-Saint-Michel. Following that, we were to spend two days at the Bricourt. That was the well-wrought plan. That's far from how it worked out.

Some instinct prompted me to ask our driver to wait until we were safely in our rooms. Carrying luggage, we presented ourselves to check in at Les Terrasses only to be told that they were fully booked; some miscommunication had taken place, sorry. But we've booked you and your party into the "annex." "No need to be concerned. It's fine." This was told us by the receptionist of the main hotel.

It was far from fine. It sat about fifty yards down the road, and we had to climb two narrow flights of winding outside stone steps, luggage and all, assisted by a young boy no more than ten years old, before we arrived at the check-in desk. There it was, cave-like, one exposed light bulb swinging lazily back and forth over the desk, a desk which had been commandeered by a woman who could have been a stand-in for Vampira. "Your rooms are on the third and fourth floors. Here are your keys. Follow the boy. Help him with the luggage."

Liz was game as always. We started the upward trudge. Indeed our room was three new flights up, all to be taken on the outside, winding stone steps. The boy stopped, unloaded the few bags he had, stepped into the hallway and pushed open the first door at his left. There, much to my unbelieving horror was a room, no larger than nine-feet square, with a steel-frame single bed pushed along one wall. A 40-watt bulb dangled from an exposed wire added to the fading outdoor light wanly seeping through a half-open window, and a horde of flies, alive, dying, some already dead, carpeted the windowsill, the floor and the bed sheet cover. This chamber of horrors gave out to a tiny bathroom with a tiny basin. Water was leaking from a faucet. A toilet engineered for the narrowest of bottoms completed the décor.

Liz, philosophical as ever, said, "Well, I guess we can manage for one night. I'll just skip dinner. I'm not going to risk my life again on those stone steps."

Liz had never been more reasonable. "Oh no—we're getting out of here," I said.

Happily, there was a phone in the room. I called our driver and asked him to stay put. I then called the manager of the Bricourt, our next-day accommodation and asked if we could be squeezed in that evening. His answer was a truly sorry "no," but he had a thought. He called a friend at another hotel not too far from the Bricourt and a kindly fate intervened, I firmly believe, on Liz's behalf. Yes, there were two suites available for the evening. We booked them. I asked my new good friend at the Bricourt to call arrivals at the Dinard Airport to see if Andrew could be found and re-directed. The cards were now running our way. Andrew was found at the baggage pickup room. He and Corinne were gathered up and deposited at our new sanctuary, the Maison Tirel Guerin.

We enlisted the young boy again, dragged our luggage down the many flights, this time with the help of our driver. I returned the room keys to Vampira, who received them with a look of complete unconcern. The avenue below was teeming with homeless tourists, evidently much less queasy than I. Our rooms would be resold in less than a minute.

We met Andrew and Corinne in the lounge of the Tirel, toasted our deliverance and then spent two brilliant days in their company. The Bricourt, our residence the following two days, was fit for royalty. What a stupendous time we had in Brittany. Liz truly lived a completely normal life. We toured the roadside, visited ancient ruins, some not so ancient, such as an underground cave that the local people lived in during the Nazi occupation. We dined every evening at a superb restaurant.

We flew back to New York on June 29, this time departing from Rennes.

Liz had a chemo treatment on July 1. Her CA125 reading was 23. Once more we were hopeful that the end might be around the corner. We had dinner at home that night. Liz arranged the mandatory manicure with her old standby, Rose Syrkin, the following afternoon. We left for Montana the next morning. The next number of weeks were spent either at Tranquillity or at Triple 8. Liz saw Dr. Weiner on the 11th. He checked her blood counts.

All was well. He scheduled her next chemotherapy for July 29. He once more reduced the dosage of Taxol-platinum that was being administered.

We returned to New York on Sunday, August 3, landing at MacArthur Airport in Islip so we could have a few days on Fire Island. We were both on a subdued high. Liz had a PET scan the 7th. Good result. We were back to hopeful finger-crossing. We flew back to Montana on the 8th, in time to be witness to the heavy smoke clouds at Tranquillity as a forest fire was in progress.

Liz had e-mailed Kim in mid-August. This was the very first e-mail Liz had ever sent. We had purchased a strikingly handsome, wide-screen Apple computer, which sits elegantly on her desk. She loved looking at it. "Isn't it gorgeous?" she would say. "Someday I'm going to use it to store photographs. For now I'll be happy just to go back and forth with Kim." This was the first of many to follow:

"Hi Kim, Well the FIRES *forced us to have a wonderful Caille & Paté picnic!!! Delicious!!! So we are doing it again tomorrow night and we are looking forward to it. They really are very good. Thank you again. I prepared them as they told me on the can, on the bread etc. and we were both surprised at how appetizing and yummy.*

"How do you like my e-mail??? I'm there, but it takes me forever to type a letter, and not being able to spell does not help. All love to all of you. Liz."

The Swan Valley area in Montana was under siege to fire that summer. The state itself had been fire-swamped following years of dry weather and reduced harvesting. Tranquillity and the entire Seeley Lake–Condon area were surrounded by national forests, and a fire, soon to be named the Crazy Horse Fire, was out of control. It threatened to sweep across Lindbergh Lake Road and envelop the summer homes in the area. Impenetrable clouds of smoke and ash slowly rolled our way. We both felt duty bound to be with Rip and Leanna, our new managers at Tranquillity. The ranch was equipped with a sophisticated firefighting system and easy access to pumping water from our small lake if necessary. Rip insisted that he drive us to Triple 8. We acceded.

Dr. Weiner's staff administered the next treatment on August 26. He reduced the dosage once more. We spent the next few evenings at home.

We were back in New York on September 9. Liz saw Dr. Pasmantier on the 10th for a routine visit. He decided that a laparoscopy was in order. "Let's take a look at where we really stand."

The laparoscopy was performed on the 16th.

We met with Dr. Pasmantier on the 23rd and had a happy chat. We discussed the favorable results of the laparoscopy. They showed no further encroachment of the disease. The disease was controlled, at least for now.

We had another good luck dinner that evening with our close friends, Jon and Stephanie Reckler. They were in the process of searching for a new dog, one that would be exotic enough to stop strangers while you were walking the creature, but unpredictable enough to keep strangers at a distance.

Liz, pleased to be with them and extra pleased at the good news received that day, said, "Exotic, like my disease, unpredictable like my disease, but controllable." We lifted our drink glasses. "Cheers."

We flew back to Montana the following day.

There was no treatment in September, nor would there be in any of the following months of the year. There would be a bone density test at the end of October, a mammogram in November, and blood drawn in mid-November. The year was ending. Liz's CA125 at year's end was 24. It appeared, that at least for now, Liz had beaten back the colonizer seeds and that her digestive system had not been further undermined.

The last months of 2003 had been routinely eventful. That year the October board meeting was largely taken up with the structuring of the new Red Lodge web site. We spent time in Montana. We visited Omer and Jeanette in Santa Fe. We flew to Chicago for a day to visit my daughter, Nancy. We spent customary time in Fire Island as well as St. Barts. And then back to New York on December 2 to hear and see the first reunion of Simon and Garfunkel, super favorites of Liz. She was especially devoted to Paul Simon. His *Graceland* recording had been an essential accessory to enliven Liz's time on the treadmill. She rarely sang, but I would find her treadmilling and yowling, with her earphones strapped to her head and Paul Simon on disc keeping the tempo upbeat. We ended 2003 applauding the return of Simon and Garfunkel and had good reason to hope that Liz had "normalized."

"Normalized," in Liz's world, required that she carry a case with her on all trips, a case that harbored her medications: Celebrex for arthritis; Fioricet for migraines; Ativan to combat nausea and vomiting; Mylanta, Prilosec, Gas-X, all to combat acid "indigestion"; Fiber Con, another therapy for "regularity"; Ambien for sleeplessness; Benadryl; Dulcolax; Diflucan; Compazine and whatever other medicines that had been prescribed for any new ailment. And there were new ailments, osteonecrosis for one, a disease of the gums, which necessitated amoxicillin to combat it. There were a number more of these small vials, lined up like soldiers, awaiting assignments. Always at hand was Liz's small jar of Carmex, an indispensable cold sore remedy. Since we traveled so frequently, she had three small carrying cases; they each were packed with the latest assortment of required medications. It's unnecessary to point out, but I will nonetheless, that each case was beautiful and packed only after a great deal of thought. Nevertheless, when faced with a crisis, it was never easy to find precisely what was needed. With it all, and despite the almost constant adjustments that the medications served, it had been an encouraging year.

On August 13, my seventy-seventh birthday, Liz had sent me a note written on the back of a photograph. There I stand, blabbing away, bedecked in a bright green shirt. Liz wrote: "Green is your color. 77 is your age. Talking is your gift. Bright is your future...because we all know you will live to be 100! But as long as I'm around, that gives me more time to love you... with all my heart, Happy Birthday Darling. Your devoted wife, Liz."

Two weeks after Louise's death in 1993, we flew to Barcelona. Liz wanted to stand in front of Gaudí's magnificent, soaring Sagrada Família, "Expiatory Temple of the Holy Family." The rapture that drove Gaudí to design his church had been so visceral that the work was still reaching to the sky, unfinished at his death in 1926. Liz stood before the building, enraptured herself. It was a gesture for her mother, an affirmation of her love for the beautiful. Here Gaudí had designed a temple, beautiful for its own sake, a temple for all the people of Barcelona and the world. Liz felt that beauty was Gaudí's deity. The temple remains unfinished today. I think about that and wonder if there is a greater truth evident in incompletion. The work is eternally in process, and then, one day, succumbs to time and the elements. And the new begins.

CHAPTER EIGHT, 2004

TWO THOUSAND FOUR, the year Liz was to turn seventy-five, began quietly. We were in St. Barts for virtually the entire month of January. We returned to New York for a PET scan on the 20th, all fine. Liz's eye surgery happened on the afternoon of the 20th. All went well. She saw Dr. Zweifach again the following day. Additionally, the 21st included an appointment with Evelyn, her dental hygienist, and then an afternoon appointment with Dr. Magid.

On the 27th of the month, Liz e-mailed Kim a somewhat out-of-character note. Liz rarely acted as an advisor. Kim and Christophe were faced with a decision as to where to live. Their dilemma was being sure that William, their son, would have a comfortable home.

Liz summed up the quandary, and then opined:

"I would not hesitate too long about what to do...Next fall squeeze into a small place in Paris with your husband. Or, find a place in not such a chic area but with enough room for the family. I'm a great believer in husband and wife staying together and letting the children adapt. They are usually better for the experience. And for realizing that they are NOT number one."

Liz at her seventy-fifth birthday—Liz Red nails, Liz Red smile.

And she ended:

"But it should be the both of you together! A bientot, and with love, Liz."

Liz was quietly and I believe thankfully aware that her seventy-fifth birthday was on the near horizon. She would celebrate her seventy-fifth birthday on March 31. It was now five years since that deliriously joyous evening in St. Barts.

Gwen Satterfield, Liz's personal assistant, and I had planned a surprise party. Gwen had been with us since 1990. Before that she had worked for the company as a clerical assistant to the design department. She is a large, handsome woman in her fifties, willing to do anything to please Liz. She handled all catalog ordering for Liz, all of Liz's photography development work, all subscriptions, travel details, whatever and whenever Liz needed her help.

The party was held at Daniel on 65th Street in Manhattan. Gwen had arranged everything: invitations, the menu, flowers, seating and hotel accommodations for people we had had flown to New York. What an evening had been planned. And what an evening it turned out to be. And most amazingly, it was truly a surprise.

"This isn't the room we generally sit in," Liz said to me as we walked toward the party room. "No, it isn't," I said. "But there's something I want you to see." I opened the door and there sat and stood over forty people, all shouting, "Surprise, surprise!"

Liz put her hands over her face and began to weep. And then Ronnie Odrich, her periodontist, a fly fisherman and clarinetist supreme, who led a trio for the evening, began the music. Alex was there, feverishly smiling and brandishing his guitar. He was sitting in for the first set.

Gwen and I had arranged for three tables of about fourteen people per table: our closest friends, our closest family. Liz sat at the head table, her brother Omer at her right, Bill Conway at her left and Lorna Daniels, Liz's mother's companion, sat just across the way. And Liz's beautiful corn yellow hair, her very own, framed her lovely face.

When I spoke with Bill Conway at the end of August this year, I told him that that evening, Liz knew she would be back in treatment on April 2. He was not aware of that, despite the fact that he sat beside Liz the entire evening. He was stunned by her ability to put that aside. He commented on her "exceptional beauty." In retrospect, he felt she seemed to show "a kaleidoscope of emotions and distractions, but trying very hard to stay focused on her guests. She felt it important to make all of her guests feel that they were important to her."

Her brother, Omer, sat at her right. She said nothing to him about the bad news we had just learned.

We had seen Dr. Pasmantier on March 23. We had waited for blood test results before the next step. Liz's CA125 had been 63 in February. We knew that we were nearing the end of a period of remission. The March number was now 102. Liz was feeling well, but Mark felt it would be too risky to allow the disease to get too active. We were still in the earlier stage of a track one assault. Therefore it was necessary to counterattack before the cancerous seeds established too strong a hold. Liz's treatment would resume in April, on the 2nd, just a few days after her birthday. We kept the sour news to ourselves. On April 2, as scheduled, she resumed treatment: Taxol-platinum, once every three weeks. Liz and I had flown to Montana to attend the Montana Heritage Project Student Conference on March 28 and then back to New York. Liz's arithmetic, never too precise, indicated to her that she might soon be seventy-five. She asked me for confirmation. She disliked rushed trips, but the project was too important to her to miss. I confirmed that on March 31 she would be seventy-five. We belonged in New York. Gwen and I continued orchestrating the movingly beautiful evening of the 31st.

Anniversaries are double-edged events. They announce the passage of time, always coin not redeemable other than in memory. Two thousand four was such an anniversary for Liz.

The evening of her new chemo treatment we again had dinner with Jon and Stephanie. They had been at the party and were now being told of Liz's return to treatment. We told them about our strategy of recollection, of going back ten years in time. And then followed the story of our 1994 reunion in Hong Kong. This was a celebration of the unusually close relationship we had with a major Hong Kong vendor, Jeffrey Fang, and his tal-

All Our Eggs in One Basket—Jeffrey Fang, the man with the eggs. Liz and Art and team, 1984.

ented wife, Chris Ma. We were to celebrate an event recorded in a happy photograph, all of us grinning, Jeffrey seated behind a basket filled to the top with Easter eggs. The caption reads, "All Our Eggs in One Basket." What that meant was that Jeffrey's knitwear company, the largest holder of export quota in Hong Kong, would allocate that quota to Liz Claiborne Inc. We were an honest, dependable company. We trusted one another.

Liz and I had gathered the group responsible and invited them to fly with us to Hong Kong. Along the way, we made fueling stops, a repeat of an earlier stop at the most northerly island of Japan, Hokkaido, at the air strip at Sapporo. This was a stop that Liz found tremendously entertaining. We slid to a stop at the end of the runway and, in less than a nanosecond, forty-some-odd, nimble, Rockette-like men arrived, each smothered under a brilliant yellow poncho, held the gas line in place, dropped the line in unison, reeled it back to its stand and disappeared.

We were then off to Kamchatka, a volcanic peninsula, snow-covered, long and narrow, lying off Russia's far-east coast. The field personnel on the ground were one notch less skilled than those in Ushuaia, or perhaps more hostile in intent. We passed over the landing strip, descended and were advised to land directly into a facing mountain. We asked for a repeat after we pulled up and circled around, and were then given the same instructions, a bit more testily this time. So we naturally assumed there was a language barrier and the pilots landed as they thought best.

After we had come to a stop, a towering official, beaver-capped, loden green coat virtually touching the ground, documents under his arm, climbed aboard. He motioned Liz to get out of her seat as that was where he wanted to be. Everyone aboard murmured, "Push Liz out of her seat? Never."

Liz smiled her bewitching smile. The official was unimpressed. It strikes me as possible that this was the first time in her entire lifetime the smile had not won the day. She moved.

Terry Feldman, a brilliant (with numbers) assistant who worked for me in line-planning projections, then in her late twenties, pretty in her own voluptuous way, consumed this official with her eyes and played the charmer. He checked our passports and grumpily departed. Terry followed him outside. He bestowed a permissible Russian smile at her and shooed her back aboard. That was our Kamchatka adventure.

Everything that followed, the reunion, the dinners honoring us, the protestations that we were very much missed and that Hong Kong would never again see the likes of us, made the descent into Kamchatka a worthwhile adventure.

Later in the year, toward the end of May, we journeyed again to Provence with Omer and Jeanette. We followed our standby route through Provence, a day or two here and there revisiting places we had found of interest in the past. We parted from the two of them on May 30 and flew on to Crete. We had been told that Crete was famed for its horseback riding along its beaches and its colorful people, and that one lifetime is not complete without visiting the fabled 3,000-year-old city of Knossos, capital of legendary King Minos. The ruins of Knossos, proof that such a city had existed, had been described as essential to see. Just as at the Alhambra and similar to our walking experience on Mont-Saint-Michel, Knossos was overrun with tour buses, in this case largely full of people from Germany. Inexpensive tours linking Germany and Crete had become big business. It was unlikely that anyone could get to see the ruins. There was litter everywhere. Children, as they always seem to, were running loose. The rest of the trip was a bit underwhelming. Most of the horseback riding was on tarred surfaces. Our charismatic guide, Vangelis, net-fringed head cover and all, was elusive when we needed him and intrusive when we did not. Our inn on the water was beautifully austere, our room tasteful and comfortable. We never forgot that part of the trip. The dining room, however, was completely forgettable. It was packed with large people, speaking simultaneously so that you walked into a bedlam of roaring thunder only to discover that the meal was served buffet style, that the line was deep and seemed glued to the ground, and that the food seemed to have been flown in from a Munich beer hall to accommodate the guests. We decided to forego the meal, found a few apples and returned to our room. We slept well. The next morning we flew back to the United States and Fire Island.

Chemotherapy 5—Taxol-Platinum 4/2/04 to 2/7/05

The period after Liz's seventy-fifth birthday party was relatively free of dramatic events. That events were not dramatic, however, was no indication that the disease was not at work. By now Liz had accepted that she was a cancer patient, for better or worse, for shorter or longer duration, but always subject to blockages and incidents. "Normal," Dr. Pasmantier had said.

On April 5, she had e-mailed Kim:

"The only downer is that I am back in chemo. It was expected, but such a nuisance. Managed to put it off till after all of the festivities, family etc. It was such fun. Poor Art was exhausted after all the planning, but he and Gwen pulled it off! Love to all…Liz."

She e-mailed Kim again on April 12:

"Yes, the treatments were expected: it was a question of when, not if. Art keeps hoping, bless him, but I have ovarian cancer and it is chronic. Treatment will be ongoing; but it IS treatable. All goes well, not to worry. Lots of love…Liz."

And on May 16, she e-mailed Kim:

Hi Kim—here is a smoke signal! These last two weeks have been weeks that were; and would rather not have again. I just opened your e-mail! But basically I am a mess. Dentists by the hour, chemo and painfully bad reaction (this time), more dentist to rebuild what the other had destroyed, physical therapist. You name it! Yuck. But worse, I ignored your son's birthday…Am very sorry about that. Please tell him to forgive me. I will make it up sometime when things are calmer. Everything is really OK, just too much at once, that's all. We are at the moment in Fire Island & it is beautiful, sun shining, temp in the 70s (sixties here on the ocean). Art deep into a four-inch book out on the deck. We will be around thru late June or early in July, except for a trip thru Spain (if all goes well)—Madrid, Bilbao, and Barcelona. Ten days at the most…In the meantime love to all…Liz.

Liz, who rarely sounded off other than to me, and often not as vigorously to me as she could have, was having a difficult time. The major problem again was her digestive tract and the possibility of blockage. Chemotherapy and its attendant activities, including blood tests, a heart check and visits with her endocrinologist, were added to her time in the dentist's chair and her regular sessions with Dr. Pasmantier.

She did attend our board meetings in mid-May. And, no matter what other time-interrupters she had to endure, nothing interrupted a scheduled appointment with Rose, her manicurist. Now two of Nicholas Piazza's carefully wrought wigs traveled with us.

The pressures described to Kim were beginning to ease. We resumed dinners out and scheduled Dr. Miskovitz for a GI series after our return from Spain. The trip was still on. And what a fulfilling trip it was.

Spain was a perfect gift to compensate for the price paid earlier that year. We stayed once more at the Ritz in Madrid, a hotel so self-assured in its worldliness and elegance that the staff is relaxed and helpful. We found the hidden and discreet bar at the rear of the lounge, bantered with the bartender as we waited for our table on the veranda and toasted one another—every moment to be as precious as all the moments we had already lived together. And so the trip went. We had a splendid suite overlooking the Guggenheim in Bilbao. We took a day trip to Guernica, now a peaceful village just as it was the afternoon of April 26, 1937, when a Nazi swarm of airplanes, pilots throwing bombs from their cockpits, incinerated the town, killing over two thousand people, mainly women and children. That was the plan. The colonel in charge of this "tactic" called it a perfect victory. Slaughtering civilian populations from a distance had been introduced into modern warfare. Miraculously, the ancestral oak tree and the assembly house it stood next to survived.

It is difficult to describe in words the emotions we felt. Out of such misery the village had bloomed again, as if time and events had not interceded. Hand in hand we walked through the assembly house, now a museum, and realized, without speaking, that such would be our own destiny, to perish, return to the earth, and be reintegrated into the cycle of life. T. S. Eliot wrote, "In my end is my beginning." It was a ponderous thought I carried with me for years. Liz and I had become citizens of Guernica, a place of renewal, of victory in defeat.

We had stood in front of Picasso's enthralling painting in Madrid, strangely alone. A small group of students had eyed it for a moment and moved on.

• • •

We were back in Montana in July. Dr. Weiner had recommended a physical therapist, Anne Ripley. Liz picked up on that immediately and made a string of appointments with Anne. During this period, Liz's weight continued to drop. Her appetite was generally good, but her ability to consume favored foods in satisfying quantities continued to diminish. Dr. Weiner had found her a bit anemic and prior to treatment on the 17th gave her a booster. Treatment was routine.

I met with Anne Ripley this past September. She was surprised, she told me, that Liz lasted as long as she did. "I tried to draw her out, but, as you know, she was very private. I never saw her discouraged, even though I could see she was tired. She talked about her son and her love of Lindbergh Lake and how hard it was to maneuver there. She was fun to work with, to have had the honor to work with her."

Liz's e-mails to Kim, the first at the beginning of July:

On this end of the Atlantic, everything is going well, including my treatment (though there are bumps in the road). Art is busy as ever and planning our social schedule around people who have something to do with our foundation programs. It's all I can do to remember the names from season to season! Lots of love to the Brindel family, and especially to its senior member, (Kim) 48—WOW, do you realize how young you are?? Liz.

At the end of July she e-mailed:

All goes well here, just got over my last blast! Sun's shining here in Canyon Creek and the temp, just right! What could be bad? Give my love to your fellows. Liz.

July brought additional encouraging news. Her CA125 had lowered to 76. Liz's sessions with Anne Ripley continued to be helpful. We spent August in Montana as well, alternating between Tranquillity and Triple 8. We had visitors in abundance, all of those who had canceled the year before because of the fires and, in addition, Lisa Milton, Liz's cousin once removed, and her husband Tom; and Alex and Christina, their marriage still on hold.

On the 27th of the month, Liz had e-mailed Kim:

"All's well, the treatments have gone smoothly this beautiful, fireless summer, slow to knock the numbers back but on the whole routine maintenance. Alex and Christina just arrived at Tranquillity (we are at Triple 8) but they will join us here on Saturday, am looking forward to seeing them. Art had a nice quiet birthday, unfortunately not quite as quiet as he might have liked. My cousin (once removed) arrived with her new husband that evening, but he (Art) was a great sport. August is the 'guest' month…All those canceled out last year!!! He is neck deep in all kinds of involvements. Foundation etc. All love from the 2 of us to the 3 of you. Liz."

September was an all-Montana month. On the 13th, Dr. Weiner's staff gave Liz the sixth chemotherapy treatment in this cycle. A booster dose of Neupogen followed on the 14th. That was followed by the traditional stop at Hair Hair.

Hair Hair is Helena's top-of-the-line beauty shop complete with all the now-required indulgences: massage room, soft, float-away music, a range of improvement products that are guaranteed to improve any part of your body other than your mind. The owners, Joe Hrella, the strikingly good-looking partner of David Brown, good-looking in a less dramatic way, were by now admirers of Liz and friends of mine. This September, the routine continued: an Anne Ripley workout and then a late afternoon stop at Hair Hair. Liz would see Robin Burk, trustworthy manicurist, and I had a trim and a sage discussion with Joe. And then, we enjoyed the calming and satisfying sit-down at the Windbag Saloon.

I spoke with Joe a number of months ago about the hair treatment he and Robin had been giving Liz. "For Liz," Joe said, "her loss of hair was one of the more emotionally painful consequences of her cancer treatment. That's not unlike most women. Most wait until hair loss is so obvious that they must get a wig, or tie a scarf around their head. Not Liz. Distressing as it was, she was prepared. Of course, when her hair had grown back during remission times, we did some bleach touchups. She really trusted New York on the bleaching. But she always made it her business to look great. We all loved her."

Liz went back to town the day after her last Hair Hair appointment for some not overwhelmingly necessary shopping at Albertson's, but she so enjoyed zipping about in the Boxster that another fifty or sixty miles was considered a lark. It may have started as a lark, but the arrival of an armed but amused police officer the following day at Cabin A of Triple 8 changed the mood of an otherwise sunny morning—"Liz Claiborne?"

She nodded, "Yes."

"Is that your car over there?" he asked, pointing toward the Boxster. Liz nodded yes again, thinking whatever could the Boxster have done?

She found out at once. "I'm going to have issue you a citation. You scraped someone's car yesterday in the parking lot of Albertson's and left the scene of the accident. You shouldn't have done that." He began writing the citation. "You'll have to appear in the Helena City Court."

Liz frowned, not in disbelief, because in Helena that would have been a wasted frown. "But I didn't feel anything. I didn't hear anything. I didn't know I had scraped another car."

"Too bad, lady," the officer said. He handed her the citation, wished her a good day and took off.

The headline appeared in the *Independent Record* on the 28th. "Fashion icon apologizes over fender bender, pays $140 fine." "Fashion designer Liz Claiborne learned the perils of cutting corners last week when she was cited by Helena police for leaving the scene of an accident." The story ended with Liz saying, as she had been prompted to, "I apologize to whoever it was I scraped inadvertently," she said. She continued to shop at Albertson's.

• • •

I am now in St. Barts, alone at Terra Nova. I find working here congenial, unpressured and drenched in reminders of Liz. It is December 21, 2007. Alex and Christina are here and staying in the guest house. They leave after Christmas. Neil and Karen will be here tomorrow and will also be a part of our Christmas festivities. We have a small tree wrapped in blinking lights, standing precisely where a tree has stood each year that Liz and I holidayed "en famille" or alone.

No script of Liz's dialogues with her supportive team would be complete without the comments of superstar hygienist Evelyn Melian, "the great Evelyn," according to me (she was always booked months in advance). Evelyn is another early member of the Liz fan club. I spoke with Evelyn in September of 2007. I asked how Liz had handled the endless implant work. This is what she said, "She was always peaceful, serene, always seemed accepting, graceful. She was easy to love. She was inspirational and courageous. When I would ask her how the treatment was going, depending on the current circumstances, she would say, 'I'm fine,' or 'not so great, but I'm hopeful.' She never tried to hide anything. She always kept it simple, and never ever felt sorry for herself. She was a very special lady."

My dialogues with manicurists began in St. Barts. I had decided to start with Francoise Rannou, Liz's St. Barts manicurist, pedicurist, hair trimmer and all-around island newscaster, before recounting my talks with the various other manicurists who were so essential to Liz. All of them came to adore her. All of them coated her nails in their own version of Liz Red. None knew it as Liz Red. None knew how famous the color was.

I would often be in the living area at my desk waiting for Liz to be finished so I could be trimmed. The women seemed to do nothing but jabber in high-pitched bubbly French, every topic worthy of guffaws. Francoise specialized in revealing the exotic behavior of her clients. They all seemed to stay at the most expensive hotels on the island. Liz specialized in finding it all hilarious. I asked Francoise if they ever talked about Liz's cancer treatment. "Ah, oui. I would ask her how she was doing, and always, always, fine, fine, fine."

I had also spoken with Robin Burk of Hair Hair in early October on the telephone.

These are her words as I transcribed them:

"She was one of the most beautiful women I ever saw in my life. When she came in, and this was after I hadn't seen her in a year, she asked about my children before we talked about anything else. She remembered my daughters' names, Lacey and Belle, and all the things about them I had told her. She remembered everything about them I had told her. She even sent them shoes from her own dress-up box. They treasure those shoes. Liz will be with me forever. There was always such a light about her and she always gave me hope. She just wouldn't let the cancer get her down. The two of you have been such a gift in my life. I was particularly depressed and worried about how my life was going until I met Liz. She turned me around. The one thing she did talk about was how she missed normal eating. She had started eating lightly and often said this bothered her."

My first manicurist dialogue was with Rose Syrkin. Rose had been doing Liz's nails for years and years, first when Rose was at Saks and then later when she moved to Sothy's Nail Salon.

"I didn't know she was Liz Claiborne until after I read the obituaries. She was so down to earth, so lovely, so modest. She was really great, always caring, always on time. At the beginning of her chemo she told me about it because she was bald and had to wear a cap. But she never mentioned it again. She was very, very caring. She talked so nicely about her family. I miss her a lot. I knew how really bad things were when she made an appointment for me to do her nails in the hospital. That was June

21. She wanted to set up an appointment for a pedicure but I was going on vacation. She said, 'OK, when you get back.' Her spirits were so high. She had hope. I was sad to see her. When I saw the papers, then I got to know my Liz died."

• • •

Rose was not the only person who had never identified the patient in room 252 as Liz Claiborne. When I spoke with Dr. Miskowitz on October 24, he admitted that the first time he knew her professional name was in a conversation with Dr. Angie Eng, internist and gastroenterologist, who had covered for him the weekend of May 19, 2007. Liz had been hospitalized on May 15. At that time, numerous CT scans had been taken, including one of her bowel area to determine whether or not there was any blockage in her digestive system. The scan showed negative.

Liz had assured me the previous evening that she was feeling well and that I should take an early morning walk in the park prior to coming to the hospital. I did and came to deeply regret that I did.

Someone had prescribed another CT scan of her bowel area despite the negative reading four days earlier. It was to take place the late morning of Saturday the 19th.

I was never made aware by anyone that this was to take place. The nurse on the floor that morning was determined to follow the prescription irrespective of the patient's circumstance. She had insisted that Liz drink a glassful of oral contrast liquid. Sandra sat and watched as Liz tried to force the liquid down. I arrived and grabbed the glass from Liz's hand and insisted that the whole process stop. Liz had already forced about two ounces down. The nurse called the laboratory and in moments two attendants showed up with a wheelchair to take Liz down to the lab. I went with them. The scan was done and Liz was returned to the room.

To this day I have not been able to determine who did the prescribing, but there is no question that Dr. Pasmantier is the lead doctor for his patient and no treatment can or should be applied without his consent. He has no recollection of prescribing the scan. This may have been a stand-in's thought that it might be a good idea to check for blockage. All lead oncologists are covered on weekends by another oncologist.

The scan was negative for blockage.

A few moments after Liz was put back in bed she began to shudder, rolled over on her side and vomited a torrent of blood. It seemed to pour ceaselessly out of her throat.

Dr. Angie Eng, working the weekend for Dr. Miskowitz, was quickly called. It was our good luck that she was in the area. She came at once, put her arm around Liz, and told her this was not unusual, the blood came from inside the stomach, and the accompanying diarrhea was also not unusual. She was wonderfully calming. She assured us that the vomiting was not concerning. Imodium was prescribed to relieve the diarrhea.

Later, Dr. Eng told me, "In the short time I was with her I sensed that she was well put together. She never fell apart. She asked for help appropriately. She thanked people for helping her. She had a sense of dignity, a very dignified woman and all this with a puddle of diarrhea in front of her."

This was the patient in room 252 who Dr. Eng reported to Dr. Miskowitz as Liz Claiborne.

The same Liz Claiborne, the fashion icon who had inflicted a "scratch and scuff to the right rear bumper of Jessie Lesofski's 1992 Chevrolet Blazer in late September of 2004," was nonetheless going to be honored by the University of Montana on the evening of October 6. She and I were recognized as great entrepreneurs, whose story might inspire Montanans and students at the university. Liz felt well, looked radiantly beautiful and delivered her speech to an audience of more than two hundred at dinner.

She spoke about how scale could and usually did defeat principle, why she felt scale and time had rendered style and design bothersome irritations that impeded the rushing of product to market. In a sea of mediocre, repetitive clothing, fashion itself had become a competitive display of wealth, no longer of taste. It was perhaps her lovely softness, the sorrowful cadences in which she spoke, that stilled the roomful of people. Somehow she crystallized for her audience the intensity of her sense of loss, her sad conviction that not only were the barbarians at the gate, they were now in the temple. I had never heard her speak so movingly.

The applause that followed her words started slowly, and then swelled to a crescendo.

The next morning we had a classroom on campus grounds to ourselves for open discussion with students interested enough to be alert and ready by 9:00 AM. We had a large group, perhaps fifty young people. We all felt very much alive that morning, glad to be with one another, certain that we would be asked straight questions, and the young people certain that we would do our very best to give straight answers.

We saw Tom Weiner and staff on the 11th. Liz's CA125 was down to 55. By mid-month we flew from Missoula to MacArthur Airport on Long Island. We were in the city on Monday and Liz, once more, was scheduled for a week of doctor appointments: Dr. Buchman, Dr. Pasmantier, Dr. Magid, Dr. Zackson. We weekended at Fire Island and came back to the city for more of the same. The week ahead, the last week of October 2004, had some additional stops for Liz: Dr. Litvak, our restorative dental expert, and Dr. Zweifach for a routine check. November was routine, or what we now considered routine. Liz had chemotherapy on the 9th, followed by a few evenings at home. It was becoming more difficult to spring back into action. When the weekend arrived we spent an eventless and much-enjoyed number of days at Fire Island. Foundation board meetings were held on the 15th and 16th and all went well. The rest of the month went by without incident. We left for St. Barts on Thanksgiving Day and were thankful indeed to find ourselves with Patrick and Patricia Montanari, he our villa manager and she his very pretty and professional wife, celebrating the evening at Maya's.

Earlier in the month Liz had e-mailed Kim:

"On the personal front things plug along, slowly but surely; though it has gone very well this summer and hope it will continue…All love and all that, Liz." And then again on the 26th: "We had a wonderful evening at Maya's with Patrick and Patricia. Good dinner!!! All love to you all. Liz."

Most of December was spent in St. Barts with a short hop to New York for chemotherapy on the 7th; a somewhat unsettling CA125—71 ("normal fluctuation," Dr. Pasmantier said). Liz received a booster on the 8th. We returned to St. Barts the same day. We had dinner out every evening from the 9th to the end of the month, that is, except for New Year's Eve. We had dinner on our observatoire, the beautiful outdoor stone deck overlooking St. Jean Bay and out to sea. Again we lingered to watch the fireworks that closed out 2004.

We would gladly repeat that year—perhaps not the Albertson's event—but it was a year that all in all had been positive. As Liz said in an e-mail to Kim, "It has gone very well this summer and hope it will continue."

This is the Christmas card she sent me at the end of the year:

"Another year has slipped by, never boring, never dull, always an adventure with my friend, my husband, and my love. A Merry Christmas & Happy New Year. Let's have another one. Your loving 'present' wife. Liz."

CHAPTER NINE, 2005

ST. BARTHÉLEMY RISES from the sea like a clenched fist. Its knuckles are its hills and small mountains; the creases between the fingers its beaches, reefs and inlets.

It is a leeward island, sitting at 18 degrees north and about 63 degrees west. Its many beaches and reefs are washed by waters from the Caribbean on the west and the Atlantic Ocean on the east. It therefore sits in the path of oceanic disturbances as winds off the African coast come blasting westward during the hurricane season. We had experienced a few of these howlers but, all in all, felt living on St. Barts was well worth the risk of an occasional heavy dousing.

The island was discovered in 1493 by Columbus and he named it for his brother, Bartolomeo. There were no indigenous people to be absorbed. The island soil, despite a great deal of rainfall, is arid and gives a potential farmer little reason to try to farm. But its deep-water harbor, Gustavia, named naturally enough after King Gustav of Sweden, and its twenty shallow-water beaches have made the island a paradise.

The island was chiefly populated by people from Brittany and Normandy, but a minister of Louis XVI sold it to Sweden in 1784 for trading rights elsewhere. The French took it back one century later. Yet the name Gustavia remains as a reminder of the days when St. Barthélemy was a cargo stop, a hideout for sea rustlers, later a fisherman's port of call and now one of the most beautiful islands in the world.

The island has many small villages. St. Jean, overlooking St. Jean Bay, is one of them. It was there that we purchased a villa in 1984. We bought the villa the same day the realtor showed it to us. It was beautifully situated, and beautifully decorated. But the open design of the villa permitted gale winds and heavy downpours when the weather turned rainy and windy as it often did in St. Barts. We were forced to enclose the living space by dragging the villa's heavy doors closed and securing them against the weather.

We often looked longingly up the hillside, particularly at the highest point, a rocky, empty plateau. It was during a serious hurricane in 1987 that the house that was to provide the site of our atelier was seriously damaged. It was put up for sale. We bought it and then we bought the land on which Terra Nova was to be built. Terra Nova became the main residence. And then, over the years, we acquired the land to build a gymnasium, and shortly thereafter, were able to buy a guest house as well. The main residence dominates the complex. The atelier is downhill and to the south. The gymnasium is downhill and to the north. And the guest house is at the base of the hillside, a bit below the gymnasium. We had completed our own sanctuary.

Two thousand five started quietly enough. Liz was feeling well enough to have dinner out virtually every evening. We were in St. Barts for the first days of January, then up to New York for treatment. We saw Dr. Pasmantier on the third for a not-so-routine talk. The numbers were under control, but the continued bombardment of the chemicals was further reducing the elasticity of her digestive system.

The CA125 count had been 71 in December. The reading in January was 56.

There was no alternative but to continue fighting the numbers. Chemotherapy was administered on the 10th. Liz had now been a cancer patient for six years, the disease and the treatment coming in and out like tidal waves.

There were adjustments to be made all along the way. She was now spending more time adjusting hearing aids. Another of the side effects of chemotherapy is an assault on one's hearing. It was another thing to attend to—batteries and the reliability of the hearing aid itself, since components never stayed active as long as the guarantees asserted they would.

On the 17th, Liz had e-mailed Kim:

"But we are in sunny climes again and all goes well. Very quiet after the Christmas tumult! Liz."

We were back in New York in early February. The first Friday was packed with essentials: a multigated acquisition (MUGA) scan; Evelyn, dental hygienist superb; Rose for a manicure and pedicure; Dr. Zackson, eminent endocrinologist; dinner and a quiet Super Bowl weekend.

Chemotherapy took place on the 7th. CA125 was now 68. She was holding her own, but no better than that. We returned to St. Barts. The month was essentially a St. Barts month with dinner at Maya's almost every evening.

March found us back in New York for chemotherapy on the 2nd. We had a number of early appointments on the 3rd and then went back to St. Barts. The new CA125 reading was 63.4. Again Liz was holding her own. But we knew the disease well enough by then to take little comfort in the status quo. A stubborn presence of the antigens despite the ongoing chemical counterattack was not truly a status quo.

The month seemed routine enough. We returned to New York on the 30th and had chemo scheduled for the 31st, her birthday.

Liz had e-mailed Kim:

This year, it's chemo, not a lush party! Please tell William I attacked his 'fig' jam [a birthday present] *instead of giving it to our guests* [Neil and Karen]. *It's worth the bad conscience!* DELICIOUS. *Love, etc. Liz."*

April started quietly. Then it changed very suddenly and explosively. On the evening of the 9th, Liz became violently ill. She was on her hands and knees throwing up with no relief and suffering from severe cramps and headaches. She was totally wiped out. She slept for an hour or so until morning. Patrick, the property manager, carried her to our car and we drove her to the St. Barts clinic. St. Barts has no hospital. The clinic, small and understaffed as it is, is the avenue to fast medical attention. Maya met us there and within a fairly short time Liz was admitted. She was given one of the three patients' rooms in the clinic, and after the usual process of admittance, she was hooked up to saline solution and hydration began. By then, Liz had recovered sufficiently to be alert and responsive.

She was kept at the clinic for three days. Her main sustenance was apple sauce and soups that I would bring her from Maya's. The rooms in the clinic were frigid. We wrapped Liz in as many blankets and bedcovers as we could find, but she shivered throughout the experience.

We were home by the 12th and Liz, as in the past, rebounded. By the 15th, we were back at Maya's for dinner and she was able to have dinner out until the morning of the 18th, when we flew back to New York.

Dr. Julian Decter, the oncologist covering for Dr. Pasmantier, insisted that we immediately go the East River Medical Center for various scans and analyses. After Liz had undergone the tests, we waited and we worried. All the technicians who walked by were judged by their frown lines and they all seemed to be frowning. But the results when they came were far from alarming. Liz had a touch of pneumonia.

I am astonished now, as I sit here in St. Barts on December 23, 2007, at Liz's amazing resilience. We had lived that week at the end of April in 2005 as though nothing had gone amiss. I had e-mailed Kim on May 14:

"Long, long story but with an unclear story line. We had an extremely uncomfortable reaction to the last chemo, that of March 31. Herself lost weight but has been regaining her strength. Chemo is on hold as the oncologist confers with his colleagues. The purpose is to change direction and approach the problem with a new treatment. At the moment Liz is vigorous, cheerful, and looking for a change of pace. More when more is available. Art."

And Liz e-mailed Kim the following day:

"Hi Kim, Finally getting to my computer, it's been a busy few weeks, trying to fit all my other doctors in so as to clear this coming week for a possible chemo. He's thinking of a new cocktail, good news to me. I've about had it with Taxol! So has my body! The numbers are up, of course [136—my note], because I have not had chemo in 6 weeks! Heaven, but not good for that nasty little intruder! We'll know more when he returns from a conference. What a bore. Yesterday was beautiful here in Fire Island. Love to you all, happy sunshine. Liz."

Chemotherapy 6—Cisplatin & Gemzar 5/18/05 to 9/26/05

Dr. Pasmantier, after conferring with his colleagues, had determined that a change in the treatment was necessary. We met with him on May 18. A new chemical cocktail was introduced, the formidable combination of Cisplatin and Gemzar.

Cisplatin is another chemical of the platinum family, widely used for patients with a form of ovarian cancer. Gemzar is still another chemical that is often used as a booster with Cisplatin. It is considered to have a synergistic effect on the strength of the Cisplatin. The frequency of application is left to the judgment of the oncologist. The side effects of this mixture can be extremely uncomfortable. This was the schedule that Liz was to follow: Cisplatin in combination with Gemzar the first week; Gemzar booster the second week; followed by a third week free of treatment. Then the cycle would begin again.

The intent was very obviously to attack the disease more aggressively, which of course meant attacking the patient more aggressively.

The second evening after treatment was a misery for Liz. She had cramps, headaches, nausea, the more and more frequent nemeses of treatment. The following day, I ferried her back to Dr. Pasmantier's office where she spent the greater part of the day being hydrated.

So the weeks went: a pallid comeback, board meetings, a few dinners out, but by and large Liz remained exhausted.

On Friday the 31st, we had her admitted once more to New York Hospital, and this time she endured a lengthy and painful waiting period, first in the waiting room of Dr. Pasmantier's office, sitting in a wheelchair with agony written all over her face. It was a nightmare seemingly without end. The office was seething with activity, and Liz waited and waited. For the first and only time during the years of battling the cancer, she mumbled loud enough for me to hear her, "It isn't fair." It wasn't the disease she referred to, nor the pain alone, but the totality of pain and being forced to sit in the waiting room in a wheelchair. Liz, an old patient, was obviously waiting in agony.

I never heard that again.

We eventually received the forms we would need to get her admitted to a room in the hospital. I wheeled Liz the three blocks to the hospital, Nancy the stalwart nurse with me.

Then, again, we waited and waited, it seemed endlessly, for a room to be cleaned and readied for the next patient, Liz. Once settled in the room, she went through the traditional tests to assure that matching blood would be made available and, after another endless wait, four units of blood appeared and revitalization began.

The next months were as uncomfortable and depressing as any previous period. The schedule, rigorous and oppressive, continued with only a little letup to accommodate Dr. Zweifach and laser eye surgery in early June. Otherwise, it was unrelenting.

Dr. Pasmantier wanted to hammer away, hoping that the more aggressive treatment would tame the beast. But the numbers did not cooperate, nor did the patient's ability to withstand the onslaught. We were in Montana for the continuation of the new treatment from mid-July to early October.

Despite the stormy seas that had been tossing her fragile body about, Liz sent me an anniversary card on July 5. We had been married forty-eight years. "7/5 Next Year! And this is something [a gift now forgotten] to help with the 'burden.' Til many more anniversaries. Thank you for all your help, support and love all these years! With all my love, your wife, Liz."

• • •

In August, Liz's CA125 had lowered to 100. But the side effects of the aggressive treatment were making life an ongoing battle with exhaustion and digestive problems. She had required hydration at the end of July after passing a particularly difficult evening. Tom Weiner was always available by phone, and we had added some new medications that brought some relief.

There were some manageable periods—mid-August on to the time we left for New York at the end of the month so that Liz could have a spinal injection to ease her aching knees. We had dinner at the Montana Club in Helena for my birthday. Liz, at dinner with me, was present enough.

September brought no relief. The CA125 count was now 99.6. The October number was 90.6. We were still at a standstill with the cancerous invaders. Liz saw Tom Weiner on October 3 for the short Gemzar treatment. We left for New York on the 5th.

Liz had once more gritted her teeth and fought back. She would not permit herself to abandon the fight.

On October 8 she e-mailed Kim:

"The minute we hit New York, it's tests and doctors! We are in Fire Island, yuck weather! The tests were good but the body needs some pepping up, a transfusion on Monday. So I expect to feel a lot better by Monday night! I have been dragging and now I know why! The shots were just not enough anymore. We are off to dinner with Nevio on the mainland, a very nice steak house. I'll have some beef! I'll write more later. Love from us two to you three, Liz."

On October 26, the treatment was changed.

When I spoke with Mark Pasmantier this past September 12, 2007, we discussed the switch to Genentech's Avastin, to be administered once every two weeks. Avastin's reputation is a bit wobbly, being deemed a drug difficult to regulate. Mark saw no alternative, he told me. "It seemed to me that the side effects of the Cisplatin-Gemzar treatment were getting out of control. She had been in treatment a long time. Most people don't live that long. She tolerated treatment like a younger person."

Chemotherapy 7—Avastin 10/26/05 to 7/20/06

Liz and Avastin had an agreeable introduction to one another. Her CA125 was 74.6 by the end of October and 72.6 toward the end of November.

November was to be one of the more important months in Liz's non-chemical life. Alex had proposed, as Liz would say, "en fin," and Christina, with no hesitation whatsoever, was swept off her feet.

It had been agreed that the marriage rites would take place in the United States to accommodate Liz. The summer had been one of the most difficult of times for Liz, the most difficult she had thus far experienced. A second, more formal wedding would take place in Germany. But, it seems that due to the enthusiasm of both bride and groom, that intention was forgotten. The wedding took place in Germany. I knew that whatever the terms, Liz would crawl if she had to, but she would not miss her son's wedding. We packed the essentials, two of her most trusted wigs.

The date, or rather dates, had been set: November 17 and 18. There would be a civil ceremony the first day, which only the nearest and dearest would attend. We attended. It was civil enough, with two efficient bureaucrats, a young amiable woman and an attorney-like multilingual functionary driving the process. The room was small and austere. The woman's table was on a raised platform with the interested parties standing behind the betrothing couple. The main event took place the following day.

We had flown charter from New York into Stuttgart. We ferried a number of people with us: Neil and Karen; my sister, Gloria; Leslie Claiborne, Jeanette's daughter and Omer's stepdaughter, and her husband, Chris Townley. The trip any other way would have been impossible for Liz. We stayed at a comfortable hotel in Stuttgart. We had an excellent driver, which was fortunate, since the wedding and the attendant festivities were scheduled at sites at least forty-five minutes outside of Stuttgart.

We arrived the evening of the 16th, all feeling well. The 17th was civil ceremony day, followed by a ride back to Stuttgart and a small family dinner with the Mirams (this being Christina's maiden name) and the now fully wedded couple, Alexander Girard Schultz and Christina Miram-Schultz. We dined at our hotel's restaurant. Everyone smiled a great deal. Lore, Christina's mother, even laughed with great heartiness. She spoke and understood English well enough to be an enthusiastic participant. Klaus, Christina's pleasant-in-the-extreme father, could only smile. He speaks little English, does not risk his life flying about in airplanes, but, as it developed the following evening, he is a tireless, rotating dancer. Twirling, spinning, smiling, Lore would not be outdone. Liz and I were our friendly adaptable selves and when the evening ended, all left, not euphoric, but untroubled.

We had wandered around Stuttgart during the afternoon. Liz had two objectives in mind. Stuttgart is the home of the mighty Daimler company and the likewise mighty, but a bit more arrogant these days, Porsche company.

We stopped at the Porsche showroom. Salespersons were seated behind desks hidden in semidarkness, all the better to leave ample space for the Porsche variety of splendid, costly-enough-to-please-an-oil-baron vehicles. We were ignored. Liz had hoped to ask how she might be able to swing the sun visor about on her Boxster. It was fixed in one place and could not be coaxed to move left or right. The salesperson she found said in perfect English, "The visor is not moveable." He returned to his reading.

That ended that. We next found a jovial woman who had just returned from lunch and now stood behind a counter in the center of the showroom floor.

"Perhaps you can help me," Liz said. "Of course," the woman responded. "I'm looking for a stroller. I understand Porsche strollers are excellent." It appeared, from what we had been told, that the willing bride was carrying a person-to-be, that person would possibly arrive in early June and yes, we could purchase a stroller, accessorize it to Liz's taste, prepay and have the Porsche people hold it until informed that the coming inhabitant of the stroller had arrived.

Friday, November 18, was the official church wedding day, to be followed by a reception.

Liz and I sat, hand in hand, in the second row at the church. The church itself was Lutheran spare, a confessional church it was called for shadowy reasons that go back to the Hitler years. I was not alert to details that day, but as best I can remember there were about two hundred people in the church that afternoon. Alex and Christina were seated in front of the minister, side by side. I could not help but consider the feelings that Omer Villere Claiborne, a man whose life experiences with Germans and Germany had bred in him a lifelong dislike for Germans, and Alex's Jewish father, Ben, would have had upon viewing this scene. Liz, who had lived for a time through the German occupation of Belgium, and I, who had lost my grandmother, aunts and cousins in Auschwitz, stared at the couple in front of the minister. They were both of a different generation, with different cultural awareness, essentially blameless.

Alex, when asked in German if he would accept Christina, answered with as large a grin as he could inflate: "Ja!"

From there on in we were swept along with the others: first the congratulatory hugging and kissing, then to the loading of buses to take the invited to the reception hall some forty minutes away.

I remember that evening as a nonending raucous event. Liz and I were both exhausted, but pleased that we had made the effort to be there. We sat at a front table and watched Lore and Klaus pivot and spin to the live music. Alex had invited the members of the group he plays with often, very fine Italian blues and jazz men, and they played for hours. Occasionally, there was a break so that Alex could point to a table and describe those seated around it. Enthusiastic applause followed.

So the evening went along as we awaited the cutting of the cake. Wedding cakes did eventually get cut and parceled out to the happy murmurs of the crowd. And then we left. Alex had played a few more sets than originally intended, but, in his and Christina's case, it seemed a certainty, at the time, that you only get married once.

We left Stuttgart the following morning. Alex was married, Christina was pregnant and, from Liz's standpoint, all was right with the world. Alex would not face an increasingly lonely future. She had lived to see this on track, and now the child in Christina's womb was another solid reason to keep herself alive.

That Sunday, November 20, 2005, was a restful day. Liz was in fine condition for the board meetings the 21st and 22nd. These dates had been cleared months in advance to assure that each trustee, busy as he or she might have been, could wedge in meeting time. Liz was well enough to join us all for our customary dinner at Le Bernardin at the end of the first day's meeting, but she had to pass on the second morning meeting. She had been scheduled for an MRI with Dr. Rappaport, the neurologist. This was more of a ruling-out process than not, and the results did affirm that neurologically, Liz was fine.

December had arrived. We were still very much in the game. We returned to living a normal life: dinner with Neil and Karen, weekends at Fire Island, a heavy protein dinner with Nevio.

• • •

Neil and Karen joined us in St. Barts for Christmas dinner and left the following day for Cuba, a favorite haunt of Neil's. Alex, and Christina, in the early stage of pregnancy, came down the following day and stayed in St. Barts for about ten days. All went swimmingly well. We had a sumptuous New Year's Eve dinner in our circular dining room, drank champagne and faced the year 2006 in the best of moods. Our departure for New York for chemotherapy was on January 5. Our return to St. Barts was on the 7th. Alex and Christina had returned to Germany. Liz and I went back to New York for chemotherapy on the 20th and then back to St. Barts on the 21st. It was a busy schedule but that didn't trouble us then. The time had been spent with family and that suited Liz.

I had not been as assiduous a card sender as Liz had been over the years. To make up for the lack of cards, one year I hired a seaplane to fly a "Happy

Birthday" sign over our Fire Island house. But I did send a card to Liz via e-mail at the end of 2005. This was the message:

FOR FAMILY HOLIDAYS AND ALL TOGETHER DAYS
FOR LIZ CLAIBORNE ORTENBERG
WITH ALL HER IMPERFECTIONS AS PERFECT AS CAN BE
FROM HER ADORING HUSBAND NOW AND FOREVER
ARTIE ORTENBERG—NEWARK, NEW JERSEY
DECEMBER 25, 2005

The message is as appropriate today as it was then, so appropriate, I feel, that it's worth repeating. Neil and Karen, now married, Alex, Christina and baby Elias, now eighteen months old, have all joined me for Christmas this year, 2007. We are all in Terra Nova. I find this St. Barts home saturated with Liz's presence. I am too often reminded of the torturous evenings she endured. The joy and beauty of this wonderfully conceived complex have slipped away.

I had last seen Alex and Christina on October 23 of this past year. Liz had been gone for four months. Rather than plan a traditional memorial for Liz, I had arranged an evening at Le Bernardin in one of their private rooms.

The invitation read: "The Liz Claiborne and Art Ortenberg Foundation and its trustees invite you to an evening dinner remembering Liz and her love of the creatures she worked so hard to protect." We invited the directors and board members of conservation groups, field biologists and botanists from around the world. Many of the invitees were people with whom we had been working for years: Dr. Peter Raven of the Missouri Botanical Garden; George Schaller, probably the most renowned of field biologists; Graham Harris from Patagonia; Ullas Karanth from India; Alan Rabinowitz, jaguar, tiger and big cat expert; David Quammen, author, naturalist and dear friend from Bozeman, Montana; and many others.

We met at six o'clock, were all pleased at the attendance and sat down to dinner about an hour later.

On one wall, clearly visible from any angle in the room, was a screen on which we played an excerpt from Liz's unforgettable appearance at the Designer Roundtable at Liz Claiborne Inc., a performance that is unbelievable now in its display of Liz's naturalness and radiant charm. It had been delivered on April 27, 2007. The segment we showed was of Liz holding her arms up and dancing to the rhythm of the stately movement of giraffes and ele-

231

phants. A DVD of the event now exists. That afternoon was another of the many sublime moments in her life, sublime moments that she shared with us. I will later describe that event more fully.

About ten feet west of the screen was a double life-size blowup of a photograph taken on our first trip to Alaska. There stands a determined Liz, her legs planted on the ground of a swirling rapid stream, the water half-boot high, a camera gripped tightly in one hand, the other pointing directly ahead. Gates Helm, newly acquainted aficionado, was the photographer.

I attempted a few welcome words, but I went falsetto, as I often do when speaking about Liz. Bill Conway, at our table, took over. And then the room opened up. John Robinson of the Wildlife Conservation Society followed, and then more and more people spoke homage to Liz or, in many cases, homage to Liz and Art and the work we and our foundation had accomplished.

Bill, as is his custom, is now in Patagonia with Graham Harris. I received this e-mail from Graham today:

"Bill tells me you are in St. Barts, the first time back without Liz. How difficult for you. But the things she did live on in so many ways and in so many places. With fond wishes, Graham."

The evening of the 23rd was a magical evening. It was an evening that can never again be replicated. I liken it to a one-time assemblage of great instrumentalists whose presence was uniquely self-motivated.

George Schaller e-mailed the following day:

"Dear Art: All the way while driving home last night, Kay and I discussed what a marvelous evening it had been and how happy everyone was to honor Liz in that way. She will remain in all our memories. Tomorrow I head back to Tibet and my thoughts will be with you both. The little Buddhist tangkha wheel of existence can be mounted flat as a painting. I wanted you and Liz to have a small remembrance of the lovely dinners we have had over the years, and as a token of gratitude for your help and friendship. Do please keep in touch and take care of yourself. Kay and I send our warmest regards. George."

I had arranged for Alex and Christina to fly in from Germany and for Neil and Karen to attend as well. Nancy had had a bout with surgery and was unable to be with us. I wanted them all to know who we were, what we had dedicated ourselves to for many years and how we were judged by our peers.

Alex, a few days later in conversation with Jim Murtaugh at the foundation's office, told Jim how impressed he had been with the work we've done in Africa.

Liz and I had made five trips to Africa: those in 1987, 1988 and 1990 have been described. We had thought of the 1995 trip as the "Alex" trip. The last one in 1996 to Botswana, via South Africa, now seems more a South African trip than a safari. It really was both.

But that first trip in 1987 with Jim was the year of Liz's epiphany.

"Epiphany" is a serious word; it implies a "divine revelation," something transcendental, suddenly seeing a burst of light and finding a worshipful essence worthy of self-dedication. I think that to Liz it meant something akin to that, not just an "awakening" or "insight," but a fresh appreciation of the fullness of life. The mind's eye retains a library of stunning and transforming images, I believe, until life's end. Liz indeed experienced her epiphany on that first trip.

This had been a heady immersion for the two of us. Not only had Liz been reborn, not only had the symbol and reality of elephants become the core of Liz's religion, but we now knew where a major part of our future efforts would be directed.

One afternoon, after the event at Le Bernardin on October 23, Alex told Jim that 1995, the year he came to Africa with us, perhaps not quite an epiphany, nonetheless was "the happiest year of my life." It had also been a beacon year in our lives. Not only had we once more luxuriated in the viewing of Africa's wild animals, but we were also about to meet TJ, a creature of overwhelming beauty whose story, poignant, and in the end cruel, merits telling.

• • •

I've chosen to record the story of Liz's enduring love affair with tigers as a part of the continuum of human affairs. All incidents in life, I believe, are a sequence of rapidly moving still lifes. Since it was in Billings, Montana, that Liz discovered her tiger, Billings is a logical starting point.

Frederick Billings, lawyer, shareholder of an ambitious railroad company, ascended to the presidency of the Northern Pacific Railroad in 1879. Though a quiet, laid-back Easterner, Billings was a big man, in Joe Howard's words, long before Joseph Kingsley Howard, a Montana journalist, wrote them. Fred Billings may not have been "tall, wide and handsome," a description Howard felt described the state of Montana, but the description nevertheless fit this handsome, bearded, nature-loving man as it did the city that was to be named Billings. In 1882, the name of the eastern terminus of the new railroad was dubbed Billings, and it wasn't long before it became the largest, most aggressive, self-conscious city in the state.

The town commissioners realized upon the city's centennial in 1982 that one of its missing amenities was a zoo. What could be more appropriate than to designate a site and plan the building of a Montana-flavored zoo with wolves, elk, antelope, deer, marmosets, wolverines, foxes, burrowing rodents, even a handful of ferrets—the skittish and long-nosed members of the weasel family? Frederick Billings was long gone, but the zoo would be a reminder of Billings' sophistication. Filling the zoo with entertaining and educational exhibits was a long process and it wasn't until 1995 that the star attractions were in place—Siberian tigers. The purity of the zoo had now become secondary. Attendance and revenue were now primary. The tiger, not a creature indigenous to Montana, was to be an attraction. And, indeed, the tiger brought people to the zoo.

Two years earlier and five jet hours to the east, the seeds of our Billings trip were planted. In 1993, Dr. Jay Kirkpatrick, a reproductive physiologist and specialist in wild animal sterilization, had been invited to Fire Island to see what he could do about the white-tailed deer population that infested the western end of Fire Island. In years that were very cold, the Great South Bay froze over and thus this long sliver of sandbar, on average eight miles south of the southern coast of Long Island, became infested with white tail deer, "so brazen they walk right up to you," an editor of *The Fire Island News* complained. The deer loved Fire Island, particularly our community, Saltaire, which was only six miles from the mainland. There were no predators and, just as significant, no competitors. Grasses grew and were consumed. Birds, other than gulls and crows, went elsewhere.

Jay phoned and came to visit. He hoped that Liz and I, among others, would help to fund a long-term program. Jay soon found out that long-term financing was not his only problem. There were many citizens who objected to the whole idea. The program got off the ground, sputtered and died. It lost momentum within a few years and was forgotten.

234

But Jay didn't forget us. And we certainly didn't forget him. So when he called from Billings and asked Liz and me if we'd like to stop at the zoo and meet TJ, the zoo's three-year-old Siberian tiger, and if she had arrived, Nadia, his six-year-old intended mate, we dropped everything, left St. Barts and flew to Billings. This was early 1996, the year Liz fell madly in love with tigers.

Jay is a short, quiet, husky man whose speech is slow, "Pennsylvania like," one of his assistants claimed, but then "Pennsylvania like," to Montanans, refers to anything east of Billings. He is bespectacled and will remove his glasses and use them as an emphasis prop as he makes a point. He is one of the most thoroughly dedicated and convincing people Liz and I ever knew.

We were caught in an airplane schedule that limited our time, so as soon as we arrived at the zoo, we ran out to the cage where TJ sulked about. Nadia was asleep, but not in the cage. The idea was to mate TJ and Nadia, but that wasn't TJ's idea. He either wouldn't or couldn't. He was a zoo-bred tiger, young and very badly confused. He had been born at the Denver Zoo. His mother found him easy to ignore and his handler coddled him. It seemed that TJ had no idea that he was a beautiful tiger. But Liz certainly did. The hopes for a TJ and Nadia consummation were never realized. TJ was either aloof or frightened. He was shipped to St. Louis and a new male, Prince, was brought in from Minneapolis. Nadia didn't accept this male and off she went to be replaced by Luna. I've lost track of the next sequence in Nadia's life.

I talked with Jay a few weeks ago and the saga of TJ goes on. Jay ran into him, quite by accident, in Columbia, South Carolina. Jay was visiting a local zoo, and there, caged alone, was TJ. He recognized Jay and came to the bars of the cage and rubbed his body back forth, back and forth. Jay told me that he was moved to tears and had to turn his back on TJ. He made up his mind to forget TJ forever.

Liz never got over TJ. Neither did the foundation. Liz taught us to love elephants because of their behavior and she taught us to love tigers because they are so supremely beautiful. Our board members have added field knowledge, long experience and their own individualized love for the creatures and their love of Liz. That love was as free and easy as a friendly conversation.

Liz had put her camera away in Billings. She spurned photographing a caged animal. She saw it as an act of violence. But having become a woman happy and free on safari, she used her camera in Africa to tell stories that words could not capture.

. . .

Botswana was the safari destination of our last trip to Africa, late September 1996. It was the last leg of a lengthy trip through South Africa. The country is awesome, from Table Mountain outside of Cape Town to Durban on the northerly coast and inland to Johannesburg. The wine country is gorgeous but at times difficult to appreciate. A staccato of gunfire would sweep the road as modern-day highwaymen forced cars off the road. Liz, like a lucky charm, somehow seemed to be protected. Somehow our car was always a number of car lengths ahead of the fusillades.

We flew from Johannesburg to Botswana, a landlocked country in the southern part of Africa with an extraordinary abundance of wildlife. We started our safari at Maun, a town from which we flew by helicopter, in glaring sunlight for once, to Chobe National Park. There we set up camp and prepared for a number of days of viewing and photographing. Botswana is famous for its immense variety of animals and their accessibility. The safari was successful; all went as planned. Our tenting quarters were comfortable, there was a dearth of stinging insects and the camp itself was clean and well managed. On the way back we flew low over the Okavango Delta, the world's largest inland delta.

We never returned to Africa. Perhaps the delta, so lush and full of life and movement when in full tide, so forlorn, empty and bleak after the waters have vanished, serves as a metaphor for the oscillations of life and death. In its death is its beginning.

Goodbye to Okavango—goodbye to elephants—goodbye to Africa.

CHAPTER TEN, 2006

JANUARY 2006 STARTED with chemotherapy in New York on the 3rd, Avastin now being the chemical of choice. We had returned to St. Barts on the 5th. Alex and Christina were leaving for Germany the following day. The baby was due in June. They planned to look for an apartment in an area not too far from where Christina's parents lived. Christina would take a leave of absence from teaching. Alex would find gigs in Europe and Liz and I, especially Liz, would continue to be supportive and agreeable. So it went.

The routine I refer to has to be understood in context. Even though her appetite was strong and many foods appealed to her, her ability to retain food in quantity continued to diminish. Her weight loss continued. Her energy became more easily depleted. And her CA125 numbers were not improving. They were, according to Dr. Pasmantier, "creeping up." The January reading was 120. The Avastin treatment was serving one purpose and the side effects were tolerable. But the treatment, admittedly, was not curative.

The e-mail she sent to Kim on January 6 was chatty:

"Alex and Christina are leaving for what I imagine will be their home in the near future. Am so glad we all saw each other. They are both so enthusiastic about the baby. They may need some advice down the road...Liz."

There were other chatty e-mails. It would no longer be her health alone that occupied Liz's mind; the child-to-be changed that. Not entirely, of course. Liz was genuinely thrilled that a baby was on the way and that Alex was to become a father. But Liz was not a typical grandmotherly type, not a baby-bouncer or fondler, or knitter of tiny clothes. And I certainly had never been enchanted by little children. Babies had and have little appeal for me.

February brought us a gratifying experience. We were honored by the Wildlife Conservation Society at a private dinner. We were honored, we believed, not as much for the funding we had provided over the years, but for our personal involvement with the biologists in the field, our close and demanding analyses of outcomes, our willingness to change course, to adapt and never to insist on that ineffable thing called success.

It was a game but weary Liz who was honored that evening. Her poise and bare-knuckled vigor were typical of the Liz everyone admired.

Her CA125 continued its creep, now to 125. March's figures continued the upward direction. The reading was 137.

Liz had chemo on March 1, the same day we got the reading. We resumed our St. Barts commute.

Off went another chatty e-mail to Kim full of the news of the day other than Liz news: "I never quite know where we are. Next week here and the following week in NY, Fire Island and Montana!" She ends by saying, "Now I must run down and do my treadmill before going to the airport! Much love to the 3 of you, Liz."

We made certain of our return early on the 13th. Lisa Lockwood, feature reporter and writer for *Women's Wear Daily*, had scheduled an interview at our apartment to commemorate the company's thirtieth birthday, an improbable length of time for an apparel company to exist. *Women's Wear Daily* was planning a special section to pay tribute to Liz Claiborne, both the person and the company she had founded. There was a full-page picture of Liz as she had been, hand on hip, a hint of a smile and brandishing a huge black cross. The headline read, "YOU'VE COME A LONG WAY, BABY!"

Liz had indeed come a long way. The article appeared on March 27, four days before her seventy-seventh birthday.

She was far from finished. On the 6th of the month, Liz had received a "thank you" letter from Anne Cashill, Vice President of Corporate Design and Merchandising at the company. Liz had accepted an invitation to speak at its Designer Spotlight Meeting on the afternoon of Thursday, April 27.

Anne Cashill had pointed out, "We feel that our designers would be delighted to have the opportunity to hear more about the founder of our company, your career and viewpoints." We were later to refer to the event as the Designers' Forum. That appearance became the magical coda to Liz's explanation of herself and her work. I've referred to that brilliant event earlier when Liz had emotionally equated elephant and human extinction.

Her meeting with the designers that afternoon was never forgotten.

The *Women's Wear Daily* insert appeared on March 27. Liz had another Avastin chemo session on the 28th. Her CA125 was now 125, not encouraging, but not alarming. This was an acceptable status quo: elevated numbers perhaps, but the less draining side effects enabled her to function.

She e-mailed Kim on April 7:

"Re 'WWD,' Thanks Kim for both your card and your comments on 'WWD.' Art was very pleased that you saw what he was trying to do with the interview, and she got it right and it was printed correctly. I just think it was a well done piece...I was very pleased. No it was not sunny on the 31st [Liz's birthday] but it was very nice, we were in Fire Island before going to Helena for what may be our last Heritage Student Conference, then back to New York then to St. Barts. Whew! Enough traveling for a while. Love to you all 3, Liz."

April whizzed along with chemo sessions and manicures. Evelyn discovered that Liz had a gum disease, osteonecrosis, another bothersome and painful affliction that required antibiotics and additional pre-bedtime rinsing—all this in addition to a blue plastic mouthpiece Liz had to wear when sleeping. She had begun to grind her teeth in her sleep. Another darned nuisance.

• • •

I am now, at year end, December 31, 2007, reliving the days that had prepared Liz for the afternoon of April 27, 2006, Liz's magical interchange with those assembled to meet her in the company's auditorium. The space was packed to overflowing, standing room only. Her company had turned out en masse to hear her. This was to be one speech (she disliked the word) that she wanted to write on her own, no suggestions from me and no corrections. She began the writing in Montana, wrote and rewrote, and then, quite incidentally, read a profile of Pete Seeger, the legendary folk singer and musician. You can find it in the April 17, 2006, edition of *The New Yorker*. That gave her the hook she was looking for.

The life of Pete Seeger was the model she had followed. She started her speech with that model, and felt that whether her audience knew Seeger or not, they would get the point. She expressed the essential truths by which Pete Seeger, unfailingly, ordered his life. He was condemned as a communist. No matter. He believed in justice and love. He expressed his sense of justice through his music, derived originally from the skills and love of music of his family. He wanted to sing and play the banjo, and he knew he had to hone his skills to communicate more intensely with his audience. So he practiced, and he played, and practiced more and played more and he reached and captivated his audience. That was Liz's first big message: "Find your star, find what you believe in as a designer and then make darned sure you know how to implement that vision as effectively as possible. Keep at it! Don't surrender to despair. Don't give up; talent and determination working together will get you to your star."

I was not in the audience, deliberately. But I've seen the film of that afternoon many times, seeking further clues, finding nothing I hadn't known, but becoming overwhelmed by her poise, her beauty and how aware she was of how poignant these moments were.

She reached out and into her listeners. A wave of good feeling covered the room. Liz's focus was as intense as was her desire to be clear and to be understood.

So she spoke as plainly as she could, slowly, distinctly. The story of the beginning of the company was important to her and it was important to her that she get one major principle across, that she and I strongly believed the company must have a skilled, talented and flexible engineer as a partner, one who would work positively with Liz. Manufacturability, fit, fashion relevance and dedicated taste would emerge from the partnership of design and engineering.

"We ran a small ad describing the partnership offered. We had many responses," Liz said, "but when Len Boxer walked in wearing a Prince of Wales black-and-white checked suit, I knew he was the one."

Indeed, he was the one.

She then described the life that she and I were now living and her love

Liz at her appearance at the Liz Claiborne Inc. headquarters on April 27, 2006, with Dana Buchman (top left), the impresario of the event.

for the host of creatures that live on this planet. She described our first trip to Africa and the early morning she had left her tent to view the passing animals and the undulation of the giraffes. She smiled and moved her arms side to side. She described the elephant clan and her discovery of the bewitching compulsion that kept an elephant herd under the death-defying care of the matriarch. And then came the memorable moment. She broke into tears, wiped them away and apologized for her emotional outburst. "If we can't save these magnificent creatures, then we can't save ourselves."

When the forum was opened to questions, Liz was asked what her thoughts were about the change in the company's direction after she had left. Her answer was pure Liz. In essence, she respected the right of management to manage as it saw fit. She had no quarrel with the company.

That afternoon and the day of her courageous, clear-eyed meeting with death remain, in my mind, among her greatest moments.

Oh yes, there was an aside that was not spoken. It is written on the paper that she had used to shape her talk. She has just told about her epiphany on her first trip to East Africa. She wrote, "So that's what we do now!"

She had been in chemotherapy for seven years. Her CA125 was 125. She looked wonderfully well. No one but she and I knew that she was somewhat pasted together. She and Mr. Piazza had done wonders with her wigs. That afternoon there was not a word about cancer, not from her or anyone in the audience. That afternoon she was cancer free.

I met her and we went home together. She was exhausted, but pleased. She knew she had connected. And then we went through some flopping about the apartment as I tried to help her remove her boots. Our floors are cement and slippery. It seemed like a good idea at the time but has proven a costly indulgence. This time the bootjack kept slipping. I was on my hands and knees, tugging at a boot. I kept falling and landing on my backbone. After what seemed to be an interminable, fruitless struggle, the boots were off.

"Success," she said. "See, we can do it if we make up our minds to do it." And I remember just nodding and smiling.

Our reward that evening was dinner out at 66, a gourmet Chinese restaurant, with Neil and Karen.

Liz's further reward arrived hand-delivered a few days later. The company had put together a memory book and a DVD of the event. (We have distributed dozens of that DVD. It is a treasure.)

Anne Cashill wrote to Gwen Satterfield, Liz's personal assistant:

"Dear Gwen: It was such a pleasure, for all who attended, to have the rare and special opportunity to hear from Liz Claiborne. Everyone was moved by her personal story, her struggles, her vision, and the development of the Liz Claiborne brand. Her clear message about being passionate about product connected with everyone in the audience. It renewed the spirit of the Liz Claiborne designers and reconnected them with the original brand vision. It made us proud to be working for a brand with such a rich heritage. It was extremely inspirational to be in her presence. Many of those who attended have called me to thank me for making the arrangements for her visit. Thank you, Gwen, for helping on your end. It was a magical day here at Liz Claiborne."

Chemo on May 9; Avastin continued. Eye surgery, a simple cataract procedure, had been scheduled for later in the month. Her vision had been blurred. The procedure was routine. The month, other than that, was filled with doctor's appointments: Hartman, Buchman, Magid. We again tried to keep activities routine with dinners out and weekends at Fire Island. The eye surgery, her general weariness and her inability to eat as she would have liked made the last Fire Island weekend of the month a tough one for Liz: nausea, headaches, vomiting, general wretchedness. Nevertheless, she slept it off and we stayed at the beach until Tuesday.

Her CA125 was now 196, not too surprising since she had skipped one treatment in deference to the eye surgery.

Our May board meetings went well. We had invited Martin Meredith to be our guest the first morning of the meeting. Meredith is an English journalist and historian who had just published a book, *The Fate of Africa*, an accounting of the status of all the new African nations liberated by their colonial rulers from the 1960s on. The book was a somber read. We were interested not only in the political and societal aspects of new nationhood, but what effects he thought this would have on the fate of wildlife.

He had earlier written a book called *Elephant Destiny*, a history of the relationship between men and elephants, which asks the burning questions: "What is to be the destiny of the elephant? Will elephants survive only in zoos and nature preserves? And what can we do about it?" This book was to become constant reading for Liz. We had invited Meredith to dinner as well. Meredith was fascinating company. Dinner was a success.

The following evening we had dinner again with Iain Douglas-Hamilton and his film-making daughter, Dudu. It was another successful evening. We talked elephants. We asked about Boadicea and were pleased to hear that she was still alive and still in charge, a bit more tentative, but still in charge.

May was coming to an end. The past two months had been fulfilling, reasonably active and reasonably comfortable.

June 2006 started with a spinal shot on the first. Chemotherapy continued, on the 8th and the 22nd. Liz had a PET scan on the 27th and, according to Dr. Pasmantier, the results were "pretty good, even showed some improvement."

The first days of June, however, had been considerably more portentous than reviewing a parade of numbers.

On June 6, Elias Schultz, normal and beautiful in every way, was born. He emerged, screeching, furious at the disarrangement of his young life. Alex, camera in hand, recorded every moment. He still does.

Liz had a grandson! She had won another round in her struggle to stay alive, viable, functional and effective.

July 5, 2006, we had been married forty-nine years. Remarkable. We celebrated the way we enjoyed celebrations the most—together, quiet, alone, the two of us, at Le Bernardin. She handed me a card, about four-inches square, cut from a file folder. We lifted our glasses to toast one another, a toast of gratitude and hope. "To us," we said, a toast we had repeated through the years.

This is what the card had written on it: "HAPPY ANNIVERSARY," printed four times on the face side, each printing differently colored:

HAPPY ANNIVERSARY

HAPPY ANNIVERSARY

HAPPY ANNIVERSARY

HAPPY ANNIVERSARY

And on the back:

I LOVE YOU!

I LOVE YOU!

I LOVE YOU!

"I could not duplicate the frame," Liz wrote. I had seen a nine-inch-square sign with a thin black enamel frame that said, "for sale—$50." The sign was in the back corner window of a small store on Madison Avenue. I had commented, months ago, that I'd like to own that sign. Fifty dollars was about all I felt I was worth at the time. Liz tucked the comment away and months later tried to buy the sign. Her note to me continued, "The owner would not sell me the original so she did the best she could!" The sign read "For sale." There was no price. "I LOVE YOU, Your loving if difficult wife! Liz, 7/5/06."

And now, on July 5, 2006, married forty-nine years, Liz and Art as one person, despite the fierce toll of time and disease, were still very much in love, alive and planning for the future. In retrospect, the story is commonplace: two people who had married early and insensibly, met one another, fell in love, sought a clearer understanding of themselves through years of individual psychoanalysis, and then, against all odds, ended up sipping lukewarm beer in Bay St. Louis, as wife and husband, or more precisely, Liz and Art. We were more and more obviously inseparable and, with the passage of time, we were, to all intents and purposes, becoming one entity—thus, one designation: Liz and Art.

I was a garment industry executive. Liz was a clothing designer. It was through connections made at college that I ended up, unlikely as it was, in the dress business. The company I worked for also had a successful sportswear division. The fact that I was a friendly hire would protect me for a while, but unless I could grow the volume of the dress department, I knew my days were numbered.

Liz, at that time, was married to Ben Schultz. She had just given birth to Alex and had returned after one week's leave. Juniorite, a manufacturer of junior sportswear, was the company she had been working for. She found a new designer in her design room.

Juniorite had run a sportswear ad in *The New York Times*. I saw the ad. I thought the clothes were terrific and that it might be a good idea to hire a sportswear designer to give our dress line a sportswear look. I had no idea what that meant, but it sounded good to me. I made some calls and discovered that Liz Schultz had been the designer. So I hunted her down and set up an interview.

The moment we met, I knew something important was happening. We had an affair, or rather, we fell in love. Our first line, me as department head, Liz as new designer, had been conceived, it seems now on reflection, as a romantic statement. It flopped. I was fired. But she was asked to stay on.

Liz retold the story of that event at the Designer Roundtable in April of 2006. There was nothing to think about. It was clear to Liz what she had to do. "If you fire him, I'm leaving," she said. And she left.

That was in 1955, the year Alex was one year old. Liz was in the process of being divorced and I was spinning in circles, out of work, in psychoanalysis, a general catastrophe of a person. Liz was also in psychoanalysis, working to support herself and her child. Liz, true to her nature, despite the uncertainty of the outcome, stayed with our affair. There is no false modesty in my bewilderment. Why? I think now of Dr. Buchman's comment, "She knew she was loved and you would do anything for her." Despite being harangued by friends who said, "They never leave their wives!" and the like, Liz waited for me. This is a story I've told here before but I think deserves repetition. She worked for virtually every cent she had. She lived in a walk-up apartment. She had thus far brought up her child alone and had never lost sight of the need to hone her skills, to learn and to grow as a designer.

Yvonne Stephens was Alex's babysitter at that time and all-around home assistant. I spoke with her recently. She said, "I can see her now, standing at her easel, drawing, designing. Often she drew little pictures of Alex. She always worked so hard."

We were married on July 5, 1957. The documents show us married in Bay St. Louis, Mississippi, a city that was open for divorce business twenty-four hours a day, seven days a week. Bay St. Louis is no longer what it was; Katrina did it in. I had two children from my previous marriage, Neil and Nancy. Liz had one child, Alex.

Liz and I had spent the evening of the Fourth of July in New Orleans. I had just returned from Ciudad Juárez in Mexico, via El Paso, Texas. Ciudad Juárez was a divorce factory in those days. I had flown in from New York via Birmingham on a DC-3, crossed the border at El Paso, slept a few unwashed and restless hours at the Hotel Sylvia and was then whisked off to the divorce gymnasium. I was in the hands of a local, highly disinterested abogado, a local lawyer skilled in divorce work. I went through some sleepy formalities, was seated at a desk, one of perhaps a thousand in this endless plain of a gymnasium, had some papers stamped, turned over some money and, magically, I was a free man.

Liz had divorced the hard way: with contention, tough lawyers and no child support. I had agreed to responsibilities that made life tough on Liz and me, particularly on her, for the first five years of our marriage. She essentially supported me. If she didn't work, we were in trouble. Most of my income had been earmarked for my former wife and our two children. That knot was loosened five years later. My former wife remarried. Now there were the children to be supported and neither Liz nor I felt it should be any other way.

We met at the New Orleans airport on July 4, both exhausted. I was somewhat ambivalent. Liz was determined, pleased and ready to dance in the streets, exhausted or not. And she did. She was ready to dance in the streets and it didn't matter with whom or where. She was happy. She had waited two years, as she later told Kim, and now the wait was over.

The next morning, July 5, Liz took an early bus to her parents' home in Pass Christian, about twenty miles east of Bay St. Louis. Louis, my best-man-to-be, and I slept in New Orleans on the hottest night of the century, and woke up late the next morning to find Louis hungover. Our assignment was merely to drive to the Pass and take Liz and her mother to Bay St. Louis, as all were now members of the wedding party.

We were late, unconscionably late it seems, but there she was, patient, determined and beautiful in a longish dress of cotton lawn, sprinkled with printed violets. I still see her there in that so unlike-Liz dress, forever smiling.

Her father shook my hand, wished us all luck and went fishing.

The wedding itself was performed by Judge C. Delius Rhodes in a tiny room that seemed to have been constructed after the dining room table was in place. All four of us were crammed into a separate corner. The Rhodes children were watching television in the next room. This was a non-sentimental, hello-goodbye affair. Just as well. The temperature was boiling, so there was nothing to do but hike over to the veranda of the Bay St. Louis Hotel and sip lukewarm beer.

• • •

We waited more than fifteen years to start our company. Liz insisted that not until Alex was twenty-one and somewhat self-supporting would we take that risk.

We knew from the beginning that whatever we did, we would do it together.

Late in 1975, an opportunity came along. We passed. The product and market position would have been overly traditional. After fifteen years of secure work at Youth Guild, a division of Jonathan Logan, the mother company wanted to set Youth Guild afloat. Youth Guild made sensible but tasteful junior-sized clothing, all manufactured in the United States. Did we want to buy in? We decided no. Let's do something new, something Liz, on our own.

Thus, "Liz Claiborne Inc." was incorporated in January 1976 with three founding partners: Liz Claiborne Ortenberg, Designer; Arthur Ortenberg, Operations; and Leonard Boxer, Production.

It was long after we married that we became Liz and Art, not until we had started the company. Of course, we were called Liz and Art by friends, but in the context of being two separate people. We were not then Liz and Art as a single entity. We had hired our first staff at the end of 1975, assuming that we would raise the necessary funds to formally incorporate. It wasn't easy. But it was done. We moved into my consulting office at 80 West 40th Street, an old building erroneously attributed to Stanford White. I had been a textile and fashion consultant for a number of years, had acquired some prestigious accounts, and, as was the case with consultants in general, was not overworking. Nor was I particularly stimulated by the work. Liz had become more than a little annoyed when I would call her at Youth Guild, urge her to remove the pins from her mouth, close the door behind herself and stop working for the day. This could be as late as eight o'clock in the evening. A solution, of course, was for us to be in the same business. And that's the way it worked out.

Eighty West 40th Street, very much in the Beaux Arts style, as was my second-floor space, sits on the southwest corner of 40th Street and Sixth Avenue and faces Bryant Park. The park still serves as a major platform for fashion shows.

I had converted my consulting space, approximately 200 square feet, into a three-wedged design room with an accounting area (my ten-foot-long butcher block table). We had built a small showroom at the east end of the space, one step up, carpeted, with bins at each end for the sample line. Folding screens separated the design room from the accounting office.

Anita Boxer, Leonard's wife, came aboard pro-bono as my accounting assistant, as new to the game as was I, both of us now intense readers of *Basic Accounting*. Whatever Anita, who had never worked a day in her life, lacked in skill, she more than made up in her bubbly spirits.

My experience, broad and lengthy as it had been, never immersed me in the details of budgeting, cash flow control and banking relationships.

Howard Olian, a close friend and producer of woolen goods, dedicated a small room in his building where Leonard could work. The room was a short block from 80 West 40th. In a room no more than twelve feet square, Leonard did first patterns and readied designs for production. We managed a short-term lease on a warehouse in Karlstadt, New Jersey, where we would receive fabric for production. Neil, Alex and I, as needed, would be our piece goods handlers and stackers, hand-carrying seventy-yard bolts of fabric to the cutting table.

We were in business. Even though we had no credit line as yet, nor any banking relationships other than our personal accounts, friends in the textile industry advanced sample yardage and accepted inventory orders. We used our own funds to purchase a few sewing machines and redecorate the space.

By February 15, 1976, we had amassed, with great difficulty and much compromising, the funds from investors to incorporate the business: $255,000, of which $75,000 had been invested by Liz, me and Leonard—$25,000 each.

Our first hire was Nancy Valentine, a large, robust woman, skilled and sensitive in pattern making, draping, and being able to translate a designer's sketch into a wearable garment. Liz had worked with Nancy earlier and they had tremendous confidence in one another. Nancy knew that Liz knew what she wanted and had a professional understanding of how goods are produced. Liz knew that Nancy was on the same page that she was. They worked in a tiny space behind the sewing machines. We had built a clever table with a drop leaf: all up, and it was a cutting table; leaf down, it became a design table. The relationship lasted until Liz left the company. Nancy stayed on. Our next hires were sample hands, four skilled women, all of whom remained with the company for years. We bought sample cuts, we had short runs of fabrics made to order, we did everything we felt necessary to get off the mark in as convincing and professional a manner as possible. Our next hire was a lovely young woman, Andrea, who was both fit model and show-room model. Liz would be our salesperson. Every evening, Liz and I would

Liz, Art and their first skilled technician, Nancy Valentine, in 1994.

oil the machines. I would clean and restock the bathroom. The two of us would sweep, vacuum and get the space ready for the next day.

This was our space for the first year of the company's life. Liz, always on the lookout for feedback, was avid to show merchandise or sketches and swatches of merchandise planned to any knowledgeable buyer who would work with us. We sought straight talk, even if it hurt. Bob Salem and Mel Schneck of the Associated Merchandising Corporation were staunch friends. Ed Roberts, president of J. L. Hudson Company, flew to New York specifically to review our line when his buyer was too ill to do so. Dottie Kaplan of The May Company also reviewed the line, looked us squarely in the eye and said, "Very nice. It won't sell. It's overpriced."

"Where should we be priced?" I asked. "At least one full price range lower," she said. And that was when it occurred to us that the markup margin going in was not the crux of the matter. It was your maintained margin that counted and if you ran your company properly, if your merchandise was superb, as ours would be, and if your cost of doing business was controlled, then there was no reason that your maintained margin should not be satisfactory. And that's the way it became for the years thereafter.

It wasn't long before we grew out of the space. We rented two additional floors, the fifth and sixth, put a new and more spacious showroom on the fifth floor and used the sixth-floor balcony for design. There were more sample hands and a roomier space for Liz and Nancy. Liz hired our first sweater designer for a category destined to become tremendously important. We were becoming an item house as well as a collection house.

We expanded the second-floor space for our first batch of young planners and statisticians—basically a group of young, well-educated people who reported to me. But actually we all reported to Liz because that's where the line planning began and the intricate game of putting the pieces together and delivering a product began. Bob Abajian, a designer in the market whom we had known and respected for years, later became Liz's backup designer.

Years later, the company made a promotional film, and Bob's voice described the art and mechanics of our design process. He said, "Despite the many components and despite the number of hands involved, the line looked as though it was painted with one brush." That was the point.

We worked each day until fatigue set in. Then I would call out, "We're going out to dinner. Treat's on us. Who's game?"

"Monte Rosa?" someone would ask. "Of course." And then we treated everyone to dinner. Monte Rosa was on the same street as our apartment.

It had become a sign of distinction to have dinner with Liz and Art as often as possible. We both liked the placement of our names; the sweet sound of "Liz" and the more aggressive "Art."

We were now "Liz and Art." We were told repeatedly that over time we had evolved into one being. Our work together had grown into a trusting interdependency.

Gene Landrum, the doctorate student and author of *Profiles of Genius*, provided a rousing, climactic overview of the power of being Liz and Arthur. (That's his usage, not mine.):

"According to Liz and Arthur, 'our model of a successful entrepreneur…is the man or woman who has a successful business and a successful marriage.' They had had both. Arthur was always the administrative and chief operating officer of the company while Liz saw to the designs. A former marketing director for the firm refers to Arthur as 'the wizard of Oz, because he's the man behind the door—intellectual and godlike, introspective but dogmatic. He makes pronouncements. Arthur is outgoing while Liz is shy. She is serious. He jokes a lot. She watches the details, he watches for the big problems. She manages by doing, he by teaching. They were a great team.'"

Newlyweds, Paris, 1957.

Liz said it for me in her commencement address at the Rhode Island School of Design in 1991. "My husband claimed his role was to carry the banner and lead the charge.

"He certainly did."

• • •

The summer of 2006 was preparation time for a visit to meet young Elias, our grandchild. July 7 and July 20 were days on which chemotherapy would be administered. Avastin was still the drug of choice. Chemo had been scheduled to bracket our trip. Liz's CA125 was 100.

We were met at the Stuttgart airport late in the day of the 8th, billeted at a nearby small hotel, slept another exhausted evening, breakfasted in the hotel and were then whisked off by cab to the Schultz condominium in Wilheim Teck, a well-ordered, thriving village in the hills of southwestern Germany. There was much busyness at the Schultz home that morning and there would be for our entire stay. Christina was a forty-year-old, first-time German mother and Alex was a total novice at this kind of work. I am not a fan of little babies, even large babies, so my visit, other than at dinnertime, was somewhat unsettling. But, for Liz, there he was, the living proof of continuity. She held him, a bit tentatively, but she was enraptured by every moment of contact. Liz did not behave at all like an omnivorous grandmother, more like a jeweler holding a fine gem. Alex, an adventurous chef, cooked dinner every evening. Nothing could be routine, as Elias had no routine other than to shriek when hungry, be quiet when being fed and either be quiet or shriek when being held or walked about.

We left on July 13, stopped in Shannon for old times' sake and spent the afternoon and evening at an old favorite haunt, Dromoland Castle Hotel.

In the past, every return trip from Africa included a stopover in Shannon, a luxurious bath to trade the soil of Africa for the cheery water of Ireland and then dinner in the room or up in the main dining room, blazered and neck-tied. I was always proud of being the escort of the most beautiful woman in the room. So it was that evening.

At a Jonathan Logan party, 1965.

Clockwise: The founders of Liz Claiborne Inc. at their farewell from the company, 1989; in St. Louis for an award in 1991; and photographed together after leaving the company, 1991.

Clockwise: In Provence, a turn in the road that became a marker, 2002; at the Pont du Gard, 2002; and on Mount Cook, New Zealand, 1990.

At Tranquillity Ranch for *Architectural Digest*, 1992. Photograph by Robert Reck.

We were back in New York the following day, with chemo due on the 20th. The 19th was a dentist day and she saw our restorative expert, Harold Litvak. I was with Liz. As she rose to get out of the dental chair, she jammed her right thigh into the chair's extended arm. Blood began to gush out, really gush out. She quickly grabbed a towel, pressed it on the wound and began to laugh, a natural, easy, far-from-hysterical laugh, while the technician and the young woman at the phone board began screaming. I called our dermatologist, who was in, who could see Liz at once and who, great good fortune, had his office across the street. We hobbled over and, as Dr. Stier told me later, "it was a superficial laceration, but what wasn't superficial was what she taught me about handling wounds. She's a thorough expert." Liz did slow, careful, professional work, whatever it was or however long it took.

My son Neil and his fiancée Karen were married on Sunday the 23rd. They were married in Montauk, Long Island, a three-and-one-half hour drive in each direction, particularly on Sundays when the traffic is heaviest. Liz gave it her all, brought a stunning change of clothes and, despite her fatigue, beamed and radiated love and affection throughout. We couldn't quite make it through the dinner that followed the marriage vows. The trip home was torture for her: nausea, trying not to vomit, a recurrence of cramps and the whole gamut of distress. We got her to the apartment just in time and the evening ended. Liz finally fell asleep. Somehow she felt well enough the following morning to take off for Montana.

We saw Tom Weiner at St. Peter's on August 3 and, following the script, he administered Avastin. Her CA125 had begun to elevate. It was now 664.8. It was apparent that the Avastin treatment was becoming ineffective. Despite the elevated number, Liz had rebounded. Avastin had protected her from the more painful effects that other corrosive chemicals, previously administered, had inflicted. But now the track-one loss, the re-colonizing of the cancerous seeds, was on an unimpeded march.

She had things she wanted to do that August. Nevertheless, Tom found Liz much the same in outward attitude. She discussed her condition in as matter-of-fact a manner as possible, almost as though she were talking about someone else. I was with her. I knew she had important things to do, so she was downplaying her discomforts. Yes, she mentioned the headaches, the loss of appetite. Well, her appetite, she said, was fair. That wasn't the case, I knew, but she would make it the case for the near term.

It was time to consider abandoning Avastin. On the whole, Liz had re-acted well to the chemical. Avastin is considered to be a maintenance drug that rarely gives a patient more than a five-month reprieve. Its efficacy lies in its ability to reduce the severity of chemotherapy side effects while main-taining the patient's ability to control the disease. Liz had been on Avastin for close to ten months. The sobering realization that Avastin would no longer be the chemical of choice was painful to accept.

Dr. Pasmantier and Dr. Weiner conferred and decided to switch back to Gemzar in combination with another platinum-based chemical, Carboplatin.

But the month of August lay ahead of us and Liz had plans and the de-termination to pull them off.

After the early August treatment at St. Peter's, we drove off to see Anne Ripley. Liz determinedly went through her physical therapy exercises. Af-terward, she kept her manicure appointment with Robin Burk. This time Robin also cleaned the fuzz off the top of her head. I met Liz at Hair Hair, having spent time at the Red Lodge Clearinghouse office. It was haircut time for me. After all, I was preparing to celebrate, if that's the word, my eightieth birthday. We then went off to the Windbag Saloon for a hamburger. Liz, de-spite a high CA125 reading, picked her way through the food. I then fol-lowed Liz to the Pan Handler, an upscale purveyor of tasteful kitchenware to fill every need, perceived or real. The Pan Handler is conveniently lo-cated across the way from the Windbag, and is another popular tenant on Helena's famous Last Chance Gulch.

This particular early August was a time in which Liz's appetite was the appetite of a normal person, but was also a time when her ability to consume was greatly diminished. She had lost none of her zeal for any kitchen item that she might, someday, find a need for: a grill pan, for instance, or a mini-cocotte out of the endless offerings of Le Creuset. The Le Creuset color ranges were tasteful and exciting. I would haul a heavy bag back to my parked car (on this day we had come to town in two cars—Liz in her beloved Boxster and me in my respected Mercedes wagon). When the shopping spree ended, she would head off first to drive back to the ranch and I would follow her. We acted as though, irrespective of the numbers, she was going to get better.

I believed it. Liz would get better. She plunged into busyness. She avoided thinking about the disease. She thought about other things.

Neither of us found it strange that Liz would drive into Helena with Kathy on a number of the days to follow for some additional shopping and ordering at the Pan Handler.

We lived at Triple 8 for practically the entire month of August. The new treatment wasn't to be administered until the end of the month.

Liz and Kathy pored over recipes, oblivious to the narrow range of meals we would prepare at home. She didn't care. She loved food, she loved reading about food.

Liz's busyness was largely focused on making plans for my birthday. We drove to Tranquillity, invited Bob and Ellen Knight to join us for a quiet dinner at home. That's what Liz had led me to believe. But she, who had planned and pulled off an ambitious surprise party for my seventieth birthday, had major plans for my eightieth on August 13, 2006.

She had called Eric Ripert, grand chef and partner at Le Bernardin, and arranged to have a surprise dinner for four flown from New York to Missoula, where Rip Grubaugh, our ranch manager at Tranquillity, would meet the dinner and the chef for the party, Leo Marino. Eric had planned to be chef for our evening, but a command performance in Oregon dictated otherwise. Leo, his sous-chef at the restaurant in New York, would be a top-grade replacement. He was given the assignment, but then things went awry. Leo missed his flight out of JFK in New York. The food, however, had been put aboard and arrived at the Missoula airport. When Rip discovered that we had food in Missoula, but no chef, he called the airport and made arrangements to have the food refrigerated. Gwen, back in New York, always ready for a dilemma, got Leo on a plane leaving New York three hours after the one he had missed.

Rip drove through the Tranquillity gate at two o'clock on the morning of August 13. He had picked up Leo and they had the birthday dinner in hand. The food was further refrigerated and all went to sleep. The surprise had been deleted from the surprise party, but not the delight of the evening ahead.

I must repeat, fully astonished and now of mixed feelings: Liz's CA125 was 664.8 that evening. She knew the number, as did I from our meeting with Tom at the beginning of the month. Liz drove the number out of her mind and acted as a cancer-free hostess that evening.

The new treatment and a demanding application schedule would begin at the end of the month. We both knew that even more difficult times lay ahead.

If you had been with us that night, you would have suspected nothing amiss. There we were at six o'clock, with Bob and Ellen Knight, Liz and me toasting one another with Dom Perignon champagne. We listened to easy jazz music, Jack Teagarden and Vic Dickenson, trombone players, primarily because John Knight, Bob and Ellen's son, is a jazz trombonist. We chatted about the weather, political irritations and our concerns about the severity of the past few fire seasons. I remember so well the lightness of the evening. There we were, four well-fixed adults drinking champagne, about to share a superb dinner, compliments of Eric Ripert. He refused payment. Even though it was my birthday, all efforts were to please both Liz and Art.

Liz had been in e-mail communication with Mandy Moser, the special events director at Le Bernardin. On August 8th and 9th, they made sure that the necessities of this dinner would be in place: china, spices and herbs, fruits if needed. After seeing the proposed menu, Liz e-mailed Mandy once more:

"My goodness! Bravo! Does Eric really think we can eat all that? But we will certainly taste it all. Tell Eric that Art will be very touched by his exceedingly generous gift. Liz."

Here's the menu:

Canapes
Layers of Thinly Pounded Yellowfin Tuna, Foie Gras and Toasted Baguette
Shaved Chives and Extra Virgin Olive Oil
Crispy Soft Shell Crab on a Bed of Jumbo Lump Crab Meat in a Fragrant
    Coconut-Lime Broth
Wild Alaskan and Smoked Salmon, Baby Watercress, Yuzu-Tomato Vinaigrette

A Tribute to Gaudi
Pan-Roasted Monkfish: Confit Peppers and Fiery "Patatas Bravas,"
    Chorizo-Albarino Emulsion
Special Dairy-Free Dessert—to be decided
Petit Fours
Special Birthday Cake

I was moved beyond tears. I was overwhelmed by my gratitude to Liz and Eric and the knowledge, once more, that I was the most fortunate of men.

We returned to Triple 8 the following day. Liz had pulled it off, fatigued as she was. If poring over recipes with Kathy didn't turn her mind away from her discomforts, she would speak with Kathy and me about Martin Meredith's book, *Elephant Destiny*. Oh, how she loved elephants. She would sit on the deck of our cabin, Cabin B, and read and then fill us in at dinner. She told Kathy about her epiphany at Kichwa Tembo. There she was twenty long years later, speaking as though the experience was new and had just occurred.

Triple 8's eminence on a high hill affords a 360-degree view of gorgeous landscape: hills, mountains in the distance and a tree-lined ancient stream bed. Our cabin complex, astride the apex of one of the higher hills, reinforces the sense of freedom and timelessness that we loved.

For Liz, there was another powerful reason for her love of Triple 8. She was a person who loved to cook, despite the infrequency of her opportunities to do so. And she loved her kitchen at Triple 8. It was truly hers. She designed it without interference from anyone, including me. The views through the windows, the placement of basins, ovens, refrigerator and freezer, working areas, storage areas, dishwasher—everything a proper kitchen should have—she arranged for at Triple 8.

That was far from the case at Tranquillity, where she had inherited a ready-made kitchen. That was acceptable as long as Jerry Watson worked for us as manageress of Tranquillity. She and Liz got along well. They respected one another's kitchen and cooking skills. But when we changed managers, the female of the duo was either no cook at all, or so tentative a cook that others had to be hired to take over. The kitchen became a carousel without music, just grunts and shoves. The storage areas, refrigerators included, were best left alone; all items were stored helter-skelter, a geography of storage beyond Liz's tolerance.

The kitchen at St. Barts, on the other hand, is dark and mysterious. It had been my idea to use Brazilian dark wood facings and cupboard doors to enhance the monastic look. The equipment is so high tech and cold that it adds another reason to be at Maya's every evening. If not that, at holiday time we would hire a chef for the evening and dine in the turret room. But when the hard times came and most foods were difficult to digest, Liz would have soup in bed.

I was now beginning to understand the fun she had cooking, teaching, experimenting at Triple 8. She was looking forward to more time in the kitchen with Kathy, more pans and covered dishes, more of what a kitchen should house. But the disease was making her fight every inch of the way.

On the 17th, after a hard night, we took her to the hospital for hydration. She was now more often paying the price for trying to live a normal life.

Chemotherapy 8—Carboplatin & Gemzar 8/31/06 to 9/28/06

As I recall the session at which the change in treatment was discussed, I'm not at all surprised at our lack of curiosity. What were these chemicals? Gemzar, described earlier, bizarre as the name may seem, is a commonly used chemical mix in ovarian cancer treatment, as are the numerous platinum blends, Carboplatin for one. In this case, it was to be used because its side effects, particularly nausea and vomiting, would be less severe than those of Cisplatin. As to its effectiveness, that remained to be seen. But we both knew that the toolbox was emptying. We would just keep busy doing other things. Our excellent physicians would work it out. We would accommodate and go from there. We would try to live as normal a Montana life as we could.

The new chemical cocktail, Carboplatin and Gemzar, was to be administered much like Cisplatin and Gemzar had been. The first week, Carboplatin and Gemzar were administered consecutively on the same day; the second week, just Gemzar was administered; followed by one week off. The new treatment would begin the end of August.

Liz's CA125 was 1,134 on August 31. Once the disease swamped the Avastin, Liz was defenseless. She might waiver, she might stumble, but she would not give up.

The treatments continued as scheduled in September, with the designated chemicals infused on the 17th and then another treatment on the 28th. Liz was soldiering on. For the very first time in this battle, I felt ambivalence, uncertainty, impending loss.

Liz e-mailed Kim on the 23rd:

"Puff, Puff. Glad to hear from you, Kim! We are well, though at the moment it is my second day after treatment and I am a little 'groggy,' so this will be short. I'm back on the more traditional treatment but it seems to be working! This summer was

a little mixed up, not knowing what and when, and we are selling Tranquillity. Just too much! We spent most of the summer here at Triple 8, which I love anyway. It's close to Helena and hospital and doctor etc. I am so into babies that I can hardly picture a 7th grader [Kim's son, William] around 12½–13 years, I would guess... Much love to all, Liz."

September 28 was the next scheduled treatment and it seemed to go smoothly. We had learned over the years of chemotherapy that the day of treatment is generally untroubled, the second day a little less so, and then the effects become more potent. September 30 was a Saturday night.

Liz had gone up to the kitchen early and told Kathy that this would be her night to cook. "You just sit and watch and if I need anything I'll ask for it," she said. When I spoke with Kathy this October, she said Liz was very "devil may care." "She seemed to have had it with restraining herself. She was doing a stir-fry and I would be the assistant."

When I came up to dinner I got the message immediately. Liz was on a tear and I wasn't going to stop her. I think back now and wonder just what I could or should have done. She ate well, but didn't stuff herself. She drank two glasses of wine. She wasn't shaky, just angry. She would not permit interference. Who would not have been belligerent after years of disappointments, constraints and pain?

We made it down the twenty-nine steps to Cabin B, our sleeping and living cabin. Then the nightmare began. We spent the greater part of the evening in the bathroom, she throwing up, a creature so pathetically vulnerable and out of control. Her body was so depleted of energy that she lost consciousness and finally slept. In the past, we had lived through mini-episodes, some not so mini, of this nature. I thought she would sleep and, as in the past, recover.

She didn't. At about one o'clock in the afternoon, I tried to wake her, but she was in a stupor. Irv drove up to the cabin and we got Liz into the Mercedes and took off for the hospital. Luckily, I had reached Dr. Weiner and he met us at the entrance to the emergency room. There were no formalities. Five minutes later, she was in a room. Fifteen minutes later, she was being hydrated. Now we had to find a way to unblock her. She was CT scanned. The undigested food lodged immovably in her digestive tract had to be removed through a nasal tube to the stomach. Slowly, she came out of it. She opened her eyes, panic-stricken. All memory of events had been wiped out. And then, within a few hours of restless sleeping, Liz returned.

She was in the hospital for ten days. We went back to Triple 8 on October 11. She weighed ninety-five pounds.

Brian and Sandra came by every afternoon at five o'clock, brought me a drink, some nuts and some cheerful talk. I ordered the hospital dinner in the evening: grilled salmon or grilled chicken, salad, vegetables, fruit—all for $7.50, no tipping, exact amount required.

Liz's spirits had risen. Dr. Weiner stopped by every afternoon and was encouraging. The nurses were all professional, congenial and, most importantly, on call. The Cancer Center is one flight down from the patients' rooms. The pharmacy is right down the hall.

This episode was very disappointing. But Liz would not permit herself to be driven to giving up. As soon as we returned to Triple 8, we began to make the uphill, twenty-nine-step journey from Cabin B to Cabin A less challenging. We started by building a wooden handrail on the wall that leads from our bedroom in Cabin B to the foyer and exit door. There are four steps to negotiate. Solving that problem was easy. More difficult by far was climbing the uphill steps from Cabin B to Cabin A. The route used over the years was up the steps. We built a handrail and added lighting each foot of the way. Liz did the measuring and the specifications. The next improvement was to dig a circular road from Cabin B's door to Cabin A. Once the road was in, we would buy a golf cart to negotiate the distance. I insisted on this fairly major and long-term construction job because I could not trust Liz to ask for help when she desperately needed help. Only a short while before, I had found her crawling up the steps, pushing her tray ahead of her, step by step.

"Why didn't you ask me to do that for you?" "Because," she answered, "I didn't want to bother you again. I don't want to become an ongoing burden."

That's how the road came to be. I'll find a way to use it if I'm still around when my own "one-hoss shay," as Liz had described herself, begins to lose a piece here, a piece there.

Chemotherapy 9—Carboplatin 10/19/06 to 1/16/07

Tom scheduled the next treatment for October 19. He had spoken with Dr. Pasmantier and recommended dropping Gemzar from the menu. Liz seemed unable to tolerate the side effects. Mark had reservations as to the effectiveness of the treatment without Gemzar, but they decided to give it a try. So the 19th became a routine chemo day: 12:30 at the hospital, 3:30 at Hair Hair, and a full dinner at the Windbag Saloon. The first two nights were a little difficult, but controlled. Medication stopped the nausea. There were no cramps, and then with each succeeding day she felt better and better. My notes are as affirmative as they had been for a while: the 23rd, "much better"; the 24th, "feeling very well"; the 25th, "VERY WELL"; the 26th, off to see Tom who seemed pleased with her progress.

I was on a modified high when we returned to New York on the 27th. For now, the Carboplatin alone seemed effective. Dr. Pasmantier was dubious. Without Gemzar, he felt, Liz would soon lose ground. Liz was cautious, grateful for the short period of feeling relatively well. She knew, and I also knew but refused to absorb the knowing, that the game had changed. The end of the effectiveness of Avastin had emptied the toolbox. The choices of treatment had now become limited to chemicals already used, but in more massive doses and administered with greater frequency. The side effects would be more debilitating. Time had favored the disease, not the patient.

Liz was no longer certain that she would be able to go round-for-round with the chemicals. She was losing her certainty of being able to rebound from the side effects, including, crucially, the effect they would have on her ability to ingest food. She weighed ninety-five pounds. Her body could not live without protein and general nourishment and absorb the aggressive chemicals as well. She knew that only too well.

When I spoke with Kathy a few months ago, she told me about a poignant discussion she and Liz had had just before we left for New York.

Liz had said, "Just because I can't eat doesn't mean I don't get hungry. I dream about food, about foods of my childhood, like how my mother made grits. She put so much effort into that, ditto corn bread with maple syrup." And then Kathy said, "She just couldn't eat because she knew she would suffer."

Determination alone would no longer suffice. It was necessary, but not sufficient. It was determination, plus physical strength and stamina, that had taken Liz to the summit of Everest in 1991. Now, in November of 2006, her strength and stamina were fading. Determined survivor though she was, survival was more and more removed from her determined control.

The month started badly. The first chemo in New York was scheduled for Wednesday, November 1. Liz was far from ready. So she spent the day at Dr. Pasmantier's office, ill, nauseous, headachy, in need of hydration.

We canceled Fire Island and rested at home. Sunday evening, we did manage an early dinner with Bob and Alison. Every activity, dressing, applying makeup, fitting her wig, integrating herself to her own satisfaction, had become a slow-motion activity. Dinner out with friends, even dinner out alone was now becoming an uncomfortable, self-conscious and frustrating experience. The one exception was a boisterously friendly Italian restaurant where she ordered spaghetti to her very own recipe. Other than that, she ordered little, ate slowly, but rarely with gusto. She ate perhaps a dish of cheeses and nothing else, and watched the rest of us. She told me more than once how uneasy all this made her. She hated holding everyone to a slow pace, and then having to watch as further courses were delivered. She was not eased when I told her how much pleasure it gave others merely to be with her. And that, of course, was the total truth; being with her, exchanging smiles and nods and small or larger talk with Liz was reason enough to be happy to be at the table with her. She would not have been Liz if that satisfied her.

The weeks that stretched ahead seemed bramble-filled with tests and a struggle to hang on.

The next chemo treatment was scheduled for the 9th, and once more it was deferred. Her blood counts were low. A low white-cell count left her open to infection. A low red-cell count indicated anemia. The next scheduled date was Wednesday, November 15. The evening of the 11th, an evening we had dinner out with our good friend Ellen Daniel, ended miserably. We were at our apartment in the city and Liz again paid a price for dinner. She had been careful, happy to be with Ellen, but nonetheless she could not get the food through her system. Liz's determination was beginning to flag. It was becoming a mountainous effort to stay in the ring.

• • •

Last September I had dinner with Jamie Hellman, capable and caring nurse who worked for Dr. Pasmantier. She had known Liz since July of 2005 and was sensitive enough to relate to her patient as a person, particularly when that patient was Liz. The confidences and small signals that are exchanged in the patient's room when nurse and patient are alone are generally open and candid. The patient, Liz in this case, revealed herself as a natural, needful person.

This is what Jamie told me, "Liz had been getting Avastin. She was doing fine. Very easy-going. Her grandchild was born [June 6, 2006]. Liz was cut and dry, happy-go-lucky, but not really worried about cancer. She was matter-of-fact about the baby—business as usual. Her attitude completely changed when we started with the new weekly stuff. Her attitude completely changed, almost passive. She knew she was through but she wanted to live for you. She didn't want to leave you. She wanted to keep going and not give up. It was a struggle for me to give her chemotherapy. She had such incredible drive. I went into my office and cried."

• • •

The chemo treatment of the 15th did take place. But the digestive problems that Liz had been having prompted Dr. Pasmantier to schedule an upper GI series the previous day to verify whether or not there might be a blockage problem in her upper digestive tract. I wonder now, as I have often wondered, just what I should have done when I knew the test had been scheduled. Here was a patient being treated as just any other patient, despite the fact Liz now weighed under one hundred pounds and found cold insupportable. If you've ever gone through one of those admittedly benign tests, you know what it's like to undergo hours of being shuttled from a freezing room, where the injected barium is being x-rayed as it makes its step-by-step way to the small intestine. Then you are wrenched back to a tiny cubbyhole, wrapped in a sheet, awaiting your next assault. She was in agony. There won't be a next time, but we could have been better prepared. The real consequential payoff came later at home. Liz, fatigued and disoriented, slipped on our user-hostile floor and crashed on her hip. "Damn it. Damn it, damn it," she said. I rolled her over carefully, felt about her hip and upper thigh. There were no breaks. She finally was able to sit, I called the lobby for a wheelchair and off we went to the indispensable Falk Surgical Supplies Shop on 72nd Street and Second Avenue. Within an hour, we had her own crutches and by the time the day had ended she was able to hobble, teeth-gritted, on one crutch.

The results of the test were negative. The notion to perform the test was the right thing to do. The one-size-fits-all treatment of the patient, however, was and is wrong.

Crutch, Liz and I were at 407 East 70th Street the following morning. It was Carboplatin day, no Gemzar. We had a new CA125 reading, 268. Encouraging. She seemed to be tolerating the new treatment fairly well. I was on the lift-off pad again. I'm not sure, even now, whether I had become so fixated with the notion that Liz was going to become well that any day of normalness or what now had become normalness to me was an indisputable sign of better times ahead. Or was I deluding myself? It didn't matter then, because the objective was to stay in the game, to be convinced that if we worked determinedly, we would contain the disease.

Liz saw Dr. Zackson, the endocrinologist, on the 22nd. His job was to evaluate the secretions and distribution of the fluids emanating from the endocrine gland. She was hoping he would have a moment to chat with me, not about our Liz case, but about "things." According to Liz, there was little that he did not find fascinating and thus we were brothers under the skin. Brothers or not, I never did get to meet him. That day, I sat at the very end of a lengthy hallway waiting for Liz to emerge from his office. I see that grey, cold passageway, a side door here, a side door there, all on the interior wall. There were no ornate signs, no marquee announcements of "Important Doctor Within." Each door could have opened on a broom closet, a lavatory or whatever handy rooms are needed on a hospital floor. Thirty minutes later, the door through which Liz had passed opened. She ambled out on her crutch, turned her head and beamed a "Thank you, Dr. Zackson," and so I never met him.

Dr. Zackson is a man so highly regarded in his field that his time for amenities is limited. The important thing to me was that he was pleased with Liz's condition—pleased, of course, as it related to his specialty.

She saw Dr. Magid the same day.

I spoke with him this past September, so Dr. Magid's comments must be absorbed, by me at least, retrospectively. This is what he observed: "She was very frail, obviously losing, but still exercising. Despite everything, she was still in the game."

The next day was Thanksgiving and we celebrated, really celebrated, with Neil and Karen at Daniel, the restaurant that had provided the backdrop for Liz's seventy-fifth birthday. It was a happy evening. Liz refused to waste time in self-mourning. Each day was precious.

We stayed in town for the weekend and enjoyed two evening dinners out, just the two of us. The month was to end with another treatment that Monday, the 27th. And so it did. We were at Dr. Pasmantier's office at two o'clock in the afternoon and all apparently went well. So far, the canceling of Gemzar seemed to be working.

The last week of November went by smoothly. We looked forward to a Fire Island weekend, packed and drove out Friday morning. It was the beginning of December, the year 2006 was waning, we were in the game and Liz was where she loved to be.

• • •

Our Fire Island house had been designed by our dear friend Tom Moore, he of the Anthony Eden moustache. He was often used by Ralph Lauren as a model when Lauren wanted someone who was the very image of a British statesman casting his glance over the vast British Empire.

The house sits about fifteen feet beyond the southern dunes, facing the ocean. Tom was imaginative, courageous and totally blind in one eye and astigmatic in the other. Thus, he never received the validation of the American Institute of Architects. He was born in Jerome, Arizona. He never revealed how he got to New York or became an interior as well as exterior designer. His wife was a fashion magazine editor and their eldest son was about the same age as Alex. I had called Tom courageous because, blind as he nearly was, his great pleasure was walking to the end of a beam, perhaps fifteen feet above floor level, with his eyes sweeping the field of vision so that he could orient the structure in a way that would bring his client a maximum of visual pleasures. He gave us all a maximum of visual shudders. Tom never fell. The lay of the land around our house required multiple levels. And that's what finally made our beautiful beach house impossible for Liz to negotiate.

Friday and Saturday, December 1 and 2, passed quietly. But Sunday evening, December 3, was as painful an evening as Liz had thus far endured. The evening's vomiting and headaches and cramps and diarrhea were thoroughly chemical treatment related. Liz refused to use the bathroom next to my bed, but dragged herself from her bed to the four steps leading to the main floor level and the four additional steps leading to the downstairs bathroom. That's where I found her, on her knees, her head over the basin. And that's where we spent the evening, I on a mat outside the bathroom door, about ten feet from Liz, she on her knees at times, on the bowl at other times, until sheer fatigue put a temporary end to her vomiting.

We left the beach early Monday morning and went directly to New York-Presbyterian Hospital, where she sat in her wheelchair in the admitting room for three pain-drenched hours before she was officially admitted.

Once in the room, the process began: hydration, then a wait for four units of blood. It was no surprise that she was anemic, exhausted and dehydrated. In retrospect, I imagine I should feel more gratitude than irritation at the length of time each process took. The wait for matching blood took many hours. It was toward evening when the blood arrived and the slow process of absorption began. We were in room 812, a room to avoid. The room was depressingly dark. It was at the end of a long hall and the nursing crew was understaffed. Liz's mood, as mine, was dark with frustration. She was in this room until Thursday, the 7th. She had suffered a partial bowel obstruction, which Mark later assured her would come and go. Dr. Hartman became involved when her blood culture showed the presence of *E. coli*.

This, according to Barry, was not unusual. Thus, Levaquin, the antibiotic used to snuff out the bacteria, was on the menu for fourteen days. When Liz later ended up in the hospital on May 15, Barry suspected a recurrence of an *E. coli* infection. He was right, of course, but he was no longer dealing with a routine, to-be-expected infection.

· · ·

Longevity, not necessarily merit, qualifies one for attendance at festive reunions. Liz Claiborne Inc. had arranged a farewell dinner honoring Paul Charron, retiring CEO and chairman of the company. All former board members, willing and able to attend, were invited. We were among those still mobile and reasonably available. Nothing could have been more fitting than to have invited us as the original board members. The dinner was scheduled for Wednesday, December 13, with early drinks and dinner at the Italian Wine Merchants on East 16th Street in Manhattan. This is not a restaurant, but a tasting emporium, chic and private. The "tasters" are arranged at an interminably long, thin table, very "Last Supper-ish," with Paul Charron at center and the others branching out. I was seated at Paul's right hand and Liz was at his left. The number of former and current board members invited was about forty.

I watched Liz dress for the evening as though I was watching the assembling of an art object. She wore a short black jacket over black pants and a frilly, ruffled, white georgette blouse to give her face more dimension. She applied color carefully, and gave her makeup the attention any valuable work of art merits. She fitted her wig carefully. By now, it had become an unattached extension of herself. I, as always, was stunned by her beauty, her carriage and her ready smile.

We arrived at the dinner, perhaps just late enough to be the last arrivals. Everyone stood and applauded. I could see our old friend, Leonard Boxer, long out of sight and mind, visibly weeping.

"A toast to the queen," someone shouted, "yes, a toast to the queen." Liz smiled and nodded, embraced Leonard, then Paul, who also had begun to shed tears, and took her seat. My presence was warmly acknowledged, and I did what I could to appear to be genuinely affected by this enthusiastic show of admiration for Liz. In a sense it was genuine. One could not but admire and love, if that's the word, this walking symbol, she who had made all of this come to pass. I could not but reflect on the history of events that had brought these people to this table. They had been the self-important spawn of the founder and, as is generally the case, believed that all of the wealth thrown off by the company had been their doing. Perhaps now they understood that it was essentially Liz's artistry and integrity that had made these seats possible.

We had received the invitation a few months back. It was sent from the office of Bernard Aronson, a man we did not know, who is a managing partner in a Washington, DC–based investment company. A warm, personal handwritten note accompanied the invitation. We accepted.

Mr. Aronson sat across the table from Liz. I had asked him earlier that evening to take notes of what Liz would say when asked to speak. I knew her voice could barely carry through the room.

When her turn came to speak, she spoke so softly that I barely heard her. This is what he told me: "Her words were full of generosity. She was appreciative of having been invited to so important an event. She was proud of the company and her part in it. It was a very short speech. She was obviously frail and worn."

The following day, December 14, we saw Dr. Pasmantier. Liz was given chemotherapy. Her CA125 was 425. We went out to Fire Island for the weekend. We relied on the blood transfusion to carry her through. It did. The days that followed were manageable. On the 18th, she was active and optimistic, looking forward to the arrival of Alex, Christina and the baby and our family sojourn to St. Barts. They were scheduled to leave with us the morning of December 22.

The week of the 18th unfolded as did many post-treatment weeks, as a slow, downhill process. By the 19th, exhaustion was in the saddle. The rest of the month was a physical struggle to participate in spite of her fatigue. Fatigue or not, we left the morning of the 22nd, Alex and family having arrived. They planned to be with us in St. Barts for three weeks. Liz was pleased. I was apprehensive. Three weeks in Liz's life, at this point, seemed like a very long time.

Our Christmas 2006 dinner was at Maya's. We had a full table. Liz was her brave self. She ordered a modest dinner and did the best she could to cope with it. She was somewhat disoriented by the presence of so many of my sister's group. There was my brother-in-law at the other end of the table; Alex and Christina and Elias in his stroller; Jennifer, Gloria's daughter, and her athletic and handsome Greek husband, Fotis; his mother, who served as babysitter for their twin boys; Gloria, Liz and me. I wore green and drank scotch whisky.

Liz and I left early. She was folding. It was our last Christmas in St. Barts, our last Christmas as Liz and Art anywhere.

We ended the year in sunshine. The weather was remarkably clear. Liz lay in the sun. Alex would carry Elias up the fifty-some-odd steps from the guest house to the residence for a viewing. Unhappily, during one of these viewings, Liz jumped up from her mat and tripped. Once more her wrapping and bandaging skills were required and so she wrapped and bandaged. I managed to trip also while coming to her assistance, so she wrapped and bandaged me as well. Neither of us was very much in control. I was frustrated by the demands that Alex and his family were making on her limited energy. But this was her choice, not mine, and I went along with it. At any rate, bandaged and weary, we celebrated New Year's Eve at Le Toiny, a lovely restaurant at the east end of the island.

That Sunday, there were the seven of us—Liz and Art, Alex and Christina and Elias, and Neil and Karen, newly returned from their honeymoon trip. We all, including me, bandaged and reconciled to the way things were, had a happy evening. As Steve Magid had said, "She was still in the game."

It wasn't until this past year, November 28, 2007, precisely, that I found the courage to come back to St. Barts. I brought my files, a suitcase filled with photographs, documents, newspaper clippings—all the material I had been sorting through and collating since I started this narrative. I had a restrained Thanksgiving dinner with Neil and Karen. We all reflected on how much richer our lives had been for having been part of the Liz story.

Liz's desk sits across the room from mine. I hadn't been aware of what she had been writing and had left on her desktop before we returned to New York. That was February 11. She never came back to St. Barts. But the note I did find brought once more to mind how hopeful we had been that she would get better. There, faintly written in pencil, probably in early February of 2007:

> *Close familly* [her famous double l as in *famille*]
> *Good friends*
> *Good food*
> *&*
> *Our 50th Anniversary!*
> *Come help us celebrate*
>
> *A small gathering, family, friends and good food to celebrate our 50th?*
> *It's half a century?*

I imagine the question marks indicated that she wasn't quite sure that she would frame the invitation precisely that way. But I do know we spoke about that evening ahead, July 5, fifty years since we had sipped warm beer on the veranda of Bay St. Louis's one old, Southern movie-set hotel.

I have never waltzed, but I was going to take lessons. We actually planned to dance, to have Liz up and about and the two of us, as always, Liz and Art together, embracing.

CHAPTER ELEVEN, 2007

THE FIRST WEEK of January was a continuation of the family gathering in St. Barts, with dinner at Maya's every evening and I doing my best, unsuccessfully I discovered, to be amiable and accepting. We all returned to New York on the 10th. Alex, Christina and Elias departed for Los Angeles.

The next number of days were demanding. Liz and I, Jonah Western, Bill Conway and our staff met on January 11 at the foundation office to discuss the possibility of developing and producing an elephant film, a notion I had that suddenly had become obsessive. We met with a producer and writer who Jonah felt might create an important film. I felt it necessary and proper to dedicate a brilliant elephant film to Liz, despite the library of documentaries that already existed. I imagine it was the explosive success of the *March of the Penguins* that convinced me that an elephant story, sustained, specific and brilliantly filmed would be a fitting and enduring piece of work. It would be a Liz Claiborne film. Liz was interested, of course, but skeptical as to what we, novices in moviemaking and deal-making, could bring to the effort other than money. We did not proceed. Even had we all been enthusiastic, events in the Liz narrative were moving too swiftly to control. The two of us were anxious, and I was more edgy than ever.

Liz had e-mailed Kim on January 14, ostensibly to thank her for gifts received from Kim and Christophe, but went on to discuss the family visit:

We had a wonderful time with Alex, Christina and Elias! But I don't think Art enjoyed it as much as I did. He's so worried about me getting tired out. Elias has grown into a handsome boy and it was nice getting to know him...I think even Art thinks he's a handsome child, but you know Art and children. Elias is now seven months old and in Los Angeles. We had a wonderful family dinner with Neil and Karen (just back from their honeymoon trip) and the Schultz family. A very nice evening! Thank you again for your over generous Xmas gifts, when we did not do anything! Sorry I just was not up to much with the hospital stays. I'm afraid nobody got nothing. Much, much love, Kim and to the family also. Liz."

We saw Dr. Pasmantier on the 16th and the Carboplatin mix was infused. We left the following morning for St. Barts.

Bumpy days and evenings followed. Maya gently recommended this or that digestible food such as almond milk or certain soups. Liz was finding life more and more uncomfortable. At dinner, she often sat quietly, gazing about the restaurant, interested in the groups at other tables, diverting her thoughts from food to the drama of other lives. She was watching for the fun of it. I became impatient. I attempted to amuse her, keep her focused on our interaction. I had quietly gone out of control. I often waved for the check, impatient with myself, inwardly seething that I could do nothing to stop the obvious downhill slide poor Liz was enduring. And then we would leave, she often relieved to have made her way through dinner, sparse as it was. She walked with me to our car and she reached for my hand.

The month of January stumbled on with some good days, some not-so-good days and much time in the sun. Liz no longer had the strength to make the journey to our gymnasium, so she swam in our lap pool and I watched anxiously. She paced herself well. Her form was superb, controlled and graceful. We sat on our lounge chairs in the sun, Liz rereading Márquez and when finished, if a person is ever finished reading *One Hundred Years of Solitude*, she went on to Barbara Tuchman's *The Guns of August*. She had become fascinated by the interwar years and the self-destructiveness of human behavior. Life is so precious, she felt, that it was completely insane that human beings would slaughter one another.

We spoke of her experiences during World War II. Human beings and the predicaments of human life, so tribal in nature, were beyond redemption, she felt. Elephants! Now that's admirable behavior. We spoke about Elias and what his world would be like. We spoke as though we ourselves were free of constraints, free of personal anxieties.

On January 27, Liz sent her last e-mail to Kim:

"Well it certainly is more than a day! But that's what happens sometimes. I have had some tough days and days where I just don't feel like doing anything. But I think I'm over the wall and coming down the other side. [I have no idea what Liz meant by that. It might have been an admission that she had climbed as high as she could, and now—the come down.] *We had a wonderful Xmas with Alex and Christina and Elias here in St. Barts and a few days in NY. Everyone thinks he is adorable...I also think your idea about coaching American couples in French and French culture thru cooking lessons and then lunch or dinner is a great idea! Go, Kim, go! All love to you three...Liz."*

Now, alone in St. Barts, our anxiety about her last CA125 number, the result of the test taken on January 16, intensified. Dr. Pasmantier's office had not called, and that, we felt, was an indication that the result was poor. The lapsed time between test and result should be no more than three or four days and here we were, still waiting as January came to an end. Liz's next scheduled chemo treatment was February 13. Did Dr. Pasmantier plan to say nothing to us until then? I urged Liz to call, but she had read so much darkness into Pasmantier's silence that she couldn't bring herself to pick up the phone. Should I call? I asked myself. No, of course not. Liz is the afflicted. So we waited, and then on February 7 she called. Her CA125 was 1,250.

We flew back to New York on the 11th, had dinner with friends that night and the next. Liz had a PET scan on the 12th.

We saw Dr. Pasmantier on the 13th as scheduled. "Yes," he told us. "Carboplatin alone was not doing the job." It had worked marginally well for a short period, but it was now indicated that Gemzar reenter the game. The treatment that day was the full blast: Carboplatin plus Gemzar. The next treatment was scheduled for the 20th, one week later.

Chemotherapy 10—Carboplatin & Gemzar, weekly 2/13/07 to 5/15/07

There were no plans for a St. Barts return. The new handrail over the pool and the new grab bars in the shower room would now join the Triple 8 road, all accommodations to Liz's waning strength. We would have to endure the week and be ready for more. We remained determined to do what was needed to stay in the game, to stay alive as long as life was bearable.

There was no treatment on the 20th; Liz was back in New York Hospital again after a siege of vomiting, cramps, dehydration.

The former treatments, hydration, rest and "x" units of blood were no longer sufficient. Her body demanded nutrition. She was incapable of supplying that nutrition through normal ingestion. Dr. Pasmantier made it clear that without supplementary nutrition, there was no chance of staying alive and keeping the cancer in check. All former strategies had been played out. Liz's discipline, tenacity and will had bought the two of us a number of years in excess of the norm. Any attempt to check the cancer would be bought, if at all, at a terrible price.

The last evening in the hospital, Saturday, February 24, Liz was introduced to TPN, total parenteral nutrition. This is defined, according to Wikipedia, as "the practice of feeding a person intravenously, by bypassing the usual process of eating and digestion. The person receives nutritional formulas containing salts, glucose, amino acids, lipids and added vitamins."

In Liz's case the TPN, delivered in a pad, heating-pad sized, is hung on a rack and, through gravity and an infusion pump, is delivered to her port and from there into her body.

New York-Presbyterian Hospital affords the advantage of a wide array of medical capabilities, in this case, a physician whose specialty is weight gain. He was on call that day and night, visited Liz, noted that her saline numbers were "a bit low" and prescribed an infusion of saline solution prior to the TPN. He told us he would in all probability be unavailable that weekend as he "was moving."

Liz was now completely in the hands of others. Dr. Pasmantier had approved the TPN. I was wrapped up in the job of getting nurses assigned to our home. Blood tests were to be taken at Dr. Pasmantier's office. Jamie Hellman would be responsible for checking the nutrient levels needed.

We had moved to another level, that of life maintenance and perhaps, with some good fortune, a resumption of the chemotherapy and a standoff with the disease. How reasonable was such a hope? Again the question must be asked, at what cost to the patient? And for how long?

Elaine Spenser of Maxim Healthcare Services, our lead nurse and administrator, was over-programmed. She was dedicated and responsible but had too few nurses who were top notch at TPN infusion. She did what she could to fill a demanding schedule: Liz's treatment called for about ten hours of TPN infusion. Ideally, the infusion would begin at about seven or eight o'clock in the evening and end close to twelve hours later. We slept side by side as always, watched a movie prior to the onslaught of the TPN, sometimes during, and then, in due course, attempted sleep. The nurse of the evening, stationed either in our living room or the extra bedroom down the hall, would come in from time to time to check the flow or check Liz. When Liz needed use of the bathroom, she would often call for help and the nurse would walk with her and then bring her back to bed.

February 2007 was drawing to an end. Liz was home, and the saline solution was still being applied, not because it had been prescribed, but because it had not been canceled. The physician who had to move the weekend that Liz came home promptly went on to other matters.

I stopped the saline solution myself. I canceled it myself. She was being bloated for no damn good medical reason, but because of the system. Dr. Pasmantier and other oncologists in his position have no way of checking every detail that involves their patients' hour-by-hour care. They should.

I add this as a warning to others: be damned sure you or someone who loves the patient is monitoring the care being given.

Last September, I asked Mark about the TPN period and why he had prescribed it. Liz was a badly worn and torn mechanism. Was there really any reason to hope that the intravenous infusion would spread evenly throughout her system? I was mindful of what Dr. Buchman had earlier said: Would a patient go along if he or she knew the cost in suffering of this or that treatment? In Liz's case, the answer was yes, but she would require the option of control. I was also mindful of Liz's insistence that her "living will" be updated and safely positioned at any hospital that might house her in her last days. She was not deluded.

Mark replied, "Do you think I would have put her through the TPN if I thought the game was over? I have become humble about outcomes."

A month or so later, I spoke with Dr. Melanie Gillar. She had been strongly recommended as a physical therapist to visit Liz twice a week during the infusion and post-infusion period.

"Liz," she said, "was fairly optimistic at times that she would get better. But as the infusions continued and she became bloated, I could see that she felt that she was in the endgame. Why do we go all out with patients? My family and I had faced the same dilemma with my father. He was very obviously dying. But we left no stone unturned to keep him alive. You just don't give up. You go all the way."

I'm not convinced that this forced stretching out of someone else's life is morally defensible.

• • •

March 2007, the month that ended with Liz's seventy-eighth birthday, was a month during which Liz suffered much as a result of the prescribed TPN treatment. It was a month of ongoing pressure from Dr. Pasmantier to continue the infusions, of a number of observations and comments from others, Gwen and Dr. Gillar, for two, and for me, a month of piercing anxiety. It's hard to disentangle the sequence of events, but what follows is what actually happened and was described as such by others. I'm afraid this approach may create a jumbled view of the precise timing of each described activity, but I see no alternative.

The infusion treatment, despite the fact that it provided the nourishment necessary to absorb the weekly treatment, was a treatment that Liz dreaded. The fluids did not disperse evenly through her body. They found sacs in which to accumulate. They bloated her legs to the point that walking without assistance was difficult. She managed at the outset, but the weekly chemotherapy treatment became more and more of a devastating crippler.

Gwen Satterfield came to the apartment every day.

These are her recollections:

"In March, during the infusion period, Liz was able to get around and also fixed what she wanted to eat. At that time, her appetite was not great, but in the morning she would eat cream of wheat or apple sauce, a little bit of yogurt, a few pieces of cracker and tea. For lunch, she would have one-third cup of chicken broth, or some of Kamini's [our general cleaning woman] homemade soup. Through the day she might have a small piece of banana and tea. She liked her tea real hot. She was able to walk by herself, slowly, and dress herself and attend to herself in the bathroom. I always found

her with a book in hand, reading, or right by her side. She would call people and thank them for flowers, as she would often get them from family and friends and from us at the office on her birthday. She spoke to all six of us to thank us for the flower plant.

"The physical therapist, Melanie Gillar, had begun coming to treat Liz. Liz told me she liked that. I noticed a few times I was there they would spend time moving her legs and arms and getting her to walk around.

"Most of the time when I came, she was always sitting up at the dining room table or in the large black chair, always greeting me with such a smile. You were always with her, but she wanted to do as much for herself as she could, so she discouraged you from doing too much. I will never forget the morning of March 21. She asked me to pick up two salads from Grace's early in the morning for Alex, Christina and Elias. Neil and Karen were coming at 1 PM that day and she wanted to be sure they had something to eat. I smiled. I bought the salads early that morning and I heard they had a great time and no one had expected Liz to prepare for them, but that was so much like her, wanting everything perfect. That day did tire her out, but she told me she had been up all afternoon holding her grandson and that pictures were taken. She seemed very happy. It was in that last week in March that she seemed to me very tired and weak. Her feet and legs had swollen so from the infusion so she found it hard to walk and rise up. I noticed after that she began to use the red chair that she told me Melanie had suggested she use to get around. [We have a number of small, red leather barrel chairs on wheels—these are our dining table chairs. Liz used one for transportation.] *And it even became hard for her to put on her shoes, as with the swollen feet, her shoes and sneakers became too tight."*

March had become the month of severe decline. Gwen makes it clear how much we all concentrated on helping Liz to put food into her system. We were fighting an unwinnable battle. Liz had managed an active day with family on March 21, but that was the day following treatment; day one was usually the easiest on her system. From there on in she became more bloated, exhausted and continually uncomfortable.

Here's Gwen again on the beginning of April:

"The first week in April, the infusion stopped. Her swelling went down some and the 'leaking' stopped. [Fluid that had not been fully absorbed had been 'slowly leaking' through her skin. She required constant drying.] *By now it was even hard for her to put on her socks or get dressed, but she always tried very hard. Walking was*

very slow and most of the time she would use the red chair, as with the chemo, so often she seemed so tired and wanted to sleep."

Liz then made it clear to Dr. Pasmantier that if she died sooner because she discontinued the infusions, then that was a risk she much preferred to continuing the TPN.

She had been scheduled for chemotherapy on April 3. She was in no condition for treatment and Mark sent her to the hospital instead. She was anemic and she was thoroughly dehydrated. The loss of fluids through diarrhea and seepage through her skin had flattened her. After two days in the hospital she went directly to Dr. Pasmantier's office for a chemotherapy treatment.

The mere act of getting to the treatment room took precise planning and effort. I would wheel Liz in a wheelchair to a waiting car; we would drive to 407 East 70th, wheel Liz to the elevator and then up to Dr. Pasmantier's office, where the chemotherapy was applied. The first treatment had been on March 5. Liz had to be wheeled back for the Neupogen booster. March was the month that unraveled Liz for good. Her determination to fight back through the infusion of TPN had turned into a detestation of the infusion process. This nightmare had to be stopped. Stopped it was. Liz refused further TPN treatment. The infusions were abandoned at the beginning of April.

There was no alternative. Mark's TPN-assisted race against the disease was lost.

In retrospect, I am enraged that I permitted the once-a-week treatment, that I had not responded more forcefully to Liz's detestation of the infusions. Mark had been a convincing advocate of the treatment. I remember receiving a call in early March from Mark while I was at our office. "Hi," he said, obviously very pleased, "1,179." A few weeks later, Liz's CA125 was 1,099, then 933. Mark's hope was that once Liz's CA125 was below 500 she might be able to carry on without the TPN. He was using whatever ammunition he thought might keep Liz alive.

Other complications arose. A blood clot was discovered on March 27. Liz's left leg was now even more swollen and tender. So, added to her other evening preparations prior to sleeping, she had to self-inject a product called Lovenox. A trio of new pills was added to her daily barrage. They were to be taken according to a complicated sequence throughout the day. She still had the osteonecrosis to contend with and that required a lengthy flossing and brushing of the area afflicted. Her disciplined application of these procedures, every night, was, to me, awe-inspiring.

Throughout all this, diminishing controls of her body's functions were constant happenings. Her calmness under these humiliating pressures was again awe-inspiring. She was not humiliated. This was the only road back. She knew that she could count on me to do whatever was necessary. More important, I would do everything I could to do whatever she wanted done.

March had brought some pleasures. Alex, Christina and Elias arrived in New York on the 20th and were able to visit for two days. They were now on their way back to Germany. We unfurled a large white blanket to create a playpen area on the floor. We all watched Elias crawl about. There was little screaming. Liz held him from time to time, and quite possibly felt compensated for the wretchedness of the month. I think these days were among the few that month that brought Liz pure pleasure.

March itself, with the pressure to be ready for chemotherapy virtually every week and the Neupogen injections, was otherwise all nightmarish. Liz's body was becoming less and less resistant to infection. Neupogen and nourishment were the only tools we had to ward off infection. They proved inadequate.

I reflect on Jamie Hellman's comments about rushing to her office during a Liz treatment so she could release her own anguished feelings. We all knew that we were engaging in a danse macabre, but also that something paradoxical was happening. Liz was determined, one way or another, to live as long as she could because I, more than she, could not accept that she was dying. I was not alone. Mark and I had become co-conspirators in keeping Liz alive. Liz was showing all of us the reach of the determined human spirit.

Her seventy-eighth birthday was celebrated in the apartment. Neil and Karen came by at about 5:30 and we spent a happy afternoon together. They had brought, as her birthday gift, a lovely orchid resting in a Liz Red vase. She loved it. The preceding days had been uniformly uncomfortable. Liz had continued seeing Melanie twice a week, basically to keep her legs moving and massaged. But her growing discouragement was evident to us all.

The TPN nurses were gone. Soon the weeping stopped. Her legs were beginning to lose their bulkiness.

The weekly confrontation with the chemotherapy had already devital-ized her. Now it became even worse. Nevertheless she had prepared herself to fight back. She was going all out to try to put enough nourishment into her body to be able to absorb the chemical barrage. She had purchased a calorie counter booklet. The goal was 1,200 calories per day. She would try to climb that mountain by drinking milkshakes laced with cream of wheat, yogurt, grits, whatever she felt she could digest. We all worked at cooking and feeding her: Gwen, Kamini, a new cleaning hire, me and, at the outset, Liz herself.

At the beginning of April, Liz would appear in the kitchen, walking very slowly, to do her own cooking, usually of her version of cream of wheat. Some mornings, she would hold a small teaching class in the art of milk-shake making. But as the month went by, she ceased walking, used the red chair to propel herself and, completely knocked out, later slept a good part of the day.

She was due for her next chemotherapy on May 1. Instead she spent a good part of the day being hydrated. It was now clear that Liz needed around-the-clock nursing. We could no longer feed her without additional help. She was becoming increasingly fatigued. I called Elaine Spenser at Maxim Healthcare Services to arrange a new schedule—two twelve-hour shifts, every day, as long as needed. Liz agreed. She would cling to life by whatever means necessary. Not TPN, but by wheelchair or crawling, she would try to be ready for the next chemotherapy.

• • •

Dana Buchman and Ellen Daniel came to visit on May 2. It was a lovely day in New York. Liz was emotionally overwhelmed by their visit.

I was in the room, off to the side, where I sat throughout. Liz had asked me to detain Ellen and Dana in the outside hall until she was fully ready. I did so. I would be going to dinner after Gwen arrived to relieve me. She was due shortly.

Liz loved Dana. She trusted Dana. And Ellen had been our buyer at Saks at the time we went into business. I asked them to write down their expe-riences and feelings visiting Liz that afternoon.

Here are Dana's words:

"A beautiful sunny afternoon in May…When we got upstairs, we waited in the hall while Liz finished getting ready for us and got back in her lounge chair facing the park. She was in the room to the left [our living/dining area] *facing the big windows with the daylight and the plants and the trees. She had a throw over her legs.*

"I knew Liz had been having a hard time the preceding weeks so I had prepared myself not to show shock at her appearance. Good thing. Though I didn't show it, I was shocked to see her weak and unable to move her body easily. I had never seen Liz in a semi-reclining position except one time at Fire Island, twenty-three years before, when she was sunbathing on the beach during Designer Weekend. She looked thin and frail.

"But her skin was still beautiful and her big eyes as magnificent as ever—like soft brown pools. She greeted us with her warm, electric smile. It was still Liz. After we started talking, I forgot that she looked sick.

"There was an enormous bouquet of yellow flowers on a table in front of her. A side table right next to her held a book. Ellen and I took turns talking with Liz. I pulled a chair right up next to her and she took my hand and I held hers—also something we had never done."

Dana's account continued:

"How are you, Liz?" I asked.
"I'm OK," she said, a bit rueful, resigned.
"Are you able to sleep?"
"Pretty well."
"Can you read?"
"Not for very long at a time."
"Can you watch TV?"
"Oh, yes. (Her voice lifted.) Art and I rented a movie and watched it together."
"This is a beautiful room to sit in."
"Yes, it is. It gives me so much pleasure to look out."
Then Liz paused, and said, "I read your book. I just finished it last week." [Dana's eldest daughter, Charlotte, had been found to be "a slow learner." Dana's book described the devotion of her and her husband, Tom, in helping Charlotte to adjust and to find in herself her own value as a bright, intelligent, attractive young person.]

"*Oh, Liz, that means so much to me.*"

"*Dana, I had no idea you were going through all that.*"

"*Liz, there was no way for you to know—I didn't tell anyone.*"

"*She held my gaze and looked at me with such love and sympathy,*" Dana went on. "*Here she is feeling for me and some tough moments I had been through years ago when she was in the endgame of her long battle with cancer. That was Liz. Not a split second of self-pity or raging at her condition. Sadness and frustration, yes, but no whining. None. Amazing.*"

Here is what Dana had said to me prior to her visit:

"*Whenever I saw Liz, throughout the whole nine years that she knew she had cancer, usually at dinners with Art and Tom at Daniel or Le Bernardin, she was gracious and turned outward. Each time I saw her, if asked, she would give an update of her condition and her treatment. But she didn't go over the details and never, never speculated on her prognosis. She stayed in the present—savoring the delicious food, enjoying speaking French with her fans at Le Bernardin, asking about my family and the girls, commenting on current fashion. Her joy in life, her pleasure in living, was incredible, even when she had finished a horrendous round of chemo and knew she'd be heading into another. She always focused on the evening at hand.*"

Dana continued, describing the visit in early May:

"*Ellen and I both talked to her. She said she had bruises and lifted the throw to show us marks on her thighs, legs and hands. It was only when she lifted the throw that I realized that even in this condition, Liz was dressed with spirit and verve. Underneath the throw, which made her look like an invalid, Liz was wearing cuffed olive cargo shorts. She also had on a deep coral cable sweater. And a sporty, big-faced watch (looking even bigger on her shrunken wrist) with a bright colored band that I think Art had given to her. So stylish, even in sickness.*

"*We stayed maybe fifteen minutes total, twenty minutes at the most. When we left, Art went down with us and gave us a lift—we dropped Ellen at her apartment, then I dropped Art at Le Bernardin. He generously and thoughtfully had the car take me downtown, as he had done for so many years.*"

This narrative will take Liz and me inexorably to room 252 at New York-Presbyterian Hospital. I've already brought us all there, told the contrast liquid and Dr. Angie Eng episode, and now was Dana's last visit. It was Wednesday, June 20, six days before Liz died:

"The last time I saw Liz was at the hospital. She was much more frail, a shadow almost, with a baseball hat that was too big and kept tilting over her eye. I sat on the bed and took her hand. She looked at me and I looked at her without saying anything for a long minute. I was thinking how long I had known her, how many things we had done and experienced together, how much I had learned from her, how much I loved her. Of course, I can't know what she was thinking, but I think it was something like that too. I'll never forget her wide eyes that day, as if she were taking everything in.

"That's when she said in her slow, resonant voice, 'Oh Day-na. We had a lot of fun, didn't we?'"

• • •

We had fun of course. Success is great fun. We enjoyed success, recognition, respect and warm relationships with suppliers, customers and our own staff. All of that was great fun. Nancy Valentine had told me, "You were fair. You were always fair and said, 'If you treat people right the bottom line will take care of itself.' Liz's great talent and your fairness was what did it."

Ellen Daniel, who visited that afternoon with Dana, had been the single person most responsible for getting the fledgling company aloft. That was way back in 1976 when Ellen was a buyer at Saks Fifth Avenue. She came to work for Liz in 1983 as a fashion consultant, shopper and overall keen-eye. When we went public, Liz and I made sure that Ellen received Share Number One. She still has it.

I've asked Ellen, as well, to describe that visit on May 2. Here are her notes:

"Once we entered the apartment, Liz was in the dining room area on a chaise lounge or a reclining chair. The leg rest was up and she was smiling and dressed in an orange cabled cashmere sweater. I think from Ralph Lauren. I think she had on a khaki baseball cap and was sporting a large watch with a lime green strap! She looked as colorful and chic as usual.

"She was covered with a white mohair throw from her waist and covering her feet. She seemed happy to see us, and I could notice her special bond with Dana. She told us briefly how uncomfortable she was with her bloated stomach, when she never had one before…She asked Dana how she was doing and they chatted for a few minutes about Dana's activities.

"Liz was very interested in Dana and told her how proud she was of her accomplishments! Dana said that she could not have done any of it without the support from Liz and Art.

"She was gracious and dignified and as positive as possible under the circumstances. She appeared very sad to me to be in this condition. Life was no fun, just a series of treatments to stay alive. This could have been my perception, and sadness in seeing our beautiful and talented Liz in this condition.

"I feel very fortunate that I was able to spend a few minutes with her, as I knew I would never see her again. However, I will never forget her colorful appearance and dignified character. A very SPECIAL human being who taught me a lot about many things."

Gwen had arrived and would be attending to the sparse dinner Liz would eat. I kissed Liz and told her I'd be back early and perhaps, if she was up to it, we would watch one of our discs, perhaps Discovery Channel's *Planet Earth*. We both enjoyed the series and the discs became standard fare in room 252 a number of weeks later.

And then I left, so mentally disarranged that I never put on my shoes, but went to dinner in slippers.

As we drove downtown, Ellen on one side, Dana on the other, my mind drifted to earlier, happier times. Liz's respect for Ellen's knowledge and intuitions was enormous. I thought back to an early morning call Liz had received from Ellen, then the "contemporary" buyer at Saks Fifth Avenue. I've asked Ellen if she'd write the little story for me. Here it is:

"At the time, I had just been promoted to the contemporary buyer, out of junior dresses, where I had been buying Youth Guild. I heard via the grapevine that Liz was leaving Youth Guild to open her own sportswear company. I knew she would have a fresh approach for sportswear and the career woman. My department at the time was driven by Jones and Ellen Tracy, with many other specialty vendors.

"I remember calling Liz at home in the morning the moment I got wind of the news, and said, 'I don't know what you are doing, but we want to see it FIRST and be the store to launch it! Please tell us when we can see something and we will be right over.' I was so excited and told Max about it. He was most anxious to get involved ASAP. [Max Garelick was Ellen's merchandise manager.]

"The first ad appeared in the Sunday Times, 25th of July, 1976."

I am recounting events of a time long gone, a time when retail store business behavior was more human and trusting than now is the case. Max Garelick, a slight, yet somewhat rotund man, who seemed to smile twenty-four hours a day, offered what I imagine now would be unthinkable. He offered to prepay the shipment. I chose not to take him up on the offer.

On Saturday evening, July 24, 1976, Liz and I hailed a cab and stopped

Liz's working sketch of the jacket for the first ad.

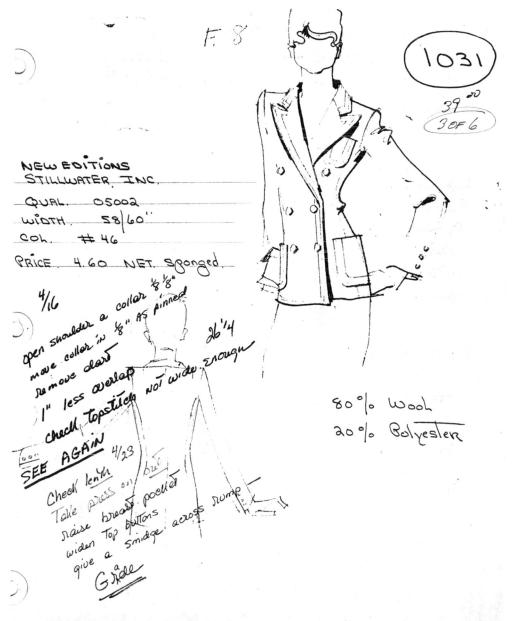

on the southwest corner of Seventh Avenue at 42nd Street. The first delivery of Sunday's *New York Times* was now on the newsstand. I bought a copy. We sat in the cab, found the ad and Liz and I sat hand in hand, dazed, too moved to speak. I was so utterly proud of Liz. The ad was of a flannel suit. Rather than the traditional grey, the color was a soft ecru that we had developed. The jacket was not single-breasted, but a jaunty double-breasted style fitted close to the body, so it would be flattering and youthful. The skirt was side-pleated and full enough to permit easy, springy walking. Double-breasted was new and risky; ecru, rather than grey, flannel was possibly even riskier. The ad was great and our risky ecru flannel suit was a smash hit.

I was remembering that rich evening, so many years ago, as I walked into the restaurant, unaware that I was still in slippers, and anxious to return home. So I made sure that dinner that evening was a fast affair. I was home before eight o'clock in the evening. We were just starting full-time nursing. Elaine Spenser would take the 8:00 PM to 8:00 AM shift and, from there on in, two nurses were scheduled for every day. Liz was now losing ground more rapidly. The once-a-week chemotherapy was beginning to prove unsustainable. Yet we tried to sustain it. I was home in time for the nurse shift.

Elaine Spenser was finding it just about impossible to line up competent nurses for every day and evening. Jamie Hellman had recommended a companion who had worked for a previous, now-deceased patient. Lyudmila Lachac, a competent, caring registered nurse who had now been with us for more than a week, sat in as I interviewed Sandra Cummings. What came across was her reliability. Yes, she could work the 8:00 AM to 8:00 PM shift, every day of the week if necessary. I hired her. She was with us to the end. She was reliable, but, as it turned out, we needed a nurse, not a companion.

Sunday the 13th was Mother's Day. Liz had been treatment-free for nine days. She felt relatively fine. Neil and Karen came to visit at about five thirty in the evening, carrying a new gorgeous white orchid that was slipped into the slender Liz Red vase that they had brought her on her birthday. Liz was delighted. We talked for a short while and then Liz's energy began to wane. She had to lie down and rest.

She looked up at me and said, "It's been a lovely Mother's Day. It was so thoughtful of Neil and Karen to come by."

I had ordered in so we could spend the whole evening together. Liz had a milkshake. We watched a little TV and then we both fell off to sleep.

And then, perhaps an hour later, I heard a crashing sound and a scream. Liz had tried to go the bathroom on her own, had slipped and fallen. She hit her head against the tub and was lying on the floor, moaning. The night nurse came running in and together we slowly lifted Liz and got her back to bed. She had to be cleaned, held and calmed. The nurse did the cleaning, I did the calming. Nothing was broken. There were new bruises on her arms and legs where she had been handled. This was another bad luck incident, not decisive, but intensely demoralizing.

The month of May had seen an ongoing retreat.

Gwen had seen it this way:

"I noticed she was getting much weaker. I sat with her a few nights when Art went to dinner. Liz would be in bed but she always wanted to watch a DVD and sometimes drift off to sleep. Most of the time, she would only want a shake and a cup of hot tea. Some nights she would want a little bit of soup, but would only take a few spoons. Through all of this, when Art returned from dinner around 8:00 or 8:15 PM, he would walk in and say, 'Hi darling.' And then he would kiss her. Liz would smile and open her eyes, always happy to see him. This to me was so special to see. I loved watching two people who I had known so many years remain so very much in love."

Liz was scheduled for chemotherapy the following day. The treatment was delayed one day and rescheduled for the 15th. Sandra and I were with her. Liz was put in one of the treatment rooms and the treatment began. I went off for a short while as I usually did, to buy food either for the evening or for Liz during the day.

Jamie Hellman describes what happened next.

"Liz had gone to the bathroom a few times. She walked. This time she started feeling weak. Nancy and Sandra were in the hall too. They put Liz in the chair Dr. Pasmantier uses when in the treatment room. Nancy and Sandra wheeled her. Liz then said, 'Jamie, I feel very weak.' Then she started a seizure and her body collapsed. I yelled for Dr. Pasmantier. Her eyes rolled up and she passed out. She started sliding off the chair. We put her back into the room on the chemo table. The bruises and scrapes on her body took place when I and Dr. Pasmantier handled her. Myrna called 911. We took her blood pressure. It was extremely low. She was shaking as if in a

seizure. She was terrified. She was agitated. She asked for you. Three people from the emergency room squad came immediately, put her on a stretcher and took her away. She was never fully conscious."

Myrna had found me. I was there when the ER people came down with Liz. I got into the van and took her hand. She knew it was me and squeezed my hand. She was regaining consciousness.

In just a few minutes we had been admitted in the emergency room and a nurse wheeled her into a side room. She had a low-grade fever. Barry Hartman was at hand. A blood culture analysis later confirmed what Barry had suspected. Septicemia seemed likely. It was likely that the seizure was really septic shock. We call septicemia "blood poisoning." It is a very serious infection that gets worse quickly. Neupogen or not, Liz had succumbed to the raid on her immune system. Barry prescribed an antibiotic, which was immediately administered.

The nurse took her blood pressure, took blood for analysis, started the hydration process and arranged for a number of scans. Because she had fallen it was possible that she had a concussion. The CT scan showed negative.

I accompanied Liz to the various scan rooms. By now she was fully alert and very much in control of herself. She felt extreme cold. But she was no longer fearful.

"Feel my nose," she said. "Freezing."

"Yes, darling, freezing." Cold was a constant unavoidable condition. She had grown to hate cold. Nose-touching and agreement could be my only response.

Room 252 was generally reserved for bone marrow transplant patients. It was empty on May 15 and Liz had the good fortune of having it assigned to her. It was clear to me that she had no intention of leaving that room. What awaited her if she recovered, if she forced nutrition? Her reward would be more chemotherapy, and neither she nor I found that outcome remotely acceptable. We didn't discuss it. We knew that room 252 was to be her last port of call.

Dr. Hartman saw Liz on the 16th. When I spoke with him this past September, he was unusually verbal for a man constantly on the run who works sixteen hours each day.

"I saw her on the 16th and by then she was alert and looked pretty good. Her white count was back to normal, her vitals were OK. Maybe septic. But she was already on antibiotics. Her history indicated that we were dealing with an E. coli infection. Then her culture showed her white cell count lowering, and 'bands' appearing, which showed 'gram negative' sepsis: bacteria in the blood, or blood poisoning. Typically there are two bacteria involved. We continued the antibiotic for two weeks and that cleared it."

Barry was all for sending Liz home. She would have none of that. I would not have permitted it. He reminded me, at times, of living according to a schedule, where crossing off activities as "done" might become as significant as what was done. I know, of course, that that's unfair. Barry, like so many other excellent physicians, is always on overload. He did, however, relate to Liz on a non-patient level. "She was always with it. We all assumed we had beaten the septicemia, since much of that problem was not acute but chronic. She was frustrated as more and more little things were happening."

Liz's first days in room 252 were given over to tests and more tests. Her energy was ebbing, her appetite was poor.

I sat in a small chair at the foot of her bed and read the newspaper to her every morning or just talked about things, always about the present. When Maureen Dowd had a few acerbic things to say, Liz would agree with as much enthusiasm as her strength permitted. Other than that, she found little in the newspapers that did not further her depressed view of human activity. From reading *The Little Prince* to her during the early days of our love life to now reading Maureen Dowd to her, almost half a lifetime had passed. My obsessive focus was to get nourishment into her body. That was not Liz's focus, not in the least. Her concern was to be warm and to rest.

During the first week, she managed to get to the bathroom, do her teeth at night and, with help, get about a bit.

Liz knew that I was hell-bent on keeping her alive. I wasn't ready, perhaps never would be. And she made it clear that nothing would induce her to go home after the infection was cured. Mark had scheduled her leaving the hospital the week of May 22. She refused. I'm sure that he actually agreed with her. She should stay where she was. Liz was fast becoming a hospice patient who we were insisting was curable. We couldn't face the thought of letting her go. One delay led to another. Mark urged her to eat, to nourish herself. She began to resent his visits.

One afternoon during her third week in room 252, Liz called Kathy at Triple 8. She thanked Kathy for a card she had sent her. They talked about new plantings for the front deck of Cabin A. And then, Liz said, "I'm not going home. I'm where I need to be." She was on the edge of the board, preparing for the final plunge.

I spoke this past August with Elisa Haber, a skilled and perceptive nurse. Elisa described the consequences for Liz of lack of protein and proper nutrition. "Fluids cannot be properly distributed," she said. "Cells leak out water. The skin becomes fragile and frequent bandages are needed to prevent more lesions, to keep her thin skin from falling off and make it possible to move her. She was willing to put up with this until she knew you felt OK about her dying. She stayed alive for you. All we could do was try to make her more comfortable." Fortunately, Elisa was able to be with Liz a number of times before Liz died, most fortunately on Liz's last day.

Over the last six weeks of Liz's life, the inevitable deterioration of her body did not foreclose her love of life. Nurses streamed in and out of room 252, often to take her vital signs: blood pressure, temperature, pulse rate. Whoever happened to be in the room listened with great intensity for the results. "130 over 60," the blood pressure nurse would shout, and then we all shouted, "Hooray!" "Temperature normal!" "Hooray!"

There were the glorious days when we were able to get her into a wheelchair. Golda and Kathy, physical therapists who had become family members, would beam, as did Liz when she finally made it. There stood Liz, teeth clenched, eyes piercing the light, eyes that would not permit her to fall back to the bed. Her cap was now floating on her head. How moving and wonderful. We all shared a moment that was romantic and victorious. Liz did that to all of us.

Then I would wheel her to the patient's elevator and from there to the sunny outdoors.

Liz had visitors, always a treat. Alex came for a number of days on two different occasions: early on and then about ten days before she died. My sister Gloria visited. Neil and Karen visited. Liz, though fatigued and uncomfortable, forced herself into high gear. Lucid, interested, as cosmetically prepared as her dwindling energy permitted, she was always beautiful.

But all the while her bronchial tubes were weakening. Soon, aspiration would become a formidable problem. As I understood it, aspiration is the entry of secretions of a foreign material into the trachea and lungs. Foreign material is a fancy way of describing food particles or liquids. Since the right bronchial tube is more vertical and has a slightly wider channel than the left tube, aspirated material is more likely to end up in this branch. Eventually, that tube gives out. Pneumonia and death follow.

The last weeks of May, even into June when her eating mechanics had to be modified, she sent me on shopping sprees for food she would have liked to eat. There was the fruitless hamburger hunt: Lucu's on Second Avenue (too meaty, too huge); then Wendy's on 53rd Street and Third Avenue, quite a trip on foot. There I stood on a long line, one of many, eventually to bark my order to a counter-person who either misunderstood or worked repetitively, à la *Modern Times*.

When I returned to room 252, gasping, barely able to hand over the package, Liz opened the bag and asked, "No tomatoes?" "I'm afraid not."

Other times, she asked for egg creams, and grilled cheese and tomato sandwiches. She felt little unease when most of the ordered food sat in the now bulging refrigerator, stuffed with yogurt, applesauce, Carnation powder packs and milkshakes of various vintages. Liz was doing her best to go along, but to a point. The pressure to eat and her strategy to avoid the pressure fed only into the ongoing deterioration of her body.

Dr. Miskowitz prescribed a video esophogram (the "swallow" test), a method of visually tracking food and liquid passing through Liz's esophagus. It was administered on June 8. The report was discouraging. Swallowing food and thin liquids would more often result in the substances migrating to the lungs. And that caused the awful, to-be-avoided-at-all-costs coughing. Oh how she feared the wracking coughing. A coughing spell could last many minutes and left her limp and drained.

I became avid to force protein into her. Gwen and I researched the availability of powdered protein and found that in all of New York City, the product was carried only by Trader Joe's on 14th Street. We had had a misunderstanding. Powdered protein in usable smaller-sized containers is available throughout the city. Gwen, because Gwen sometimes prefers the heroic to the obvious, thought I wanted a giant-sized can and that's what she came up with. She appeared in room 252, hiding the super-sized bucket behind her. We tried a spoonful in Liz's morning shake. Liz tasted the shake, swung her head from side to side and became angry. I surrendered. She was right. Life-and-death determinations were strictly hers to make.

I was with her every day, generally from about nine in the morning until six o'clock in the evening, sometimes earlier when I knew Mark would be stopping in room 252 at the crack of dawn. I carried my cell phone and would check in during dinner, when a new nursing shift came on, and would call the nursing floor during the late evenings, normally from 3:00 to 6:00 AM. I rarely stayed beyond six in the evening.

I was barely in charge of myself, intent on holding my anxiety by a tight, twisted leash. Liz understood. Though disappointed, she worried about my well-being as she kissed me goodnight. She would either continue watching whichever disc was playing or make a futile attempt at reading. More often than not, we watched one of the Discovery Channel's series covering the various geological settings in which human life adapted to the imperatives of nature. We had watched the series during the TPN misadventure. Liz never tired of *Planet Earth*. She and I had been privileged to experience a great part of planet earth, from the bottom up. We watched the discs together, holding hands. She would often smile and nod.

This, we both knew, was to be our last June together. Liz had determined, as she always had determined, to make little fuss, to accept the handling and cleaning of her body, the drying of her skin, the moistened mouth swabs to replace drinking of thin fluids—to accept all as a matter of routine, without fuss.

She had found a new friend, Dr. Raymond Sherman, a kidney specialist who shared offices with Barry Hartman. There was some question about Liz's kidney functions. Dr. Sherman made Liz a stop on his daily rounds. I've met with him once. He is a supremely ordinary-looking man, mid-fifties perhaps, kindly, courteous, completely sensitive to his patient, or, at the very least, to this patient. His medical involvement in this case was minimal, but his friendly, non-aggressive interaction with his patient was of wonderful value.

When I met with him this past September, he said, "Yes, Barry had asked me to check on Liz. She was never depressed. She was always coherent. She did not behave like a dying person."

He became a fast friend. He worked with Liz at her pace. He demanded nothing of her.

• • •

The next big event Liz was to miss was the ritual Father's Day dinner. Le Bernardin may be the restaurant of choice for Liz and me, but it has little sentimental meaning for our children. Perhaps it's a reminder of our exclusiveness. We all knew that Liz was lying alone, dying now by inches. Ben Shekroon, old friend and maître d' that evening, brought a spectacular white orchid to the table. It was in a small, square ceramic dish. The affixed note read, "Happy Father's Day, darling. How I wish I could be with you. Love, Your wife, Liz."

We spoke little at that painful dinner. There was little that any of us could freely express. Only the white orchid reminded us of the love that Liz always radiated.

• • •

Something new was being added to the daily schedule. Now follows the short, sweet saga of Daisy, a puppy of Maltese-Shih Tzu mix.

We remove ourselves from room 252 and fly back in time to the 1990s and Lindbergh Lake Road and the morning hikes we took. You leave through the gate at Tranquillity and turn left. You are now on Lindbergh Lake Road. You embark on a power walk, over hills and making angular turns, arms fully swinging, and more often than not, coming toward you was Diane Macrae Hollinger, an athletic, cheerful woman, followed by a swarm of dogs, one adorable puppy flopping away behind the rest, running to Liz, looking up at her lovingly. This was Diane's daughter's puppy dog, Pansy, a homemade Maltese-Shih Tzu mix.

Now we are back in room 252. Liz had asked for a puppy dog like Pansy. "I have to be dying to get a puppy." she said. We had never zeroed in on getting a puppy. We traveled often, moved from place to place. We both knew that the idea of a puppy dog was much more practical than the reality of a puppy dog.

The mechanics of finding a Maltese-Shih Tzu mix puppy dog was complicated, but I, who would do anything for her, managed.

On Wednesday, June 20, at 2:45 PM, Daisy, a twelve-week-old Maltese-Shih Tzu mix entered room 252. She was a remake of Pansy, many, many years later. She was being cared for by a team of patient and skilled trainers. She had been met at the airport earlier that day, given a few hours of basic training, and here she was.

Liz was thrilled. Little Daisy scampered over Liz's bed until she ran out of energy. The puppy was embraced, petted, played with and then permitted to sleep. Poor little Daisy had come a long way for a short stay.

Room 252 was far from a gloom-ridden place. There were the times when the curtain was drawn around Liz's bed and a small team of nurses did what was necessary to keep Liz dry and at ease. But there were also times when the room was almost as in a street bazaar. The barber would pop in to remove whatever stubble was forming on Liz's head. A Good Samaritan local businessman came by to offer free milkshakes. Liz tasted his product. "Too thick, I'm afraid," she apologized. He wished her well and went on to the next room. Golda and Kathy, as much family now as physical therapists, became regular visitors to room 252, spreading as much positive energy as could be absorbed.

Alex's visits were happy times for Liz. As always she somehow found the energy to immerse herself in Alex's doings and those of Christina and the baby. She stared as long as her eyes could focus at the mound of photographs that Alex always carried. The constant recording on film of his family's day-to-day doings had become his avocation. Liz loved looking at them, loved looking at little Elias with his large blue eyes and blond hair, the very picture of a perfect German boy.

Liz, with her strict code of what really counted and what could be ignored, made good use of the hospital barber. She had two head-cleaning haircuts during her stay in room 252. Hair had begun to grow back.

Thursday, June 21, was another eventful day for Liz. Appearances mattered. Rose, her manicurist, had come in the morning. Shocked as she was at the current state of the woman who had been her beautiful client for two decades, she nonetheless performed brilliantly. Liz then asked Rose when she could schedule her for a pedicure. "I'm afraid I'm going on vacation," Rose answered. "Well, then, be sure to call me when you come back," Liz said.

Daisy was due at 12:30. The weather was mild and sunny, Liz weather. Golda and Kathy helped us to get Liz into a wheelchair, another act of daunt-

less will, and we wheeled Liz to her little garden spot. We met Daisy on the lawn. Liz held the leash tightly in her hand. Daisy dashed about in all directions as though outside were a completely new experience. We asked Lisa, the trainer, to shorten the visit. Liz wanted to be back in bed, Dana was scheduled for a 4:00 PM visit and Liz wanted to be rested and ready. She knew that this would be the last time she and Dana would be together.

Here again, Dana's words:

"She was ordering dinner and reading the menu with pleasure and anticipation. She was totally in charge, voice strong, but raspy."

A word of explanation: A day or two earlier, around the 19th, Liz and I had had what you could call a "strategy" talk. "If I must eat," she said, "and you know how hard that is for me, then I'll try to eat what I really like. Why don't you get me a copy of Le Bernardin's menu?" I did. Liz called the restaurant.

Dana continued:

"Liz said, 'About thirty minutes? OK, I'll send a cab.' All of this was done with great relish. Her manicure was impeccable. We talked about past experiences. That's when she reached over to exclaim, 'We had so much fun! Didn't we, Dana?' We hugged. As I was leaving, I asked her how she could be sure that her late lunch would be picked up. She said with a big smile, 'Don't worry. Art will see to it.'"

Art did. But Gwen was the person who made it happen. She picked up the order and cabbed it to the hospital. Liz had ordered poached lobster and a glass of wine. We chopped the lobster into tiny bits and refrigerated the wine. I fed her the tiny bite-size lobster pieces. She chin-tucked and chewed and chewed and chewed. The lobster was put aside. So much for the late lunch. "Maybe it kept cooking in the cab," I offered. "No," she said, "It was tough to begin with."

Daisy visited again the next two days, the last one in a playpen so she could dash about on the floor. Lisa, the trainer, and I had dragged the components from the cab to the room, set up the pen, and Daisy wildly dashed about.

The short, sweet saga of Daisy came to an end after just four visits. Liz was drifting away, sleeping more, less mobile, more exhausted. Saturday, June

23, was Daisy's last day. By July 1, Daisy was on her way back to Plenty-wood, Montana. She had given Liz much pleasure in so little time.

Liz and I were virtually alone in room 252. Nurses came and went. Sandra sat in a chair at the far end of the room. It had become more and more of an effort for Liz to communicate. "I'm going to get you a pad," I said. She nodded. "Fine idea," she whispered.

The first-floor kiosk was sold out, so I improvised with the help of our tenth-floor nurse and made a small pad using copy machine paper. The result was a stapled together three-by-four-inch pad.

Liz beamed when I presented my pad, accepted a pencil and slowly, carefully wrote, "I love you." She became more animated. "I have some wine left over from my chewy lobster. Let's have a drink." "I'd love it," I said. I found the wineglass in the refrigerator, poured a small drink for myself. There she was, her hospital bed raised so that she was almost sitting, wineglass in hand.

She held her glass to mine and extended her arm. Our glasses met. She said, "Cheers." She smiled a soft, loving smile, a smile of good humor, almost amused. We both drank the tiniest of sips and I removed the glasses.

Liz was inexorably slipping away. It was critical that our nursing staff keep her comfortable and dry, that she be turned gently, that every motion be tender.

Claudette Devi, one of our evening standby nurses who had been with Liz for many weeks, had returned from her vacation. She would be with Liz the evening of the 23rd until her shift ended at eight o'clock in the morning of Sunday the 24th.

I later spoke at some length with Claudette and asked her to e-mail me the details of her evening shift. I've excerpted her return comments:

"Liz awoke at about 5:00 AM. She had slept through the evening. She asked for some egg cream. She also wanted me to place an order for breakfast. I told her it was too early; perhaps she should wait. She agreed and fell back to sleep. I spoke to you, Art, between 6:15 and 6:30 and I told you about her request. You told me where the menu to order from was. At 6:45, Liz was coughing, some expectoration, nothing out of the norm. She later asked for breakfast again and I asked her what she would like. Her first request was for a grilled cheese sandwich with tomatoes. She asked me to call you. Liz did speak to you, but she could not hear you very well. I ordered the sandwich. I then cleaned her up, changed her sheets and she brushed her teeth. San-

dra arrived at 8:00 AM. We both sat Liz up in bed and allowed her to eat. She only ate a small amount. She enjoyed the meal and said, 'I will eat some more later.'"

Lyudmila Lachac, known to us as "Lu," loving and trusted night nurse, had been at a Ukrainian powwow upstate. She wasn't due back until the evening of the 25th. Sharon Leyden was brought on for the evening of the 24th into the morning of the 25th. She would be relieved by Elisa Haber for the 8:00 AM to 8:00 PM shift on the 25th. And then Lu would return for the 25th evening shift through the early hours of the 26th.

Sharon and I spoke this last September. I've never met Sharon, yet she remains, I think, for all the years of my life to be, a heroine, raised to that status during her brief encounter with Liz.

"That lady was something," Sharon said. "She didn't sleep most of the night. From 3:00 AM until about 5:00 AM, she did quite a bit of coughing. But she wasn't out of control. She told me how long a battle she had had with cancer, of the years she fought it and now she was ready to go. She was not at all distressed. She asked if I was coming back and I said, 'No.' She then thanked me for taking care of her and shook my hand. That lady was really something," Sharon said again.

Dr. Sherman stopped by but Liz was sleeping. There was nothing to be done other than prescribe morphine if needed to relieve pain.

Elisa Haber, another heroine, relieved Sharon at 8:00 AM. Liz was sleeping, but managed a smile when she realized Elisa was in the room. Liz's breathing was labored; she was coughing intermittently and falling in and out of sleep.

I had arrived to sit my last morning in room 252. I kissed Liz as she lay sleeping and sat next to her on her hospital bed.

She opened her eyes and reached for my hand. "I'll be leaving you soon," she said. "I know," I said. "It's OK. It's all right." She closed her eyes and fell back asleep. She had reached the outer limits of her endurance.

Elisa wrapped Liz's legs with gauze to absorb the weeping of fluids through her tissue-thin skin. We both cleaned out the refrigerator and began the agonizing work of preparing the room for the next patient.

Liz's new good friend, Dr. Sherman, stopped by for the second time that day. Liz had spoken with him briefly, to thank him and let him know she was ready to die.

He had been conferring with Dr. Pasmantier and Dr. Hartman. Barry was to stop by later. Liz was given morphine from mid-afternoon on, frequent dosages to relieve pain and eventually to render her comatose.

I sat on the edge of her bed when I wouldn't be in the way. I held her hand as she slept. My mind was a huge empty chamber. I had claimed to be ready. I had claimed it was OK.

She suddenly opened her eyes and reached up for me. "Please, please let me go," she pleaded.

"Soon, soon darling. I promise you, very soon," I said.

I held her to me, my beautiful, ravaged wife. The morphine had taken over. She sank back, comatose as she would be to the end. I released her for the very last time.

I left, carrying with me as much of the remains of Liz's hospital belongings as I could. Elisa and I hugged and wept. We remain friends and she, Elisa, an everlasting captive of Liz's wondrous magnetism.

It's important in this account to add a note received the next day from Dr. Sherman:

"Dear Mr. Ortenberg:

Please accept my condolences on the passing of your wife Elisabeth. During the short time I was involved with her care, it was apparent that her courageous attitude, upbeat disposition and her persistence were major assets in her battle with cancer. Although she ultimately lost this fight, I believe she was comfortable, not unrealistic and dealt with the problem well.

It was my privilege to assist in her care. I hope the months and years ahead gradually ease the pain of your loss. Please convey my thoughts to the rest of your family.

Sincerely,
Raymond L. Sherman"

And the following day I received this note:

"Dear Art,

I opened the Internet this morning and read about Liz. I was heartbroken. The last time I saw you, you were encouraged by her progress. I have rarely met a person with such courage, fortitude and determination. I so much admired her, constantly positive and smiling. She always referred to you as a most supportive husband, without whom she could not have endured her illness.

You have my deepest sympathies
Mike Buchman"

She was buried at Triple 8 the following Saturday, her ashes in a Liz Red lacquered urn, as she wanted. She awaits me on a high knoll about one mile from Cabin A. We often rode to this spectacular site with its 360-degree view of hills and mountains and one lonely, stunted Ponderosa pine about twenty feet from where she rests. There is a place for me right next to her. I can only hope that she will forgive the demands I made on her to keep her alive, for my sake, perhaps more than for hers.

EPILOGUE

IRV MAUDLIN MET me at the Helena Airport in early March of 2008. It was to be a short trip. I was on the ground early enough to drive out to the ranch and spend a number of hours there. Later I would return to town and spend a late afternoon and early dinner with Dr. Tom Weiner at the Montana Club.

Irv doesn't have too much managing to do these days. The weather is his boss. I am the signer of checks, the booster of morale and the assurer of employment longevity. All of this, of course, is as Liz would have wanted it to be. Irv is in his early sixties and has been managing the ranch for about five years. He has a wide range of skills and is thoroughly honest. But he does not ride horses well and thus, one day a few months earlier, he had managed to fall off Moon, the same horse that David Quammen's new wife, Betsy, fell off two years earlier. I am told that Moon spooks easily.

Irv is a man of solid build, muscular, with ordinary good looks that match his taciturn demeanor. I like Irv and I think he respects me and tries to please me. He had dug up the ground for Liz's gravesite and has prepared a site for me a few feet to the west. I planned to visit Liz on her distant, lonely knoll, spend friendly time with Kathy and Angie, the person who exercises our six horses. I cannot think of Triple 8 or write about it in other than the possessive plural.

The phenomenon of a snow blizzard in early March in Montana, particularly at 5,500 feet, is not unusual. It occurred to me that Liz must be chuckling. Here we are again, blizzard bound.

Irv, Kathy and I met in the basement of Cabin B, our cabin. Irv had just brought a truckload of material from Tranquillity. Tranquillity had been sold in January and we had been moving leftovers ever since. We still had not moved Liz's mother's ashes and a small urn that contained some of Louis's ashes. The ground was frozen. That would have to wait, but it is my plan to have them buried to the east of Liz.

To my surprise, there were two large cardboard boxes sitting on a small wood platform. Written on the top of one, in enormous letters, was the word "Albums."

"You're kidding," I said.

"Oh no, these cartons are full of albums," Kathy said. "I thought you knew about these."

I did know about those albums. I had fussed with Liz for years to have the spines of the albums titled and arranged for easy accessibility. I had been through thousands of negatives, hundreds of mounted photographs, had catalogued and sorted for months and still had completely forgotten the albums at Tranquillity. What a treasure.

I now have on my desk a relatively thin album, titled:

Art's 70th Birthday—The Raft Trip on the Madison River, Montana

There are precisely thirty-three annotated photographs. There are Liz and David Quammen with his former wife, Kris. And there I am. We are all participating in a perilous raft trip through the rapids of the Madison River. Sure it was my birthday, but who would have guessed that Liz had arranged to have a substantial number of our family members flown to the Gallatin Gateway Inn, about ten miles down the road from our raft landing, for a surprise party? I had no idea that the perils of the raft trip, once ended, would lead to the even more distasteful perils (for me) of a surprise party.

There is one picture of me with the rafting group. The notation reads, "Is it true that people really get killed doing this?" Another reads, "Just what I've always wanted, a harmonica!" Each photograph's annotation is slyly funny.

Off we all went to the Gallatin Gateway Inn for an early dinner.

"Who are all those people?" I wondered. Liz caught that shot. Another one of me: "Alright, I promise to behave." And so on. Liz's playful humor was so perceptively on target that I cannot thumb through this album without being overwhelmed with sorrow. Time passes and life, seemingly purposeless, flows its random course. Of the couples in the photographs, four are divorced. Of the relationships, only a few remain strong. But of the people assembled, only Liz is gone.

The other albums are more straightforward: Africa—1995, Hong Kong—1994, South Africa-Okavango—1996, Israel—1987.

Overwhelmed as I was, I could not but relive my surprise eightieth birthday dinner at Tranquillity. Liz, ill and exhausted, had, by determination alone, created a magical evening. She was gay and happy and transmitted to all of us that wondrous elixir that defined her.

I visited her early that afternoon. Irv and I rode on one snowmobile through snow-covered grass, over barren soil, and forced the snowmobile within twenty yards of where Liz is buried. I walked up the hill, thinking, "Yes, darling, here we are again, in a blizzard." I stood for a number of very long minutes. And then I trudged back toward Irv.

• • •

Liz's gravesite is unmarked. Her life, however, and what she fashioned in her lifetime, aside from her glorious career, have been remarkably central to enriching the world in which we live. Yes, Liz said, it matters; brief, this tissue-thin slice of time may be, but what we do here matters.

Rocky Barker, who had been at Red Lodge, e-mailed:

"I continue to take pride in my participation at Red Lodge and the continuing camaraderie I share with others who were there. You and Liz made it happen and its positive effects still ripple through the West."

Nancy Widdicombe, a teacher at Harlowton High School in Harlowton, Montana, wrote:

"Dear Liz and Art, You have changed the world for me…The list is endless of what I owe to you both and to your support of the Montana Heritage Project. My

students owe you even more…This year, when our salutatorian and valedictorian gave their speeches at our commencement exercises, they both listed the Montana Heritage Project as their final accomplishment of their high school years!"

But it was Liz's love of creatures and the continuing work and time she gave on their behalf that I feel is her most distinguished legacy. We have heard from the Craigs.

We have read George Schaller's words.

Alan Rabinowitz, probably the most respected felid biologist in the world, has written:

"You have made a difference to the survival of many species and to the lives of many people. I add my thanks for your inspiration, guidance and friendship."

Dale Miquelle, tiger conservationist in the Russian Far East, wrote:

"It is because of people like you that I truly believe we can change the world, or at least nudge it in the right direction. Thanks so much for your stalwart support. All that we have accomplished through working with local people is due to your commitment."

And Bill Conway wrote:

"The special intensity of your personal commitment has bought time for wild creatures, and for the rest of us, all over the world."

Yes, Liz, "if we can't save these magnificent creatures, then we can't save ourselves."

• • •

Dr. Paul Miskowitz, the gastroenterologist, is an unusual man. He appears at the hospital so early in the morning that I picture him flying in through a window, cape trailing, carrying the early edition of *The New York Times* and a huge bundle of highbrow and lowbrow magazines. Liz had no recollection of seeing him at the hospital and in all probability she was right. He looked at the chart of the patient in room 252, Liz Ortenberg by name, dropped off a magazine and went on his way. Recall that when Angie Eng reported on the incident in room 252, Dr. Miskowitz, for the first time in years, realized that this patient was indeed Liz Claiborne.

It wasn't until October 24, this past year, that I was able to see him. I remember him as large, distinguished looking, compactly built and friendly.

He had accumulated a large number of technical papers and had assumed that I was interested in the mechanics of Liz's digestive system. Dr. Miskowitz, unseen by Liz, was nevertheless very much on the case. He had met with Dr. Pasmantier to investigate any method other than an oral method of getting nourishment into Liz's body. There was nothing to be done. Liz's aspiration problem could only worsen. We discussed the irony of Liz, a person who loved food, who loved living, finally being faced with no choice other than losing at last. I had said that in the sense that it is everyone's destiny to have lost.

"Lost?" Dr. Miskowitz shook his head and spoke in a low voice. "Lost? You couldn't be more wrong. She won! Yes, you of all people know that she won. She died with dignity. She showed what the outer limits of perseverance can do. She was in control of how she dealt with this tsunami-like disease. I will not forget her."

No, I thought, nor will Mark Pasmantier, who against mammoth odds struggled to extend her life, perhaps to cure her, hoping for a miracle. Nor will Tom Weiner, who at the beginning of each summer, would ask himself, "I wonder how Liz is doing? I wonder if I'll see her this year?" and then did everything his skill and caring allowed to make her life easier and better.

"No, Dr. Miskowitz," I said, "none of us will ever forget her."

We shook hands and I left. I began to write this account one month later.

Aix-en-Provence, May 2002.

ACKNOWLEDGMENTS

Despite Liz's fondness for listing names alphabetically by first name, these acknowledgments will be in traditional last name order. All those acknowledged provided light and support for Liz during her times of difficulty:

Katy Allgeyer, Kim Brindel, Chris Brook, Dana Buchman, Dr. Myron Buchman, Robin Burk, Sandra Cummings, Ellen Daniel, Rosa Dawson, Claudette Devi, Rick D'Linn, Dr. Angie Eng, Gloria Farber, Jim Gordon, Maya Gurley, Randy Gurley, Elisa Haber, Ian Harrington, Graham Harris, Dr. Barry Hartman, Jamie Hellman, Noella Hibon, Joe Hrella, Brian Kahn, Jay Kirkpatrick, Ellen Knight, Bob Knight, Lyudmila Lachac, Gene Landrum, Sharon Leland, Van Lupo, Dr. Steven Magid, Leo Marino, Evelyn Melian, Ray Minella, Dr. Paul Miskowitz, Patrick Montanari, Jim Murtaugh, Kathy Orsello, Dr. Mark Pasmantier, Mary Pearl, Sandra Dal Poggetto, David Quammen, Kamini Rambally, Francoise Rannou, Peter Raven, Dr. Jon Reckler, Stephanie Reckler, Eric Ripert, Gwen Satterfield, George Schaller, Dr. Raymond Sherman, Yvonne Stephens, Dr. Frederick Stier, Shirley Strum, Rose Syrkin, Nancy Valentine, Jerry Watson, Dr. Tom Weiner, Golda Widawski, and Dr. Eric Zweifach.